CONTEMPORARY'S

PRE-GED

LANGUAGE ARTS, READING

McGraw Hill **Wright Group**

Wright Group

Send all inquiries to:
Wright Group/McGraw-Hill
130 E. Randolph, Suite 400
Chicago, IL 60681

ISBN 0-07-252759-5

11 12 13 14 15 WDQ 12 11 10

The *McGraw-Hill* Companies

Table of Contents

PART I: CRITICAL THINKING SKILLS IN READING

CHAPTER 1 Comprehension 13

CHAPTER 2 Application 27

CHAPTER 3 Analysis 35

Acknowledgments

Excerpt on page 2 from article "Hispanics to undertake citizenship campaign" from *USA Today*, 5/4/84. Copyright © 1984, *USA Today*. Reprinted with permission.

Excerpt on page 3 by Arthur C. Clarke, *2010: Odyssey Two*. New York: Ballantine Books, 1982.

Review on page 5 of "Black Beauty" by Johanna Steinmetz, *Chicago Tribune*, D section 7, July 29, 1994.

Excerpt on page 6 from *The Stories of John Cheever* by John Cheever. Copyright © 1978 by John Cheever. Used by permission of Alfred A. Knopf, a division of Random House, Inc.

Excerpt on page 7 from *A Raisin in the Sun* by Lorraine Hansberry. Copyright © 1958 by Robert Nemiroff as an unpublished work. Copyright © 1959, 1966, 1984 by Robert Nemiroff. Used by permission of Random House, Inc.

Excerpt on page 23 from "New Mexico's Treasures: Santa Fe and Taos" by Dennis Landt, *Home & Away* magazine, Sept.–Oct., 1982. Reprinted courtesy of Home & Away.

Excerpt on page 37 from *The Skylark of Space* by Edward E. Smith. Copyright © 1946, 1947 by E. E. Smith, Ph.D., renewed 1974 by the estate of E. E. Smith. Reprinted by permission of the Viginia Kidd Agency, Inc., POB 274, Milford, PA 18337.

Excerpt on page 67 from "Flight" from *The Long Valley* by John Steinbeck. Copyright © 1938, renewed © 1966 by John Steinbeck. Used by permission of Viking Penguin, a division of Penguin Putnam Inc.

Excerpt on page 68 from "Separating," from *Problems and Other Stories* by John Updike, 1975. Alfred A. Knopf.

Excerpt on page 88 from *The Medium is the Message* by Marshall McLuhan and Quentin Fiore, produced by Jerome Agel. Copyright © Jerome Agel. Reprinted by permission.

Excerpt on page 89 from "Mining Part of Early History" in *Uplands*. Permission granted by the Dodgeville Chronicle, Inc.

Exerpt on page 102 from Yitshok Rudashevski, *The Dairy of Vilna Ghetto: June 1941–April 1943*. Translated by Percy Matenko. Copyright © 1973 Beit Lohamei Haghetaot–Ghetto Fighter's House.

Excerpt on page 103 reprinted with the permission of Scribner, a Division of Simon & Schuster, Inc., from *On Writing* by Stephen King. Copyright © 2000 by Stephen King.

Excerpt on pages 112–113 from "From Vaudeo to Video Via Radio" from *Jack Benny: The Radio and Television Work* by The Museum of Television and Radio. Copyright © 1991 by The Museum of Television and Radio. Reprinted by permission of HarperCollins Publishers, Inc.

Excerpt on page 116 from *The Complete Letters of Vincent Van Gogh* by Vincent Van Gogh. Copyright © 1958 by Little, Brown and Company in conjunction with the New York Graphic Society.

Excerpt on page 118 from "What is Poetry?" in *This Way, Delight* by Herbert Read. Copyright © 1956 Pantheon Books, Inc.

Excerpt on page 119, "Image's Exhibit Reflects the Best of Latino Art" by Margaret Hawkins, Art Critic, *Chicago Sun-Times*, October 21, 1994.

Excerpt on page 120 from a review of "A Man On The Moon" in *The New Yorker*, September 12, 1994. Copyright © 1994 The New Yorker Magazine. Reprinted by permission. All rights reserved.

Excerpt on page 121 taken from the ROGER EBERT column by Roger Ebert, Copyright © 1994. Dist. by UNIVERSAL PRESS SYNDICATE. Reprinted with permission. All rights reserved.

Excerpt on page 135 by James A. Michener, *Chesapeake*. New York: Random House, Inc., 1978.

Story "Early Autumn" on pages 136–138 from *Short Stories* by Langston Hughes. Copyright © 1966 by Ramona Bass and Arnold Rampersad. Reprinted by permission of Hill and Wang, a division of Farrar, Straus and Giroux, LLC.

Excerpt on page 142 from *Airport* by Arthur Hailey, Doubleday & Company, Inc., 1968, pp. 390–391.

Excerpt on page 144 from "A Worn Path" in *A Curtain of Green and Other Stories*. Copyright © 1941 and renewed 1969 by Eudora Welty. Reprinted by permission of Harcourt, Inc.

To The Student

Congratulations on your decision to use *Pre-GED Language Arts, Reading* to strengthen your critical-thinking skills in the areas of literal understanding, making inferences, and analyzing literature and the arts ideas. You will also learn how to read nonfiction prose, prose fiction, poetry, and drama selections.

Here is an overview of what you will find in this book, along with some tips on using the book.

Language Arts, Reading Pretest

The Pretest, found on pages 1–10, will help you decide which skills you need to work on the most. It will direct you to the parts of the book you may want to spend the most time with.

Chapter 1: Comprehension

By working through Chapter 1, you will review how to find the main idea of a paragraph and of a passage, how to identify the purpose of a selection and its supporting details, and how to use context clues to unlock the meaning of unknown words.

Chapter 2: Application

In this chapter you will learn how to apply information from one situation to a different situation.

Chapter 3: Analysis

This chapter teaches you how to recognize the patterns in which materials are presented, such as order of importance, sequence of events, cause and effect, comparison and contrast, and classification. You will also learn how to make inferences, draw conclusions, and analyze style and tone.

Chapter 4: Synthesis

This chapter teaches you how to take information from two different parts of a passage, or from a passage and an outside source, and synthesize them in order to reach a conclusion.

Chapter 5: Nonfiction Prose

In this chapter you will learn how to read nonfiction prose, recognize the difference between fact and opinion, detect an author's bias, and read and interpret business documents, articles from newspapers and periodicals, literary nonfiction, and selections about the visual arts.

Chapter 6: Prose Fiction

This chapter introduces you to the elements of fiction: setting, plot, character, and point of view. You will also learn how to interpret literal and figurative language and the theme of a short story.

Chapter 7: Poetry

In this chapter you will learn what poetry is and how to read it. You will also learn to infer a poem's meaning and understand how the use of imagery and figurative language contribute to a poem's effect.

Chapter 8: Drama

This chapter introduces you to the elements of drama. You will learn how to interpret stage directions, punctuation, and how to read dialogue. You will also discover how character and action are important to drama.

Writing Activities

Every chapter allows you an opportunity to practice different types of writing and, in this way, improve your writing skills.

Pre-GED Practice

At the end of every chapter, and sometimes more frequently throughout the book, you will find one or more passages that are formatted with five-item multiple-choice questions to help you prepare for GED-level study. The Pre-GED Practice at the end of each chapter serves as a review of the skills you have learned in the chapter.

Reading Efficiency Activities

This book contains **Reading Efficiency Activities** to help you practice reading speed and accuracy in order to achieve an optimum reading efficiency level. When you take the GED Test, you will be limited to a certain amount of time for each exam and must receive a minimum passing score to obtain your GED certificate. Because of this, it is important that you read at an acceptable rate while comprehending what you read. The Reading Efficiency Activities provide you with the tools to practice those skills and chart your progress.

There are ten Reading Efficiency Activities in this book. For each activity, you should time yourself as you read a 200- to 400-word passage and answer the 5 questions that follow. When you finish, you should record the time it took you to complete the activity and check your answers using the answer key provided in the back of the book.

Efficiency Factor (E-Factor) Chart

Once you complete a Reading Efficiency Activity, you can determine your Efficiency Factor (E-Factor) by using the E-Factor Chart on page 234. This chart provides a quick and easy way for you to determine your level of efficiency for each activity. The E-Factor takes into account an optimum reading rate and score for success on the actual GED Test. By locating your completion time on the vertical axis and your score on the horizontal axis, you can quickly determine your E-Factor. You should aim to achieve an optimum E-Factor of 100 or higher. The optimum range is located in the shaded areas of the chart.

Efficiency Factor Plotting Grid

Once you have located your E-Factor on the chart, you should plot it on the Efficiency Factor Grid on page 235. Possible E-Factor scores are listed on the vertical axis with each activity listed across the horizontal axis. Every point above 100 is shaded so you can instantly see when you have achieved an optimum E-Factor. As each Reading Efficiency Activity is completed and plotted, you can connect the dots to create a graph of your progress.

Language Arts, Reading Posttest

The Posttest, found on pages 203–218, will help you to see how well you have learned the critical-thinking and reading skills presented in this book. The Posttest consists of 40 multiple-choice questions.

Answer Key

This feature gives answers and explanations for all the questions in this book. Use the Answer Key only after you have attempted to answer a set of questions in an exercise.

Glossary

Throughout the book, key terms that are important for you to know are printed in boldface and italic type and are defined in the glossary at the back of the book.

Good luck with your studies! Keep in mind that knowing how to read and analyze various types of reading materials is worth learning for many reasons.

Pretest

The Language Arts, Reading Pretest that follows is a guide to using this book. Take the Pretest before you begin working on any of the chapters. The test consists of 20 multiple-choice questions that test the reading and reasoning skills in Language Arts, Reading covered in this book. All of the questions are based on fiction and nonfiction prose, poetry, and drama.

Answer each question as carefully as possible. Choose the best of the five answer choices by filling in the corresponding circle on the answer grid. If a question is too difficult, go ahead and come back to that question later. When you have completed the test, check your answers on page 9.

Using the Evaluation Chart on page 10, circle the number of each question that you missed. If you missed many of the questions that correspond to a certain reading skill, you will want to pay special attention to that skill as you work your way through this book.

Pretest Answer Grid

1	①	②	③	④	⑤	8	①	②	③	④	⑤	15	①	②	③	④	⑤
2	①	②	③	④	⑤	9	①	②	③	④	⑤	16	①	②	③	④	⑤
3	①	②	③	④	⑤	10	①	②	③	④	⑤	17	①	②	③	④	⑤
4	①	②	③	④	⑤	11	①	②	③	④	⑤	18	①	②	③	④	⑤
5	①	②	③	④	⑤	12	①	②	③	④	⑤	19	①	②	③	④	⑤
6	①	②	③	④	⑤	13	①	②	③	④	⑤	20	①	②	③	④	⑤
7	①	②	③	④	⑤	14	①	②	③	④	⑤						

Questions 1–3 refer to the following newspaper article.

WHY DON'T MANY HISPANICS BECOME IMMIGRANTS?

Hispanics are mounting a nationwide drive to get Hispanic immigrants to become U.S. citizens. About 5.91 million Hispanic adults in the USA aren't citizens—partly
5 because of their fear of dealing with immigration officials. They can't vote, serve on juries, work for the government, or qualify for some federal education benefits, said Harry Pachon, head of the National
10 Association of Latino Elected and Appointed Officials (NALEAO).

Saturday, NALEAO will sponsor a conference in Washington, D.C. On the agenda: a proposal to create task forces for
15 a nationwide citizenship drive for Hispanics— the USA's second-largest minority, projected to be the biggest by the year 2020. Hispanics' naturalization rate is 30 percent, compared to 44 percent for non-Hispanics, says an
20 NALEAO study.

"Citizenship used to be a highly esteemed value in the 1920s and 1930s," Pachon said. "We're hoping to revive that." The problem is most acute among
25 Mexicans—who make up 64 percent of all Hispanics. Mariana Scuros of the Mexican American Legal Defense and Education Fund said many Mexicans—with a naturalization rate of only 16 percent—don't seek
30 citizenship because they misunderstand it. "They think they have to step on the Mexican flag," said Scuros. "The Mexican is very proud of his heritage."

—Excerpted from *USA Today*, 1984

1. What is the naturalization rate of Mexicans in the United States?

   (1) 5.91 million
   (2) 30 percent
   (3) 44 percent
   (4) 16 percent
   (5) 64 percent

2. Why do many Hispanics choose *not* to seek U.S. citizenship?

   (1) As illegal immigrants, they are afraid of being turned down.
   (2) They have no wish to vote or serve on juries.
   (3) They fear dealing with immigration officials.
   (4) They don't know how to go about applying for citizenship.
   (5) They are planning to leave the United States.

3. What is the goal of the NALEAO conference?

   (1) to encourage Hispanics to register to vote
   (2) to mount a national citizenship drive for Hispanics
   (3) to raise the Hispanic naturalization rate from 30 to 44 percent
   (4) to make Hispanics the largest U.S. minority group by the year 2020
   (5) to help Hispanics who want to immigrate to the United States

PRETEST

Questions 4–6 refer to the following passage.

WHERE DO THESSE MEN WORK?

"You're not scared, are you?" asked Max, when they were about to put on their helmets.

"Not enough to make a mess in my suit. Otherwise, yes."

5　Max chuckled. "I'd say that's about right for this job. But don't worry—I'll get you there in one piece, with my—what do you call it?"

"Broomstick. Because witches are
10　supposed to ride them."

"Oh, yes. Have you ever used one?"

"I tried once, but mine got away from me. Everyone else thought it was very funny."

There are some professions which have
15　evolved unique and characteristic tools—the longshoreman's hook, the potter's wheel, the bricklayer's trowel, the geologist's hammer. The men who had to spend much of their time on zero-gravity construction projects
20　had developed the broomstick. It was very simple—a hollow tube just a meter long, with a footpad at one end and a retaining loop at the other. At the touch of a button, it could telescope out to five or six times its normal
25　length, and the internal shock-absorbing system allowed a skilled operator to perform the most amazing maneuvers [movements]. The footpad could also become a claw or hook if necessary; there were many other
30　refinements, but that was the basic design. It looked deceptively easy to use; it wasn't.

The airlock pumps finished recycling; the EXIT sign came on; the outer doors opened, and they drifted slowly into the void.
35　*Discovery* was windmilling about two hundred meters away, following them in orbit around Io, which filled half the sky. Jupiter was invisible, on the other side of the satellite.

—Excerpted from *2010: Odyssey Two,* by Arthur C. Clarke

4. What does the passage suggest about Io?

　(1) It is smaller than Jupiter.
　(2) It is far from Jupiter.
　(3) It is the same size as Jupiter.
　(4) It is a shield above Jupiter.
　(5) It is larger than Jupiter.

5. What is the meaning of the word *telescope* (line 24)?

　(1) focus
　(2) magnify
　(3) lash
　(4) stretch
　(5) drift

6. What can you conclude about Max and his companion?

　(1) They are on a geological excursion.
　(2) They have invented an amazing new method of transportation.
　(3) They are astronomers observing planets through a telescope.
　(4) They are using a device like a broomstick to travel through space.
　(5) They are trying to return to Earth from an alien planet.

Questions 7–9 refer to the following poem.

WHAT ROADS DOES THE SPEAKER SEE?

Two roads diverged in a yellow wood.
And sorry I could not travel both
And be one traveler, long I stood
And looked down one as far as I could
5 To where it bent in the undergrowth;

Then took the other, as just as fair,
And having perhaps the better claim,
Because it was grassy and wanted wear;
Though as for that the passing there
10 Had worn them really about the same,

And both that morning equally lay
In leaves no step had trodden black.
Oh, I kept the first for another day!
Yet knowing how way leads on to way,
15 I doubted if I should ever come back.

I shall be telling this with a sigh
Somewhere ages and ages hence:
Two roads diverged in a wood, and I—
I took the one less traveled by,
20 And that has made all the difference.

—Robert Frost, 1916

7. Which of the following sentences best summarizes the poet's message?

(1) It is wise to be cautious and common.
(2) Traveling in the woods is relaxing and enjoyable.
(3) It is dangerous to travel in the woods at night because you might get lost.
(4) Making choices for yourself is better than doing what everyone else does.
(5) Once you make up your mind, you cannot change it.

8. When the poet says "I took the one less traveled by, and that has made all the difference," (lines 19–20) what does he mean?

(1) He is afraid that the path he chose has made him different from everybody else.
(2) He wishes he had gone down the other path.
(3) He thinks going down the other path would have helped him fit in with society.
(4) He thinks that choosing between the two paths was a difficult decision.
(5) He knows that the path he chose has affected his life positively.

9. If the poet were faced with a difficult decision, how would he most likely respond?

(1) He would choose to do what was easiest.
(2) He would be unable to make a decision.
(3) He would do what he felt was right.
(4) He would choose the most difficult option.
(5) He would ask others for advice.

PRETEST

Questions 10 and 11 refer to the following passage.

WHO IS BLACK BEAUTY?

There is no more benign [gentle and harmless] film likely to be released this summer—this year, for that matter—than *Black Beauty,* an adaptation of Anna Sewell's
5 1877 novel about the life of a horse.

The novel, which takes place in the days when horses were valued more for work than for beauty and raised English consciousness regarding their treatment, is narrated by the
10 horse itself. The movie follows suit. This takes a little getting used to, since talking horses generally confine themselves to animation and rarely take themselves seriously even then. But Black Beauty is
15 nothing if not earnest. It's part of his charm.

"Sold?" he cries at one point (in the voice of Alan Cumming). "Every horse knows that terrifying word." Later in the story, having spotted his onetime sweetheart,
20 Ginger, he sighs, "That night I dreamed of her, of what was and of what might have been."

Black Beauty is solid craftsmanship but not flashy moviemaking. It's pretty and a
25 trifle bland, but engaging enough to entertain a wide range of ages. Best of all, it does so without trauma and without distorting the story's general message of kindness to conform to some of today's
30 political agendas regarding animals.

—Excerpted from a movie review by Johanna Steinmetz,
Chicago Tribune, July 29, 1994

10. This review is of a movie adapted from which of the following?

   (1) an earlier movie
   (2) an English novel narrated by Alan Cumming
   (3) an Anna Sewell novel that is narrated by a horse
   (4) a benign animation
   (5) a political agenda

11. According to this review, the movie's good points include all EXCEPT which of the following?

   (1) solid craftsmanship
   (2) the earnest charm of the horse
   (3) suitability for audiences of all ages
   (4) blandness
   (5) a simple message of kindness toward animals

Questions 12–14 refer to the following passage.

WHO IS TRENCHER?

"He stares at me," she said. "He sighs and stares at me." I know what my wife looks like in the playground. She wears an old tweed coat, overshoes, and Army
5　gloves, and a scarf is tied under her chin. The playground is a fenced and paved lot between a slum and the river. The picture of the well-dressed, pink-cheeked doctor losing his heart to Ethel in this environment
10　was hard to take seriously. She didn't mention him then for several days, and I guessed that he had stopped his visits. Ethel's birthday came at the end of the month, and I forgot about it, but when I
15　came home that evening, there were a lot of roses in the living room. They were a birthday present from Trencher, she told me. I was cross at myself for having forgotten her birthday, and Trencher's roses made me
20　angry. I asked her if she'd seen him recently.

"Oh, yes," she said, "he still comes to the playground nearly every afternoon. I haven't told you, have I? He's made his declaration. He loves me. He can't live without me. He'd
25　walk through fire to hear the notes of my voice." She laughed. "That's what he said."

"When did he say this?"

"At the playground. And walking home. Yesterday."

30　"How long has he known?"

"That's the funny part about it," she said. "He knew before he met me at the Newsomes' that night. He saw me waiting for a crosstown bus about three weeks
35　before that. He just saw me and he said that he knew then, the minute he saw me. Of course, he's crazy."

—Excerpted from *"The Season of Divorce,"*
by John Cheever

12. What is the main subject of this passage?

  (1) Ethel's behavior at the playground
  (2) a developing relationship between Ethel and Trencher
  (3) an argument between Ethel and her husband
  (4) Ethel's birthday
  (5) the narrator's lack of interest in his wife's affairs

13. What is Trencher's occupation?

  (1) playground supervisor
  (2) bus driver
  (3) salesman
  (4) florist
  (5) doctor

14. Which of the following best describes the narrator's feelings about Trencher's odd relationship with Ethel?

  (1) He takes no interest at first but becomes annoyed when Trencher sends roses.
  (2) He is angry at his wife for paying attention to Trencher.
  (3) His early annoyance gives way to a feeling of happiness for his wife.
  (4) He thinks the whole thing is very funny.
  (5) He is upset that Ethel is making up lies about Trencher.

Questions 15–17 refer to the following excerpt from a play.

WALTER: I want so many things that they are driving me kind of crazy, … Mama—look at me.

MAMA: I'm looking at you. You a good-looking boy. You got a job, a nice wife, a fine
5 boy and—

WALTER: A job. [*Looks at her*] Mama, a job? I open and close car doors all day long. I drive a man around in his limousine and I say, "Yes, sir; no, sir; very good, sir; shall
10 I take the Drive, sir?" Mama, that ain't no kind of job . . . that ain't nothing at all. [*Very quietly*] Mama, I don't know if I can make you understand.

MAMA: Understand what, baby?

15 WALTER: [*Quietly*] Sometimes it's like I can see the future stretched out in front of me— just plain as day. The future, Mama. Hanging over there at the edge of my days. Just waiting for me—a big, looming blank space—
20 full of nothing. Just waiting for me. [*Pause*]

Sometimes when I'm downtown and I pass them cool, quiet-looking restaurants where them white boys are sitting back and talking 'bout things . . . sitting there turning deals
25 worth millions of dollars . . . sometimes I see guys don't look much older than me—

MAMA: Son—how come you talk so much 'bout money?

WALTER: [*With immense passion*] Because it
30 is life.

MAMA: [*Quietly*] Oh—[*Very quietly*] So now it is life. Money is life. Once upon a time freedom used to be life—now it's money. I guess the world really do change.

35 WALTER: No—it was always money, Mama. We just didn't know about it.

MAMA: No . . . something has changed. [*She looks at him*] You something new, boy.

In my time we was worried about not being
40 lynched and getting to the North if we could and how to stay alive and still have a pinch of dignity too. . . . Now here come you and Beneatha—talking 'bout things we ain't never even thought about hardly, me and
45 your daddy.

You ain't satisfied or proud of nothing we done. I mean that you had a home; that we kept you out of trouble till you was grown; that you don't have to ride to work on the
50 back of nobody's streetcar—You my children—but how different we done become.

WALTER: You just don't understand, Mama, you just don't understand.

—Excerpted from *A Raisin in the Sun,*
by Lorraine Hansberry

15. Which of the following is most important to Walter?

(1) a secure job
(2) an understanding mother
(3) a loving wife
(4) money
(5) his son

16. In Mama's opinion, which of the following statements is true about Walter?

(1) He thinks too much about money.
(2) He has a degrading job.
(3) He takes his wife and son for granted.
(4) He is too young to worry about the future.
(5) He should be more helpful to her.

17. What is Walter's occupation?

(1) taxi driver
(2) clerk
(3) chauffeur
(4) waiter
(5) bus driver

Questions 18–20 refer to the following passage.

I was at first very uncomfortable in that strange country. Although I could handle the language well, I seemed to be making a lot of mistakes somehow. It was obvious that
5 people were beginning to think I was very cold, even though I felt very friendly toward them. Slowly it began to dawn on me that my sense of distance was different from theirs.

I saw a man I barely knew approaching
10 me on a road one day. He began to wave when he was still forty feet from me and was talking when he was yet twenty feet away. I did not respond at all until he was within ten feet of me: I waved. I began my hellos
15 when we were about five feet apart. I hadn't even realized that he had been waving at me from that great distance. I didn't know that he had been talking to me from twenty feet away. By the time I responded to seeing
20 him, he had already begun to think I had insulted him. Another time, when I was being introduced to someone, I extended my hand to shake his. He held my hand so long that I began to feel uncomfortable and
25 finally had to pull away. The conversation didn't last long. The man thought me impolite. My own background had taught me that a handshake should last about two seconds; his culture prescribed a handshake
30 of nearly a half-minute with the last twenty seconds more like holding hands than a handshake. Once I learned to begin waving from farther away and to hold a handshake for thirty seconds, people stopped
35 regarding me as cold. But I had to change the sense of distance I had grown up with. I had to understand that forty feet was close enough to wave and that holding hands with a stranger was nothing more than basic
40 courtesy.

18. What does this passage compare?

    (1) an American and someone from another country
    (2) waving and shaking hands
    (3) two cultures
    (4) politeness and rudeness
    (5) language and behavior

19. Why does the author become accustomed to waving from farther away and holding hands for a longer time?

    (1) he dislikes his own culture
    (2) he does not want to offend anyone
    (3) he is tired of being bothered by strangers
    (4) it is required by law
    (5) he enjoys change

20. What was the author most comfortable with at first in the foreign country?

    (1) the sense of distance
    (2) the language
    (3) changes in his diet
    (4) the new customs
    (5) the behavior of strangers

PRETEST
Answer Key

1. (4) This information is stated in the last paragraph.

2. (3) This information appears in the first paragraph.

3. (2) The third paragraph states that "a proposal to create task forces for a nationwide citizenship drive" was on the agenda.

4. (5) Since Io "filled half the sky" and Jupiter "was invisible," you can infer that Io appeared larger.

5. (4) The passage says the broomstick could "telescope out to five or six times its normal length." *Stretch* is the best possible choice.

6. (4) Lines 33–34 mention a departure. From this and the discussions of the broomstick and zero gravity, you can infer that they are traveling in space.

7. (4) The poet seems to believe that daring to be different is better than doing what everyone else does.

8. (5) The poet's path choice symbolizes a turning point in his life; the path he chose in the woods represents the "path" he chose in life. That small decision affected him deeply after he made it and from the tone of the poem the effect seems to have been positive.

9. (3) In the poem, the poet chooses the path he feels is right for him, even though it is not the more commonly chosen path. It is reasonable to assume that, faced with a difficult decision, he would do what he felt was right, regardless of if it were difficult or easy.

10. (3) The first paragraph says that the movie is based on the novel by Anna Sewell. The second paragraph explains that the novel's narrator is a horse.

11. (4) Blandness (which means dullness) is not a compliment. All of the other points are specifically made in the review.

12. (2) Most of the description and all of the conversation deal with the developing relationship between Ethel and Trencher.

13. (5) The author refers to this in line 8.

14. (1) Until Trencher sent the roses, the narrator found this relationship "hard to take seriously." But once he saw the flowers, he began asking questions.

15. (4) In lines 29–30 Walter tells his mother that money is life.

16. (1) Throughout the passage, to his mother's dismay, Walter stresses the importance of money.

17. (3) This can be inferred from lines 6–11.

18. (3) This passage emphasizes the differences between the culture of the author's native land and that of the country he visits.

19. (2) The author mentions that before he changed his ways, people he met thought he was cold and impolite. He changed his behavior to correct this situation.

20. (2) Lines 2–3 mention the author's ease with the language.

Evaluation Chart

Use the answer key on page 11 to check your answers to the Pretest. Then, on the chart below, circle the numbers of the questions you missed. Note the areas where you missed more than half of the questions. The reading skills on pages 17–65 are very important for success in GED-level study.

Skill Area/ Content Area/	Comprehension (pages 13–25)	Application (pages 27–34)	Analysis (pages 35–56)	Synthesis (pages 57–69)
Nonfiction Prose (pages 73–130)	1, 2, 3, 10		11	
Prose Fiction (pages 131–164)	5, 13, 20		4, 6, 12, 19	14, 18
Poetry (pages 165–184)		9	7	8
Drama (pages 185–201)	17		15	16

Critical Thinking Skills in Reading

CHAPTER 1

Comprehension

In this chapter, you will learn to identify two basic parts of a reading passage: the main idea and supporting details. You will also learn to use context clues to help you understand a passage.

Each section of this chapter teaches a particular skill through explanations and practice exercises. Read the introductory material first. Then read the selections and do the exercises. Use the Answer Key to check your answers. Be sure to study the explanations of any questions you missed.

The main idea is a statement that tells what the selection is about. When a passage consists of only one paragraph, the main idea is the same for both passage and paragraph. In longer passages, each paragraph has its own main idea, and so does the passage as a whole.

To find the main idea of a passage, you must first learn how to find the main idea of a paragraph.

The Main Idea of a Paragraph

Every paragraph should have a main idea. The main idea tells what the whole paragraph is about. To find the main idea of a paragraph, follow these steps:

1. Read the entire paragraph.

2. Decide what the paragraph is saying. What is it about?

3. Reread the first and last sentences. The main idea of a paragraph is usually expressed first or last.

Directions: Read the paragraph below. Put a check in front of the main idea of the paragraph.

Television feeds us a constant diet of violence and sex. When we wake up, the morning news greets us with the latest mass murders, earthquakes, and plane crashes. On game shows, the hosts and contestants trade sexy words and gestures as they smooch their way to the big prize. Soap operas serve up a menu of adultery, and agony. The evening news replays the morning news, in case we forget. The final fare of the day is nighttime television. Here we may gorge on a cops-and-robbers shoot-out or nibble on a shallow tale of lust on the ranch.

_____

_____

What is the main idea of this paragraph?

_____ (1) Television programs are not fit for young children because of the violence and sex.

_____ (2) Some of the sex and violence on television centers around disasters, adultery, and crime.

_____ (3) Game shows and soap operas promote sex more than violence.

_____ (4) From morning to night, television programs deluge viewers with violence and sex.

The main idea is best stated in choice (4). It is also expressed in the first sentence of the paragraph. The rest of the paragraph develops this idea with details of the excessive violence and sex on television.

Look at the other choices. You may have read or heard the idea in choice (1) elsewhere, but it is not stated in this paragraph. Although choice (2) is mentioned in the paragraph, it does not convey what the whole paragraph is about. The paragraph doesn't make the comparison mentioned in choice (3).

The main idea of a paragraph is often, but not always, in the first sentence. For example, we could easily move the first sentence in our television paragraph. Try it. Cross it out and rewrite it on the blank lines at the end. Now we have a paragraph whose main idea is in the last sentence. All the other sentences give supporting details.

To find the main idea of a paragraph, then, begin by looking at the first sentence. If you don't find it there, try the last sentence. In some cases, the main idea is in the middle of the paragraph. How can you recognize it? It will express what the whole paragraph is about.

The Main Idea of a Passage

You know that a passage consists of one or more related paragraphs. You have also learned that a passage, like a paragraph, should have a main idea.

How do People Approach their Careers Today?

Today, people are "career-hopping" more than ever, seeking job diversity, increased wages, and career growth opportunities. Years ago, such a concept was unheard of. In fact, may people spent their entire careers at one company, seeking a new job only if it was absolutely necessary. Now people of all ages are changing careers and employers. It is not uncommon for a working individual to change careers several times in his or her lifetime.

Rapid advances in technology, including developments in communications, computing, e-commerce, and the Internet have paved the way for many new job opportunities. However, as quickly as some technological developments have surfaced, they have also disappeared or become "extinct," contributing to even more career changes among today's workers. Staying one step ahead of today's technological trends has become a way of life for many people in the working world.

A more self-focused attitude towards employment has replaced the strong ties of company loyalty many company "lifers" felt decades ago towards their employer. Today people seek jobs that offer the best compensation and benefits, interesting opportunities for growth, and a comfortable work environment. They prefer jobs that will allow them to achieve their current goals instead of trying to find a company that can meet their changing needs for many years. This explains the recent boom in self-employed individuals who have found that being their own boss and making their own business decisions can be a very gratifying way to earn a living.

The preceding passage consists of three paragraphs. For each paragraph, underline the sentence that best expresses the main idea.

Did you find the main idea of each paragraph?

The main idea of the first paragraph is given in the first sentence. Career changes have become increasingly more common. The rest of the paragraph supports this idea with details.

The main idea of the second paragraph can be found in the first sentence. Advances in technology have contributed to the increase in career changes and job opportunities for many different reasons.

The main idea of the third paragraph also appears in the first sentence, and is supported by the other details in the paragraph, including the information about self-employment as an increasingly popular alternative to working for a large corporation.

Directions: Put a check in front of the statement that best expresses the main idea of the entire passage.

_____ (1) People should choose their careers carefully to have secure jobs in the future.

_____ (2) Thanks in part to technology and changing attitudes towards the workplace, it is common today for people to change careers many times.

_____ (3) Self-employment is becoming more popular than working for a corporation, because of its flexibility and satisfaction.

You were correct if you chose statement (2) as the main idea of the entire passage.

The Purpose of a Selection

Look back at the paragraph about television on page 14. The main idea, as you know, is that network programming serves up a steady diet of violence and sex. But the purpose of the passage is something else. The purpose is to provide information, to inform and influence the reader.

Some types of written material do not have main ideas, but all written material should have a purpose. Think, for a moment, about a recipe. A recipe does not have a main idea, but it certainly has a purpose. A bus schedule has no main idea either, but it, too, has a definite purpose. The general purpose of such material as directions, manuals, recipes, schedules, and advertisements is to be helpful to the reader in some specific way. In the case of advertising, the purpose is to persuade the reader to buy a particular product or service.

It is usually up to the reader to figure out the purpose of a selection. Rarely is the purpose spelled out in a single sentence. To find it, begin by reading the entire piece. Think about how you, as the reader, are supposed to use the information. Why was it written? What will be the result if you do what it says? When you can answer these questions, you have found the purpose of the material.

As you read the selection that follows, think about its purpose.

Water Heater

1. Set water heater at 140°F if you have a dishwasher, 120°F if you don't.

2. Take showers instead of baths.

3. Turn the heater down or off when you vacation.

4. If hot water isn't used all day or night, install a timer to turn the heater on when you need it, off when you don't.

The purpose of the passage is to

_____ (1) help readers install water-heater timers

_____ (2) inform readers about the temperature range of water heaters

_____ (3) identify the uses of a water heater

_____ (4) provide energy-saving tips

The purpose of the passage is choice (4), to provide energy-saving tips. Every sentence gives a suggestion for saving energy. The purpose is not stated in the selection. You need to figure it out for yourself.

EXERCISE 1

Directions: Read the passage below and answer the questions that follow.

For the first time in history, there are more students enrolled in colleges as part-time students than are enrolled full-time. Most of these part-time students are working people between the ages of 25 and 45; many have families.

Universities and colleges are glad to see these new, older students because they bring to their campuses a kind of maturity and determination that younger students do not necessarily possess. Because of their work and family responsibilities, older students often make better, more disciplined students than do younger ones.

Adults are in school for various reasons. Some who already hold degrees are taking courses to broaden their knowledge in a certain area. Other adults, with degrees, return to school to prepare for career changes or to get another degree. Many adults return to obtain a degree. Colleges are especially interested in such students.

Some colleges offer life-experience credits to students. They give adults credit for work they did either as an employee or as a volunteer. Other colleges shorten the amount of time students must spend in studying the basic courses in a liberal arts program. An older adult's experience is broader than that of a younger freshman; thus, it takes less time to set up a program for study.

1. Match each paragraph listed on the left with its main idea statement on the right. Write the correct letter on the line.

_____ **Paragraph 1** (a) Students attend college to get a degree, prepare for a career, or just to broaden their knowledge.

_____ **Paragraph 2** (b) Colleges often adapt coursework to the needs and experiences of adults.

_____ **Paragraph 3** (c) Colleges welcome older, more disciplined students.

_____ **Paragraph 4** (d) Colleges now have more older part-time students than younger full-time students.

2. What is the main idea of the passage?

_____ (1) There are more adult, part-time students in colleges now than ever before.

_____ (2) Older adults do better work in college than younger students do.

_____ (3) There are many opportunities for adults who wish to further their education.

_____ (4) Colleges are trying hard to attract older students.

3. What is the purpose of the passage?

_____ (1) to criticize

_____ (2) to inform

_____ (3) to evaluate

_____ (4) to persuade

Answers are on page 219.

Supporting Details

Supporting details are the facts that describe or explain the main idea of a passage. An easy way to remember the relationship between supporting details and the main idea is to picture a table. A table cannot stand without legs. Likewise, a main idea rests upon supporting information. For a thorough understanding of what you read, you must grasp both the main idea and the facts, figures, examples, and explanations that back it up, or support it.

In this section, you will practice locating facts contained within passages. The technique of scanning will help you do this. You *scan* a passage by rereading it quickly but closely to find a specific fact or detail. As you read, concentrate only on finding the piece of information you are looking for.

To find supporting details within a selection, follow these steps:

1. Read the passage.

2. Identify the main idea.

3. Scan the passage for the specific information you need to find.

4. As you scan, remember the five Ws: *who, what, when, where,* and *why.*

EXERCISE 2

Directions: Read the following passage and then answer the questions in the space provided.

Black Hawk

Black Hawk, famous chief of the Sauk Indians, refused to leave Illinois after white men arrived in the late 1700s. When the Sauk and Fox tribes gave us their lands in 1804, he would not accept the contract. He believed that the chiefs drank firewater before signing the agreement and that the white men made the Indians drunk to trick their leaders, who really did not want to give up their land.

The high point of Sauk resistance came in the Black Hawk War. In 1832, only Black Hawk's tribe remained in Illinois and Wisconsin. The other Indians had moved west to reservations. The war did not last long, and the casualties on both sides were light, but Black Hawk and his tribe were strong foes. After the Indians were defeated, Black Hawk and his sons were sent with their tribe to a reservation at Fort Des Moines.

The story of Black Hawk lives on forever in his love for the land. "Keep it as we did," he said to his captors.

1. When did the Black Hawk War take place?

   _____

2. Why did Black Hawk resist the white settlers?

   _____

3. What did Black Hawk do?

   _____

4. Who were the Sauk and the Fox?

   _____

5. Where was Black Hawk sent after the war?

   _____

Answers are on page 219.

Context Clues

When you read an unfamiliar word, you can make a good guess at its meaning from the *context*—from the way it is used and from the words around it.

If you did not know what an island was, you could probably figure it out from the context in a sentence like this:

The *island* of Hawaii shines like a jewel, protected on all sides by the blue waters of the Pacific.

The words after *island—protected on all sides by the blue waters—*give clues to its meaning.

The following example illustrates other ways to use context clues.

Barbara is stationed with the army in Germany. She is the *liaison* officer, or cooperating agent, for the German and American forces.

In this example, the key word *or* helps you to define *liaison*. The phrase *or cooperating agent* defines a *liaison* as "a person who helps two groups cooperate."

Other useful key words that help to define unknown words are *because, that is, means, such as,* and *is called.* Look at this example and use context clues to figure out the meaning of the *italic* word.

Procrastination is called the thief of time because it always results in postponing an action.

What do you think *procrastination* means? Using the words following *is called* and *because,* you could conclude that *procrastination* is the act of postponing, or putting off, something you should do.

Another way of defining a new word is to search for its opposite meaning.

I was *skeptical* about his promise. However, I had to believe what he said.

Note the key words in this example. Words such as *however, yet, still, nevertheless, but, instead of,* and *while* indicate an opposite meaning. *Skeptical* refers to "doubt or disbelief."

Punctuation marks following an unfamiliar word can also be important. Look especially for commas, parentheses, or dashes.

Don suffered from a *phobia*—an irrational fear.

EXERCISE 3

Directions: For each sentence, use context clues to figure out the meaning of the italicized word. Write the meaning in the space provided.

1. Instead of being straightforward with his views, the candidate often *equivocates.*

_____

2. In *The Bridge of San Luis Rey,* we learn about the characters through *flashbacks,* or the recalling of events from the past.

_____

3. She was Leona's *surrogate* mother; that is, she replaced Leona's real mother.

   _____

4. Kathryn Kuhlman was blessed with *charisma*. She had the remarkable power of being able to heal people.

   _____

5. Today's computers include *modular* designs, a feature that allows you to add self-contained components or units to the basic system.

   _____

6. "An apple a day keeps the doctor away" is a famous *proverb*, yet few people know that Benjamin Franklin wrote this wise saying.

   _____

7. Martin Luther King, Jr., was the *bellwether* for the Civil Rights movement in the United States. He was the one who led African Americans on the road to equality.

   _____

8. The suspected carriers of the strange plague were in *quarantine*, which means they were effectively isolated from the rest of the hospital patients.

   _____

Answers are on page 219.

Writing Activity 1

Read these three words and their definitions.

monologue—a speech or dramatic sketch performed by one person

philanthropist—one who promotes the welfare of the human race, especially by giving huge donations

genealogy—the tracing of a person's ancestors or family tree

Choose one of the three words and write a descriptive paragraph in which you use the word you have chosen, but do not define it. Instead, provide as many context clues to its meaning as possible.

Answers will vary.

Chapter Review

Questions 1–8 refer to the following passage.

WHO LIVED IN NEW MEXICO?

Bleached cow skulls remind one of
Abiquiu's Georgia O'Keeffe, of wranglers,
and hardship. And countless ristras, strands
of blazing red chili peppers, hung from
5   ranch house porches, kindle the memory of
New Mexico's fiery past.

First, there were prehistoric hunters,
some as long as 11,500 years ago. Later,
Navajos and Apaches hunted deer and
10 antelope, wove rugs, and painted pots
eventually included among the world's
collectibles. Next, the Spanish arrived.
Compelled by rumors of gold, Francisco
Vasquez de Coronado rode up the Rio
15 Grande from Mexico in 1540 with priests
following close behind. By 1599, Juan de
Onate, the first governor, was in office.

Finally, Anglo frontiersmen arrived from
the East to tie their horses in plazas of
20 towns whose older residents still today
speak a Spanish which would be intelligible
to Cervantes. From Missouri to New Mexico,
cowboys and longhorns suffered the rigors
of the Santa Fe Trail.

25 The railroad ended an era when it
pushed its pistons across the plains
beginning in 1880. Then as now, passengers
who wanted to enjoy New Mexico's
unpolluted, intoxicating air got off at Lamy,
30 a hamlet as unchanged by time as Santa Fe's
Palace of the Governors, built in 1610.

—Excerpted from an article by Dennis Landt,
Home and Away magazine

1. Which title best expresses the main idea of
    the passage?

    (1) The Spanish in New Mexico
    (2) The History of New Mexico
    (3) The Santa Fe Trail
    (4) Travel in New Mexico
    (5) New Mexico During the 19th Century

2. According to the passage, when did the first
    Spanish arrive in New Mexico?

    (1) 1599
    (2) 1800
    (3) with the railroad
    (4) before the Apaches and Navajos
    (5) after the Navajos and Apaches

3. Why did Coronado explore New Mexico?

    (1) to bring Christianity to the people
    (2) to take possession of new land
    (3) to find gold
    (4) to reach the Rio Grande
    (5) to find areas suitable for raising cattle

4. What are *ristras*?

    (1) bleached cow skulls
    (2) strands of chili peppers
    (3) ranch house porches
    (4) prehistoric hunters
    (5) Anglo frontiersmen

5. What is the main idea of the last paragraph?

    (1) The coming of the railroad marked the
         end of an era.
    (2) The railroads first pushed across the
         plains in 1880.
    (3) Pistons drive railroads.
    (4) New Mexico has clean air.
    (5) The buildings of Santa Fe are ancient.

6. What is a *hamlet*?

   (1) a railroad piston
   (2) a palace of governors
   (3) a settlement unchanged over time
   (4) a train station
   (5) a town with few people and clean air

7. What does New Mexico today have in common with the New Mexico of 1880?

   (1) fresh air
   (2) the Santa Fe trail
   (3) red chili peppers
   (4) deer and antelope
   (5) the Indian life

8. Which group was the first to come to New Mexico?

   (1) Navajos
   (2) wranglers
   (3) Anglo frontiersmen
   (4) prehistoric hunters
   (5) Apaches

Questions 9–15 refer to the following passage.

WHAT DID THE NARRATOR WANT TO LEARN?

The first thing I ever learned in the way of book knowledge was while working in this salt-furnace. Each salt-packer had his barrels marked with a certain number. The
5 number allotted to my stepfather was "18." At the close of the day's work the boss of the packers would come around and put "18" on each of our barrels, and I soon learned to recognize that figure wherever
10 I saw it, and after a while got to the point where I could make that figure, though I knew nothing about any other figures or letters.

From the time that I can remember
15 having any thoughts about anything, I recall that I had an intense longing to learn to read. I determined, when quite a small child, that, if I accomplished nothing else in life, I would in some way get enough education to
20 enable me to read common books and newspapers. Soon after we got settled in some manner in our new cabin in West Virginia, I induced my mother to get hold of a book for me. How or where she got it I do
25 not know, but in some way she procured an old copy of Webster's "blue-back" spelling-book, which contained the alphabet, followed by such meaningless words as "ab," "ba," "ca," "da." I began at once to
30 devour this book, and I think that it was the first one I ever had in my hands.

—Excerpted from *Up from Slavery,*
by Booker T. Washington

9. What is the meaning of *induced* in line 23?

    (1) helped
    (2) persuaded
    (3) allowed
    (4) taught
    (5) commanded

10. What is the best title for this passage?

    (1) How I Learned the Number "18"
    (2) My Early Education
    (3) My Job in the Salt-Furnace
    (4) The First Book I Owned
    (5) Pioneer Life in West Virginia

11. Which of the following had no influence on the narrator's early education?

    (1) the effect of memorizing the number "18" on salt barrels
    (2) the old copy of Webster's "blue-back" spelling book
    (3) his desire to learn to read
    (4) his desire to obtain a better job than his stepfather's
    (5) his mother's ability to get hold of a book for him

12. When did the narrator obtain his first book knowledge?

    (1) when he was working as a saltpacker
    (2) when he moved to West Virginia
    (3) when he obtained the dictionary
    (4) when he first saw the alphabet
    (5) when his stepfather showed him a newspaper

13. The word *procured* in line 25 has several meanings. What does the word mean in this story?

    (1) got possession of
    (2) took care of
    (3) brought about
    (4) achieved
    (5) accomplished

14. The word *devour* in line 30 has several meanings. What does the word mean in this story?

    (1) eat
    (2) destroy
    (3) enjoy greatly
    (4) prey upon
    (5) use up

15. In this story, what does the number "18" signify?

    (1) the writer's age
    (2) the number of saltpackers
    (3) the number of barrels packed per day
    (4) the number marked on the stepfather's barrels
    (5) the age at which the writer learned to read

Answers are on pages 219–220.

CHAPTER 2

Application

In this chapter, you will learn how to interpret and apply information from one place to a different situation.

Application of Ideas

One kind of inference skill is the *application of ideas*. This involves taking information from its source and applying it to another situation.

> Stress is a human condition resulting from mental or physical strain. People facing new or difficult situations often experience stress.

According to the definition, put a check in front of the situation that would result in stress.

_____ (1) a walk in the park

_____ (2) a job interview

_____ (3) eating your favorite meal

Choice (2), a job interview, would result in stress.

You applied the definition of stress to a specific situation. The key words *new* and *difficult situations* helped you find the correct answer.

Writing Activity 2

Imagine that you have just interviewed for a job you'd really like to get. Write a letter to the person who interviewed you. Say how much you appreciate being considered for the position. Emphasize your enthusiasm and your specific abilities to meet the employer's needs.

Let the interviewer understand that you are interested and available immediately.

Answers will vary.

EXERCISE 1

Directions: Read the passage and answer the questions in the space provided.

Advertising plays a vital role in the nation's economy. Americans spend more than $33 billion a year on this enterprise. No other country invests in advertising as the United States does.

Advertising is found in media ranging from newspapers to outdoor signs. About 85 percent (or 85 cents out of every dollar) of newspaper advertising is done by local businesses and individuals. Radio receives about 70 percent of its advertising activity from the local community. National advertising is a favorite approach of mail-order houses. Magazines and television have great appeal to national advertisers.

The following chart shows the top three types of media for advertising and the percentage of money spent on each.

Newspapers 30%	Television 20%
Direct mail 14%	All others 36%

Other forms of advertising include window displays, sale displays, and telephone directories. Novelties such as pencils, matchbooks, and business cards are inexpensive but useful advertising tools.

1. You want to sell your refrigerator. Where would you most likely place your ad?

   _____

2. You are president of General Gadget Corporation. You want to tell the country about the latest in your new line of gadgets. Where would you advertise to reach the most people?

   _____

3. The U.S. Postal Service has just delivered your favorite catalog. What kind of advertising is this?

   _____

4. Out of every dollar spent on advertising, how many cents does television account for?

   _____

EXERCISE 2

Directions: Read the passage below. Then put a check in front of the correct answer to the questions that follow.

How should you introduce two dogs to each other?

Adopting a dog from an animal shelter is a wonderful way to gain a pet. There are thousands of dogs that find their way into shelters each year as strays or unwanted animals. Because of this abundance, you should have no problem finding a wide range of dogs to choose from. The tricky part of dog adoption often arises when you have a pet already established in your household.

When you first introduce your new dog to your current family dog (we'll call him Fido), it is best to be on neutral territory. A public park or field will work nicely. Keep both dogs on leashes, and allow them to sniff each other to say "hello." Watch carefully for signs of aggression in either dog, and be prepared to separate them if necessary. Puffed hair along your dog's back, a tucked tail, or bared teeth are signs to look out for. If the first meeting goes smoothly, reintroduce the dogs at your home, preferably outdoors. Be aware that you may have to keep one or both dogs on leashes and/or in different parts of the house for some time as they adjust to each other.

Feeding time can be interesting when you bring a new dog into your house, especially if Fido is set in his ways, and loves his dinner, as most dogs do! Always keep separate food and water bowls for your two dogs, and place them in different rooms, if possible. Feed Fido before you feed the newcomer—it's an ego-boost for Fido, and reminds the new dog to tread lightly—he's the new kid in town!

1. Which title would be most appropriate for this passage?

_____ (1) Too Many Strays

_____ (2) New Dogs Are Hilarious

_____ (3) Warning Signs of Dog Aggression

_____ (4) Dog Adoption 101

_____ (5) A New Friend For Fido

2. According to the passage, where is the best place to introduce your dog to the new dog?

_____ (1) at the shelter

_____ (2) indoors

_____ (3) outdoors

_____ (4) in your yard

_____ (5) in a dog crate

3. Which of the following could be a sign of aggression or hostility in a dog?

_____ (1) whining and howling

_____ (2) sniffing

_____ (3) fur standing up

_____ (4) running in circles

_____ (5) tail wagging

4. Your dog growls and snaps at the new dog when he comes near his food dish. What should you do?

_____ (1) Feed the dogs near each other so they can see each other eating.

_____ (2) Separate the dogs and feed the new dog after your first dog is fed.

_____ (3) Pet the new dog and reassure it.

_____ (4) Put your dog outside to eat so the new dog doesn't bother it.

_____ (5) Change dog food brands to give your dogs some variety.

Answers are on page 220.

EXERCISE 3

Directions: Read the recipe and then answer the questions in the space provided.

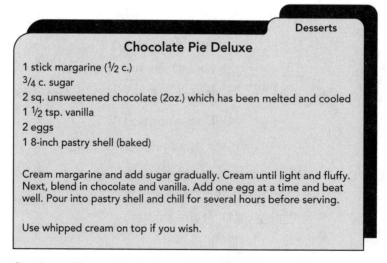

Desserts

Chocolate Pie Deluxe

1 stick margarine (½ c.)
¾ c. sugar
2 sq. unsweetened chocolate (2oz.) which has been melted and cooled
1 ½ tsp. vanilla
2 eggs
1 8-inch pastry shell (baked)

Cream margarine and add sugar gradually. Cream until light and fluffy. Next, blend in chocolate and vanilla. Add one egg at a time and beat well. Pour into pastry shell and chill for several hours before serving.

Use whipped cream on top if you wish.

1. According to the recipe, what should be done right after the margarine and sugar are creamed until fluffy?

_____

2. How many eggs would you need for two pies?

_____

3. What is the next step after the eggs are beaten into the mixture?

_____

4. How much margarine equals one-half cup?

_____

Answers are on page 220.

EXERCISE 4

Directions: Read the passage below. Circle *T* for each true statement, or *F* for each false statement.

The Great Depression

The Great Depression was a worldwide business slump of the 1930s. It ranked as the worst and longest period of high unemployment and low business activity in modern times. The Great Depression began in October 1929, when stock values in the United States dropped rapidly. Thousands of stockholders lost large sums of money. Many of these stockholders were even wiped out. Banks, factories, and stores closed and left millions of Americans jobless and penniless. Many people had to depend on the government or charity to provide them with food.

President Herbert Hoover held office when the Great Depression began. The voters elected Franklin D. Roosevelt president in 1932. Roosevelt's reforms gave the government more power and helped ease the depression.

The Great Depression ended after nations increased their production of war materials at the start of World War II. This increased level of production provided many jobs and put large amounts of money back into circulation.

The depression had lasting effects on the United States government and on many Americans. For example, the government took more responsibility than ever before for strengthening the nation's economy. In addition, many Americans who lived during the depression stressed the importance in later years of acquiring such material comforts as household appliances and an automobile.

—Excerpted from *The World Book Encyclopedia* © 1995 World Book, Inc. By permission of the pubisher. www.worldbook.com

T F **1.** "The Great Depression" is an appropriate title for this passage.

T F   **2.** The purpose of this passage is to criticize.

T F   **3.** According to the selection, Roosevelt's reforms helped the economy recover.

T F   **4.** From this passage, we can infer that hard times have a long-lasting effect.

Answers are on page 220.

EXERCISE 5

Directions: Read the instructions. Then answer the questions in the space provided.

How does a fax machine work?

Turn the machine on by pressing the lighted button on the left corner of the keypad. Then insert the document you wish to fax face-down and top-first into the document feeder. Press the FAX button at the top of the keypad, and select BLACK for a black-and-white fax, or COLOR for a colored fax using the buttons at the bottom of the keypad. The document will then be drawn through the fax machine to be scanned, at a rate of 15 seconds per page. After all pages have been scanned, dial the number to which you will be sending the fax, using the green number buttons on the left side of the keypad. Press ENTER after you input the fax number to send the fax. The ENTER button is located in the lower right corner of the keypad. You will hear the fax machine dial the number and connect to the recipient's fax machine. It will take approximately 30 seconds per page to send the fax.

1. How long will it take to send a 4-page fax?

_____

2. According to the instructions, what do you do after your document has been scanned by the fax machine?

_____

3. What step comes before you select the color of your fax?

_____

4. Which side of the document you are faxing should be visible to you when it is placed in the document feeder—the front or back?

_____

Answers are on page 220.

Chapter Review

Questions 1–6 are based on the following passage.

HOW DOES THE NARRATOR FEEL?

The words still echoed in my ears: "You're pregnant, about two months along." The doctor broke the news to me after my examination. She spoke with a thick accent. I
5 guessed that she was from India.

The people at the Community Clinic were very nice to me, especially the social worker. She told me about the alternatives. I could keep the baby, have an abortion, or
10 give it up for adoption.

They didn't know that my parents split up when I was fifteen. I ran away and met Larry. We lived together in Uptown and ran errands for his "important" friends. Then I
15 moved back with Mama after we had a fight.

I walked down Wilson Avenue back to the apartment. The heat brought people out on the sidewalks, and they were hanging from the porches. I felt that they were
20 staring at me.

I had to tell Larry what happened. I walked up the dark, musty stairway to apartment 252A. I knocked and knocked, but he didn't answer. When I rang the office
25 bell, I asked Sam where Larry was.

"Went to Texas, Sue. Left about two nights ago. He took everything with him but the roaches. Y'know he still owes me back rent. Is there . . . is there anything I can do
30 for you?" he asked with a startled look of concern.

I was shocked and turned away from Sam as I felt tears trickle down my face. Damn that Larry. Did he know too and then
35 leave me?

I ran from the building and walked to the lakefront until the locusts buzzed in the trees. They were there, yet I couldn't see them, just like my baby.

40 "Pregnant-pregnant," they seemed to say. Were they happy for me or were they mocking me? I really couldn't tell.

1. According to the passage, which statement about the doctor is correct?

   (1) She is from India.
   (2) She wears thick glasses.
   (3) She has a thick accent.
   (4) She tells Sue about available alternatives.
   (5) She recommends adoption as the best alternative.

2. How does the news of the pregnancy affect the main character?

   (1) She is enthusiastic.
   (2) She appears indifferent.
   (3) She is self-assured.
   (4) She chooses to keep the baby.
   (5) She is confused and upset.

3. How would you best describe the author's attitude toward the young woman in this passage?

   (1) indifferent
   (2) ironic
   (3) optimistic
   (4) arrogant
   (5) sympathetic

4. What can you infer about Sue's childhood and adolescence?

   (1) She was brought up in a happy home.
   (2) Her parents put Sue's needs ahead of theirs.
   (3) She and her family grew up in the South.
   (4) Sue was forced to grow up more quickly than usual.
   (5) As one of several children in her family, Sue didn't get enough attention.

5. What can you infer about Sue and Larry's relationship?

   (1) They love each other very much.
   (2) They enjoy living and working together.
   (3) They are not able to work out their problems with each other.
   (4) Larry is happy about Sue's pregnancy.
   (5) Larry wants Sue to give up the baby for adoption.

6. Why does Larry go to Texas?

   (1) He must find a job to support Sue and the coming baby.
   (2) He is behind on rent payments.
   (3) He can no longer live in their roach-infested apartment.
   (4) Larry knows about the pregnancy.
   (5) The passage does not say why he left.

Answers are on page 220.

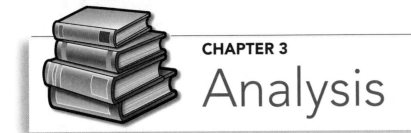

CHAPTER 3

Analysis

When you analyze something you read, you break it down into its parts to understand the whole. In this chapter, you will learn how to make inferences and draw conclusions from something you read. You will look at the patterns of organization writers use to present their ideas in a certain order. You will also study the types of words writers use (style) and the emotional bias often found in a piece of writing (tone).

Some of the ways materials are organized include the following patterns:

- order of importance
- sequence of events
- cause and effect
- comparison and contrast
- classification

Inferences

An *inference* is an educated guess about something that is not directly stated in a passage but is strongly hinted at or implied. For a complete understanding of written material, you must be able to make inferences wherever necessary.

When the main idea of a paragraph or a passage is not directly stated, you must infer it from whatever information is provided.

The main idea of the paragraph below is unstated. Notice, though, how the details help you infer what it is.

> Some drove up in beat-up station wagons and dusty pickup trucks. Other, more citified types arrived in shiny convertibles or new campers. Cousin Otis Barnett, who owned half of the county, brought his family to the occasion in a private jet. Last, but not least, came Jack and Marge Barnett, oldest living members of the clan. They gladly volunteered details about their 22 great grandchildren.

The main idea of this passage is a family reunion. Did you correctly infer it? Four generations of an extended family—young and old, rich and poor—have gathered for a special occasion. You simply put the details together to come up with the main idea. Even the vocabulary helps you—*cousin, clan, great grandchildren*.

Use your inference skills to answer the questions below based on the following passage.

Mom had come to live with us after my father-in-law died. With her came all of her huge pots and pans (she cooked for an army), her noodle machine, all her jars for canning, her pizzelle iron [a metal mold for making deep-fried desserts], her jars of roasted peppers, her superlong rolling pin. Our house was transformed—you would open a closet door and get hit with a string of garlic. Inside several drawers, seeds were growing for something that would be planted later in the garden. On the counter was always a pot of water with lupini beans soaking.

And everywhere there was flour. She made noodles almost every day—just to pass the time, she would say. You would sit down and get up with flour all over your clothes. There was flour on the children, flour on the dog, flour choking all my plants, getting into all our lungs, threatening to kill us all. Sometimes I thought we were all the filling in one big pasta.

—Excerpted from an article by Judy Esway, *New Covenant* magazine

1. Who is Mom?

_____

2. Where would you most likely find Mom?

_____

3. How does the author feel about Mom?

_____

For question 1, Mom is the author's mother-in-law. You can infer this from the first sentence, which explains that Mom moved in after the author's father-in-law passed away. For question 2, Mom would be in the kitchen because she loves to cook. For question 3, the author regards Mom as an imposition, or someone who gets in the way. You can infer this from her complaints that Mom took over the kitchen, flour was everywhere, and family members seemed to become "all the filling in one big pasta."

EXERCISE 1

Directions: Read the passage below and answer the questions that follow.

They descended rapidly, directly over a large and imposing city in the middle of a vast, level, beautifully planted plain. While they were watching it, the city vanished and the plain was transformed into a heavily timbered mountain summit, the valleys falling away upon all sides as far as the eye could reach.

"Well, I'll say that's *some* mirage!" exclaimed Seaton, rubbing his eyes in astonishment. "I've seen mirages before, but never anything like that. Wonder what this air's made of? But we'll land, anyway, if we finally have to swim!"

The ship landed gently upon the summit, the occupants half expecting to see the round disappear before their eyes. Nothing happened, however, and they disembarked, finding walking somewhat difficult because of the great mass of the planet. Looking around, they could see no sign of life, but they *felt* a presence near them—a vast, invisible something.

Suddenly, out of the air in front of Seaton, a man materialized; a man identical with him in every detail, even to the smudge of grease under one eye, the small wrinkles in his heavy blue serge suit, and the emblem of the American Chemical Society, which formed the pendant of his watch-fob.

—Excerpted from *The Skylark of Space,*
by E. E. Smith

1. Put a check in front of the statement that best summarizes the entire passage.

_____ (1) Seaton and his crew encounter strange events on a new planet.

_____ (2) Seaton meets his double on an unknown planet.

_____ (3) This city was located on a level, planted plain.

2. What effect does the disappearing city have on Seaton?

_____ (1) He is terrified.

_____ (2) He is astonished but persistent.

_____ (3) He can't decide what to do.

3. Which of the following can you infer about Seaton and the crew?

_____ (1) They need space suits to survive on the planet.

_____ (2) They want to turn back.

_____ (3) They are courageous.

Answers are on page 220.

Order of Importance

When presenting information according to its order of importance, you have two choices. Either you can build upward from a small detail to the central idea or you can work downward from the most important point. The following example starts with the most important point. The details that come next are progressively less important. The least important detail concludes the passage.

> The typical household budget includes many fixed expenses. Rent or mortgage payments rank among the highest expenditures. Next is the cost of food, always on the rise. Fuel bills also drain finances, especially during the heating season. Telephone, electricity, gas, and water cost less if families conserve usage. Finally, taxes, home and life insurance, and medical bills should be considered; they often entail only once- or twice-a-year obligations.

EXERCISE 2

Directions: Read the passage and then put a check in front of the correct answer to the questions that follow.

> Small signs of a sugar binge [uncontrolled eating] were already there. As Vana opened the refrigerator, her eyes darted from the box of raisins to the leftover apple pie and back again. Then Vana gazed at the grapefruit. Before reaching for the melba toast in the cupboard, she gently fingered the package of sandwich cookies and the new brownie mix. Although these distractions annoyed her, she felt cool and calm.
>
> On her way out of the house, Vana sipped a can of diet cola. Fantasies about swimming in a chocolate shake drifted in and out of her head.
>
> She felt herself weakening after she parked in the shopping center. Passing the bakery was too much. The sweet smells of freshly baked donuts and cakes greeted her senses. Rows of pies, sweet rolls, and cookies beckoned. This was a rendezvous [meeting] with old friends. In that very hour, Vana devoured five glazed donuts and four brownies. The diet was over.

1. Which of the following details is the most important in the passage?

_____ (1) the fantasy about the milkshake

_____ (2) the binge at the bakery

_____ (3) the meal of grapefruit and melba toast

_____ (4) the cookies in the cupboard

2. In what order are the details presented?

_____ (1) least important to most important

_____ (2) most important to least important

Answers are on page 220.

Drawing Conclusions

Drawing a conclusion is a common type of inference skill. Suppose you and a friend decide to see a movie together. You agree to meet at the library at 7:00 P.M. and then walk to the movie, which starts at 7:30.

You arrive at the library at 6:45. At 7:10, your friend still has not arrived. By 7:30, you realize that your friend is not coming. You go home.

When you decide to go home, you are drawing a conclusion. Your friend has not actually told you anything, but, based on the fact that this person is half an hour late and the movie has started, you conclude that you have been stood up and that your friend is not coming.

EXERCISE 3

Questions 1–6 are based on the following conversation.

        [in a local bar]

   PAUL: Hey, Tom! Have a seat! Haven't seen you in a long time. How's it going?

   TOM: I've just had the worst day of my life.

   PAUL: How's that? *[orders two beers]*

5 TOM: I just left the court. We split for good, me and the wife. She got the kids, the house, everything.

   PAUL: Sorry to hear that. *[passes the pretzels]* I've been there, two years ago,
10 you know.

   TOM: Yeah, at least your kids were grown. I've got little ones and a dead-end job.

   PAUL: Being a welder isn't the end of the line.

15 TOM: When you pay big alimony it is. *[pause]* She's living with lover boy, too.

   PAUL: So kill her with kindness.

   TOM: Are you crazy?

   PAUL: I've learned that much. Love is
20 bigger than anything. The hate will pass. And you'll feel better, too.

   TOM: Impossible!

   PAUL: Hang in there, Tom. I've got to get back to the office.

1. From this passage, what can you infer about Paul?

    (1) He is younger than Tom.
    (2) He is about the same age as Tom.
    (3) He is older than Tom.
    (4) He is Tom's brother.
    (5) He is Tom's father.

2. Which of the following jobs is Paul most likely to have?

    (1) insurance salesman
    (2) construction worker
    (3) teacher
    (4) druggist
    (5) auto mechanic

3. According to the passage, what is the source of Tom's troubles?

    (1) drinking too much
    (2) having a dead-end job
    (3) feeling lonely
    (4) owing his wife money
    (5) getting divorced

4. From the conversation, what can you conclude about Tom?

    (1) He will take Paul's advice.
    (2) He will reject Paul's advice.
    (3) He will think about Paul's advice.
    (4) He will share Paul's advice.
    (5) He will like Paul's advice.

5. What can you conclude about Tom?

    (1) He is pleased with his job.
    (2) He works in a courtroom.
    (3) He builds houses.
    (4) He makes a salary he is proud of.
    (5) He dislikes his job.

6. What does the word *alimony* in line 15 probably mean?

    (1) court costs
    (2) house payments
    (3) support payments made to a spouse
    (4) home-improvement costs
    (5) school tuition costs

Answers are on page 221.

Sequence of Events

Information is commonly organized according to a sequence-of-events approach. This approach lists events in the order in which they occurred. This approach is widely used in history, newspapers, and fiction. Recipes and instructions generally follow a sequence of events, too.

Certain words can help you spot a passage that is based on a sequence of events. These words include *first, second, third, finally, before, after, next,* and *then*.

As you read the following passage, think about the sequence it presents. Then put a check in front of the correct answer to the question that follows.

Brown Leather Dye: Directions

Clean old polish and dirt from leather surface. Household cleaning fluid may be necessary. Shake well with top on. Remove top, invert bottle, press applicator against shoe. Apply liberally to badly scuffed areas first; then dye entire shoe. Apply two or more coats of dye if necessary. Let dry for 30 minutes between applications. After use, rinse applicator in water, blot dry, replace top. Dry shoes overnight before polishing or wearing them.

1. According to the directions, which sequence of steps is correct?

_____ (1) Apply dye liberally. Then remove old polish and dirt.

_____ (2) Dye entire shoe before applying dye to badly scuffed areas.

_____ (3) Dry shoes overnight before dyeing.

_____ (4) Dye entire shoe after applying dye to badly scuffed areas.

The correct sequence is given in choice (4), *Dye entire shoe after applying dye to badly scuffed areas.* Choice (1) is incorrect because the passage tells you to clean shoes before applying any dye. Choice (2) is the direct opposite of the correct sequence given in the passage. Choice (3) would be reasonable if shoes were soaked, but the passage does not address the matter of dyeing wet shoes.

EXERCISE 4

Directions: Read the following passage and answer the questions that follow.

Jake and the Bear

Old Jake Cochran was a gold miner. One night, while searching for gold in the high mountains of Canada, he made his camp by a stream. Near the stream he saw large tracks. He decided they probably belonged to a bear that had come to the stream to fish. Not wanting the animal in camp, he hung his food from a tree several yards from his tent and his campfire.

Before dawn, Jake was awakened by a crashing sound. He leaped from his sleeping bag to peer out of his tent into the dim light. He saw the back of a huge, fur-covered creature rummaging through his food, which the creature had pulled down from the tree. Jake reached for his gun. First, the creature stood up and growled. Then, it turned around to face Jake, looking more like a gigantic man than a bear. It stood upright like a man, but it must have weighed at least a thousand pounds, with thick, dark fur. After staring at Jake for what seemed like forever, the creature snatched some food in its front, pawlike hands, then disappeared into the brush with a few long strides.

1. In what order did the following events occur? Number them in correct sequence.

    _____ Jake was awakened by a noise.

    _____ Jake camped near a stream.

    _____ The creature turned around and looked at Jake.

    _____ Jake saw that a creature had pulled his food down from the tree.

    _____ The manlike creature disappeared.

2. Given the sequence of events, what should Jake do next?

    _____ (1) move his food into his tent

    _____ (2) move his camp

    _____ (3) call the police

Answers are on page 221.

Cause and Effect

Writers frequently use cause and effect to organize material. *Causes,* or reasons, are presented together in one place. *Effects,* or results, are grouped in another.

You are out walking alone one night. Just as you reach a dark yard bordered by a fence and dense hedges, a big German shepherd jumps into view, barking furiously. The scare almost takes your breath away. The sound of your footsteps (cause) has disturbed the dog (effect). The dog's furious barking (cause) scares you (effect).

Think about cause and effect as you read the following passage.

The National Character

Why did thousands of pioneers move west in the last century? Some settlers wanted more space because of rapid population growth in the East. Others like Kit Carson and Buffalo Bill yearned for an adventure. Many people rushed to stake out rich new farmland or to claim a king's ransom in gold.

Even though these reasons were the most obvious ones for the movement west, the underlying basis for pioneering rests in the national character. Right up to the present day, Americans have taken pride in their rugged individualism. The settler's ability to overcome obstacles with his or her own ingenuity was essential. Today, young Americans share this heritage in their affection for superheroes.

Look at the first line of the passage. Is westward migration presented as a cause or as an effect? Reread the first paragraph. Are the reasons for the westward migration presented as causes or as effects? In this passage, the effect (westward migration) is mentioned before the causes (desires for space, land, gold, and challenge). But, in fact, the effect resulted from the various causes. In real life, the causes came first.

Certain words can help you recognize a cause-and-effect passage. Look at the word *reasons* in the first line of the second paragraph. It is an important clue. It tells you that this passage is probably built around cause and effect. Other key terms that may indicate cause and effect include *cause, effect, due to, result, because, consequence, source, outcome, basis,* and *product.*

EXERCISE 5

Directions: Read the passage below. Circle *T* for each true statement, or *F* for each false statement.

Norberto's Secret

Every day after supper was done and the baby was asleep in his crib, Norberto and Carmen sat down to the work of the night. Husband and wife became student and teacher.

As a boy, Norberto had had little formal education. What schooling he did have was poor. As he grew up, it became increasingly difficult for him to admit that he could not read. Instead, he just pretended to understand, keeping his unhappy secret to himself.

But when he met Carmen, he did not try to keep the secret from her. She understood and did not judge. She urged him to see a specialist at the reading clinic.

At first, Norberto resisted. He hated the thought of telling a stranger that he—a father, a husband, a grown man—had never learned to read. But there was something he hated even more—being unable to read a story to the baby. A good father should be able to read his own son a bedtime story.

So Norberto began to study with Carmen at home. Once he learned how to read a little, he was not embarrassed to go to the clinic. The teachers there promptly saw how determined he was. They were able to help him make maximum progress in minimum time.

T F 1. As a child, Norberto did not learn to read because his schooling was poor and irregular.

T F 2. Carmen helped Norberto because that's what the reading specialist advised.

Answers are on page 221.

Comparison and Contrast

Writers use *comparison* to show similarities and *contrast* to show differences. Apples and oranges are both fruits that grow on trees. They taste sweet and contain seeds. Because they are alike in these respects, we can compare their similarities.

But we can also contrast their differences. An apple is red and an orange is orange. An orange has a rough pebbly skin; an apple's skin is smooth. You can eat the skin of an apple, but orange peel is bitter.

Some passages use only comparison or only contrast. Others contain both. The following passage is about two brands of dog food.

PRIDE leads the pack!
Your pet knows the difference.

In nationwide taste tests, dogs of all breeds chose PRIDE over its closest competitor, Champ—67 percent to 33 percent.

Your canine friend will get the same nutritional value as with other brands. In fact, 100 percent of the daily requirements of vitamins and minerals goes into PRIDE.

The best part about PRIDE is the price. It's cheaper than Champ, but there's no difference in weight or quality. Reward your dog with PRIDE, the premium dog food at a price you can afford.

1. According to the ad, which dog food is better?

_____

2. Compare the two brands.

_____

3. Contrast the two brands.

_____

The purpose of the ad is to persuade you that PRIDE is better. Comparison and contrast are both used to accomplish this.

The nutritional information, weight, and quality are presented as comparisons. In these respects, PRIDE is similar to its competition.

The taste and price information are presented as contrasts. Dogs like PRIDE better. PRIDE is cheaper. When it comes to flavor and economy, PRIDE and the competition are nothing alike. They are quite different, and the differences favor PRIDE.

Certain key terms can help you recognize passages of comparison and contrast. These include: *compare, contrast, more than, comparison, differ, less than, alike, different, prefer, similar, on the other hand, larger, smaller, on the one hand, although, same, equal, better than, worse than,* and *both.*

EXERCISE 6

Directions: Read the following passage and then answer the questions in the space provided.

Running for Office

Peter Lopez and John Gates are running for district representative this November. Each man has striking similarities to the other, yet there are profound differences between them.

Pete and John both come from the west end of Elmwood. However, John now lives in the affluent Oak Hills section, while Pete still occupies the plain frame house where he was born. Both candidates were star basketball players at Elmwood High School. They also served in the Vietnam War. Pete and John believe strongly in their community and in their country, but Pete is a Democrat and John a Republican.

On the one hand, Pete Lopez identifies closely with the blue-collar workers and the average citizen. He is a steelworker who supports the rights of the man on the street. He has the support of labor unions and many working-class blacks, Mexicans, and Irish who live in the district.

On the other hand, John Gates receives his backing from professionals, some white-collar workers, farmers, and businesspeople of the area. A self-made millionaire in real estate, Gates gets large donations from his wealthy backers in business.

Both candidates promise the same things: better jobs, better schools, better roads, and better lives for citizens in the district. If elected, would either actually keep his promises?

1. How are Pete and John similar?

   _____

   _____

   _____

2. What campaign promises do both candidates make?

   _____

   _____

   _____

3. How are Pete and John different?

   _____

   _____

   _____

Answers are on page 221.

Classification

To *classify* information means to put it into categories that enhance understanding. Political candidates, for example, can be classified according to such factors as the office they are seeking, their party identification, and their state or district.

Classification is used in the following list of jobs showing the qualifications, salary, and employment outlook for each job.

Occupation	Training and Requirements	Salary Range	Employment Outlook
Auto Mechanic	on-the-job; vocational school; apprenticeship	$19,000–20,000	VG
Licensed Practical Nurse	1 yr. voc. school; 1 yr. hospital training	$13,800–17,600	VG
Machinist	4-yr. apprenticeship	$14,000–21,000	A/G
Postal Clerk	written exam, high school helpful	$14,600–21,000	NG
Secretary	high school or business school	$13,000–20,000	G/VG

1. Which job has the highest starting salary?

   _____

2. Which job requires a 4-year apprenticeship?

   _____

3. What is the outlook for postal clerks?

   _____

For question 1, the *auto mechanic* has the highest starting salary. For question 2, a *machinist* must serve a 4-year apprenticeship. For question 3, the job outlook for postal clerks is *not good (NG)*.

EXERCISE 7

Questions 1–3 refer to the following passage.

WHAT DOES A CHILD DO BEFORE GOING TO SLEEP?

Before adults go to sleep, they usually read, watch television, or listen to the radio. It's all very conventional. What a child uses to promote slumber [sleep] is a real surprise.

5   Take my nine-year-old, for instance. Here is a list of things I found in his bed one night. The first thing I saw was his collection of toys. His toy car lay overturned near the pillow. Spider-Man was still battling the Star

10 Trek spaceship, and two walkie-talkie batteries stood lonely and forlorn on the bedpost.

    As I rearranged the blankets, all kinds of Halloween candy spilled on the floor. There

15 were leftover Tootsie Rolls, Life Savers, and pieces of bubble gum. Mars bars wrappers littered the sheets like fallen leaves. Never one to neglect his schooling, my sleepyhead cuddled up to his world globe with nose

20 pointed north. In the educational grouping, I also found one stubby pencil and The Book of Lost Treasure.

    Finally, in the mixed category, I uncovered two volcanic rocks from our trip

25 to Arizona and one cowboy hat from Yellowstone National Park. As I turned off the light, I gently pulled a dirty sock from under his arm. I kissed him good-night and returned to my adult world.

1. According to the passage, in which category is the world globe?

   (1) toys
   (2) candy
   (3) education
   (4) travel
   (5) mystery

2. Which of the following would be in the mixed category?

   (1) pencil
   (2) walkie-talkie batteries
   (3) bubble gum
   (4) dirty sock
   (5) Spiderman

3. In which category are the two batteries?

   (1) toys
   (2) candy
   (3) education
   (4) travel
   (5) mystery

Answers are on page 221.

Style and Tone

Style and tone refer to the way writers use words. ***Style*** refers to particular types of words and sentences. Writing styles can be formal or informal, flowery or concise, dramatic, and poetic. Let's examine three styles of communication.

"Thanks for your help. You did a super job on our house." *(Informal)*

"Thank you for your assistance. Your work on our house was of the highest quality." *(Formal)*

"Your invaluable assistance has been most deeply appreciated. The fruits of your labor are sure to astound all who enter our abode." *(Flowery)*

As you can see, there are real differences among these styles; however, the basic message is the same: "You did a good job!" An informal style is characterized by short, simple words and sentences. A more formal style uses more difficult words and longer sentences. A flowery style uses very fancy words in long, winding sentences.

Tone refers to emotion. Tone may be serious or humorous, sad or happy, angry or pleasant. A writer with an optimistic outlook on a subject uses a bright, upbeat tone. A gloomy tone is likely to characterize an article by a writer with a pessimistic point of view.

Learn to recognize irony and sarcasm. ***Irony*** is a type of writing that implies that something is not what it appears to be. When people speak ironically, they say the opposite of what they mean. The million-dollar-lottery winner who says, "All this money lying around is a bit of a nuisance," is speaking ironically. ***Sarcasm*** is a tone of bitter humor. It is usually directed at a particular target. Here are the reactions of two passengers during a turbulent flight.

Passenger 1: "I haven't had so much fun since kindergarten."

Passenger 2: "Where'd they find this flight crew, anyway? The circus?"

The two passengers react in quite different ways. The first passenger takes an ironic tone, finding the whole situation more amusing than anything else. The second passenger is plainly sarcastic. The tone of bitterness toward the crew is unmistakable.

EXERCISE 8

Directions: Read the passage below and then put a check in front of the correct answer to the questions that follow.

A Driver's Nightmare

It was an evil night to be driving. The wind drove the rain in great sheets onto the windshield. The wipers could not keep up with the downpour.

Cheri drove slowly. She had left her last client late and probably
5 should have stayed in town, but Sal had demanded that she drive on to Union City. That way, she would be there for the breakfast appointment with a new client.

Suddenly Cheri slammed on her brakes.

"What was that? I thought I saw something in the road. Someone
10 crouching. I must have imagined it. Whoa, I must be tired . . . talking to myself."

Cheri had increased her speed again when she heard a pop. The car swerved savagely to the right.

"Oh, no . . . not a flat . . . not tonight—I don't even have a spare."
15 The car rolled to a stop near a ditch. She felt for her flashlight, found it in the glove compartment, and got out of the car. The flashlight beam came to rest on the tire, sagging useless against the soggy ground.

"Better try to find help."

Cheri looked through the black trees that lined the road.
20 Somewhere to her left, she heard a dog howl.

Her flashlight stabbed the darkness. She walked back down the road, head down against the driving rain. Then she saw the row of nails on the road. She could see the place where her tires had disturbed them. Someone had deliberately placed a straight line of nails across
25 the right lane.

Her eyes widened in fear. A cold knot gripped her stomach. She began to run, blindly.

1. How would you describe the style of lines 9–11?

_____ (1) formal

_____ (2) emotional

_____ (3) informal

2. What is the overall tone of the passage?

_____ (1) ironic

_____ (2) tense

_____ (3) angry

Answers are on page 221.

EXERCISE 9

Directions: Read the speech below and then answer the questions that follow in the space provided.

CITIZENS!

It is now time for the people of this country to unite themselves under the banner of comradeship, to establish a strong front against the ills that beset us all. When each person acts solely for his or her own best interest, the masses suffer. When all people work together for the common good, they all profit. I ask all people to work for the common good.

1. The style of this passage is _____.

2. The tone of this passage is _____.

Answers are on page 221.

Writing Activity 3

Write one short classified advertisement in paragraph form for one of these categories: apartments for rent, used cars for sale, child-care services.

Limit your ad to one paragraph. Don't use abbreviations. Just write several descriptive sentences about the specific product or service you are advertising. Make sure to include the kinds of detail a prospective customer would want to know before responding to your ad.

Answers will vary.

EXERCISE 10

Directions: Study the book list below and then put a check in front of the correct answer to the questions that follow.

Books to Read

LEVEL I

Daugs, Richard. *The Golden Years: Fit for Life.* Gallery Books, 1990. Gives tips on exercise, finances, and getting new interests.

Falk, Ursula A. *On Your Own: Independent Living for Older Persons.* Prometheus, 1989. Provides insights into the stresses of loneliness, finances, and physical security.

Friedan, Betty. *The Fountain of Age.* Simon & Schuster, 1993. Distinguishes what is irreversible after 40 from what remains open to choice and vitality.

Larue, Gerald A. *Gereoethics: A New Vision of Growing Old in America.* Prometheus, 1992. Assesses the impact of societal values on the elderly and how they may respond to them.

Solomon, David H., et al., eds. *A Consumer's Guide to Aging.* Johns Hopkins University Press, 1992.

LEVEL II

Berman, Phillip L., ed. *The Courage to Grow Old.* Ballantine, 1989. Presents inspirational essays on the philosophies of aging by 41 prominent men and women.

Cole, Thomas R. *The Journey of Life: A Cultural History of Aging in America.* Cambridge University Press, 1992.

Rountree, Cathleen. *On Women Turning 50.* HarperSanFrancisco, 1993. Profiles of 18 women over 50 from the fields of politics, science, education, business, and the arts.

Swisher, Karin, ed. *The Elderly: Opposing Viewpoints.* Greenhaven, 1990. Uses magazines, books, and position papers for a wide range of individuals and organizations.

Vierck, Elizabeth. *Fact Book on Aging.* ABC-CLIO, 1990. Presents hundreds of facts from housing and health care to travel and community involvement for people who are 65 and over.

1. How are the entries arranged in the two lists?

   _____ (1) in alphabetical order by author

   _____ (2) alphabetically by title

   _____ (3) alphabetically by publisher

2. Which author presents profiles of individuals over the age of 50?

   _____ (1) Rountree

   _____ (2) Vierck

   _____ (3) Friedan

3. When was the newest book on the list published?

   _____ (1) 1992

   _____ (2) 1993

   _____ (3) 1994

4. Which author would you recommend to an elderly person confronting a personal fear of aging?

   _____ (1) Solomon

   _____ (2) Berman

   _____ (3) Cole

5. Which book presents ideas on exercise and finances?

   _____ (1) *A Consumer's Guide to Aging*

   _____ (2) *Fact Book on Aging*

   _____ (3) *The Golden Years: Fit for Life*

Answers are on page 221.

EXERCISE 11

Directions: Read the following passage. Circle *T* for each true statement, or *F* for each false statement.

Taming the Wind

The problem of billowing skirts in windy plains country was no minor one, and though it was met and overcome, there is some evidence that the solution was the work of a male—none other than our old friend, George Armstrong Custer. When the Custers went to Fort Riley after
5 the Civil War, Elizabeth's dresses were all "five yards around, and gathered as full as could be into the waistband." On her first walk across the windy prairie ground, her skirt billowed like a balloon, flew out in front, then lifted over her head. His military dignity thus affronted, George immediately figured out a way to keep his wife's skirts at their
10 proper level. He cut some lead bars into strips and ordered Elizabeth to sew them into the hems of her dresses. Thus weighted down, she was able to outwit the elements while taking her constitutionals about the post. Other women followed her example, and a dozen years later all were wearing bar lead in their skirt hems on the windy western plains.

—Excerpted from *The Gentle Tamers*, by Dee Brown

T F **1.** The style of the passage is best described as military.

T F **2.** The tone of the passage is critical.

T F **3.** When Elizabeth Custer first walked across the windy prairie, her skirts were wildly blown about.

T F **4.** Other women followed Elizabeth's example.

T F **5.** George Custer's idea was for women to weigh their skirts down with metal strips.

T F **6.** Another word for *constitutionals* is walks.

T F **7.** The material in Mrs. Custer's dress measured about three yards at the waistband.

T F **8.** The other women on the plains laughed at Custer's absurd idea.

Answers are on page 222.

Chapter Review

Questions 1–12 on the next two pages are based on the following passage.

WHAT IS AUNT ROSIE'S ADVICE?

"Anger is just hurt covered over," Aunt Rosie had said. "If you want to solve the problem, stay in touch with the hurt. Don't let the anger take over or you'll never get

5 anything worked out. The ego uses anger to build a fence around itself so it won't get hurt again."

I heard the click of the door. "Stay in touch with the hurt," I told myself. I thought

10 about her advice. Les was late again. He'd said he'd be home by six. It was nearly 8:30.

Les stood hesitantly, as if I were going to throw something.

"Sorry I'm late," he said softly. He had

15 tired lines around his eyes and mouth. His shoulders drooped.

"I felt really hurt that you weren't here when you said you would be. I fixed a really nice dinner, but it's all cold now," I said.

20 "I'm sorry. I couldn't even call. The boss insisted I go out to that new construction site and settle the change of plans with the foreman. I couldn't even get to a phone to call you . . . thanks for not being mad."

25 Aunt Rosie was right, I thought. If I had hit him full tilt with anger, we'd have just had a big fight. I smiled at him.

"Well, it can't be undone now, I guess," I told him. I wasn't feeling angry anymore.

30 Les put down his briefcase and drew me into his arms. "Tell you what," he said, "How 'bout Friday night, we'll go out to eat—just to make up for tonight's ruined dinner."

"OK," I agreed. Then to myself I said,

35 "Thanks, Aunt Rosie, you were right. If you want to solve the problem, don't let anger take over. Stay in touch with the hurt."

1. According to Aunt Rosie, what is the best way to prevent problems in a relationship?

   (1) Don't let anger take over.
   (2) Control the hurt.
   (3) Call when you're going to be late.
   (4) Get your anger out into the open.
   (5) Stay in touch with your partner's feelings.

2. Which inference CANNOT be drawn from the passage?

   (1) Aunt Rosie is a busybody.
   (2) Aunt Rosie is a wise woman.
   (3) The author loves her husband.
   (4) Les did not intend to make his wife angry.
   (5) Adults can learn to change their patterns of behavior.

3. What is the main idea of the passage?

   (1) Inconsiderate behavior can destroy a marriage.
   (2) Aunt Rosie can't resist interfering.
   (3) Anger is pain in disguise.
   (4) The author is overworked.
   (5) Les is overworked.

4. Suppose a neighbor carelessly trampled some flowers you had just planted. What would Aunt Rosie most likely advise you to do?

   (1) Say nothing and plant new flowers.
   (2) Confront the neighbor and demand to know how a person could be so careless.
   (3) Send the neighbor a letter requesting that the person replace the flowers that were destroyed.
   (4) Insist that the neighbor repay you what the flowers cost.
   (5) Quietly tell the neighbor how this carelessness has upset you.

5. What is the style of this passage?

   (1) poetic
   (2) flowery
   (3) informal
   (4) dramatic
   (5) formal

6. According to Aunt Rosie, what does the expression of anger result in?

   (1) divorce
   (2) solving problems
   (3) staying in touch with the hurt
   (4) nothing productive
   (5) clearing the air

7. Why was there no big fight?

   (1) Les finally came home on time, for a change.
   (2) The author expressed her disappointment calmly and truthfully.
   (3) The boss let Les call home.
   (4) Aunt Rosie intervened.
   (5) The couple went out to dinner.

8. What expression of feeling did Les expect from his wife when he came home late from work?

   (1) fear
   (2) anger
   (3) calm acceptance
   (4) amusement
   (5) understanding

9. Why did Les come home late from work?

   (1) He went out for a drink with friends.
   (2) He stayed in the office to catch up on his work.
   (3) He felt hurt about a previous argument.
   (4) He had to do work for his boss.
   (5) He made a habit of working late each night.

10. From the passage, what can you infer about Les?

    (1) He is a construction worker.
    (2) He is a real estate agent.
    (3) He is a architect.
    (4) He is a landscaper.
    (5) He is a retail salesperson.

11. How would you describe Les's frame of mind as he came home late from work?

    (1) angry and confused
    (2) sorry and hesitant
    (3) hurt and depressed
    (4) belligerent and angry
    (5) calm and happy

12. How would you characterize the writer's tone?

    (1) optimistic
    (2) angry
    (3) confused
    (4) gloomy
    (5) amused

Answers are on page 222.

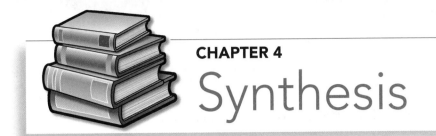

Synthesis

The GED Language Arts, Reading Test will require you to answer questions about a passage by analyzing parts of it and gathering information about the passage as a whole. Synthesis is one way of thinking—requiring us to analyze different parts of a passage to understand it as a whole, or apply information from outside the passage to increase our understanding of it.

When you answer synthesis questions, you will combine all of your observations and understanding of a passage, and add to that your own personal knowledge and world experiences to achieve a higher level of understanding.

In this chapter, you will focus on the following:

- studying the way a passage is organized

- looking at the choices an author made when he or she wrote the passage, including: the tone (or mood) of the passage, the point of view of the passage (who is the speaker), and the purpose of the passage (what did the author intend to express when he or she wrote it)

- making connections between different parts of the passage

- applying extra information (or information you know already) to the information provided in the passage

Now, let's practice the skills you need to answer synthesis questions.

Tone, Point of View, and Purpose in a Passage

Tone

In some synthesis questions, you will be asked to describe the tone of an entire passage. To do this, you will have to read the passage carefully, and decide what the mood of the speaker seems to be based on the language he or she uses and the way the author arranges these words in the passage.

EXERCISE 1

Directions: Read the following passage and think about the speaker's tone.

How is Pap feeling?

Pap wasn't in a good humor—so he was his natural self. He said he was down to town, and everything was going wrong. His lawyer said he reckoned he would win his lawsuit and get the money, if they ever got started on the trial; but then there was ways to put it off a long time and Judge Thatcher knowed how to do it. And he said people allowed there'd be another trial to get me away from him and give me back to the widow for my guardian, and they guessed it would win, this time. This shook me up considerable, because I didn't want to go back to the widow's any more and be so cramped up and sivilized, as they called it. Then the old man got to cussing and cussed everything and everybody he could think of, and then cussed them all over again to make sure he hadn't skipped any, and after that he polished off with a kind of a general cuss all round, including a considerable parcel of people which he didn't know the names of, and so called them what's-his-name, when he got to them, and went right along with his cussing.

He said he would like to see the widow get me. He said he would watch out, and if they tried to come any such game on him he knowed of a place six or seven mile off, to stow me in, where they might hunt till they dropped and they couldn't find me. That made me pretty uneasy again, but only for a minute; I reckoned I wouldn't stay on hand till he got that chance.

—Excerpted from *Adventures of Huckleberry Finn* by Mark Twain, 1885

1. Which word best represents the tone of the speaker in this passage?

_____ (1) disappointed

_____ (2) confident

_____ (3) humorous

_____ (4) embarrassed

_____ (5) excited

2. How does the speaker seem to feel towards Pap?

_____ (1) affectionate and loving

_____ (2) amused and comfortable

_____ (3) afraid and intimidated

_____ (4) surprised and worried

_____ (5) impressed and amazed

Answers are on page 222.

Point of View

Some authors may choose to have an outsider (someone who is not taking part in the events of the story) narrate (tell) the story. Other authors may choose to have one of the characters in the story tell about what is happening, as he or she participates in the events.

EXERCISE 2

Directions: Read the short passages below, and try to determine who is telling the story. Write an *O* in the blank if it is an outside narrator telling the story. Write a *P* in the blank if the narrator is a participant in the story.

_____ 1. Mrs. Pocket was sitting on a garden chair under a tree, reading, with her legs upon another garden chair; and Mrs. Pocket's two nursemaids were looking about them while the children played. "Mamma," said Herbert, "this is young Mr. Pip." Upon which Mrs. Pocket received me with an appearance of amiable dignity.

—Excerpted from *Great Expectations* by Charles Dickens, 1861

_____ 2. Albert went away regretfully, but the drayman and some of the Methodist ladies were in Mr. Holliday's yard, packing chairs and tables and ice-cream freezers into the wagon, and the twins forgot the sick cat in their excitement. By noon they had picked up the last paper napkin, raked over the gravel walks where the salt from the freezers had left white patches, and hung the hammock in which Vickie did her studying back in place.

—Excerpted from *Old Mrs. Harris* by Willa Cather, 1932

_____ 3. And right there he'd stay, watching that door like a hawk until I came through it again. Well he'd just have to watch it for a while; I was doing the best I could.

—Excerpted from *The Sound and The Fury* by William Faulkner, 1929

_____ 4. And she told her sister, as well as she could remember them, all these strange Adventures of hers that you have just been reading about; and, when she had finished, her sister kissed her, and said "It *was* a curious dream, dear, certainly; but now run in to your tea; it's getting late." So Alice got up and ran off, thinking while she ran, as well as she might, what a wonderful dream it had been.

—Excerpted from *Alice's Adventures in Wonderland* by Lewis Carroll, 1865

_____ 5. We were there for many hours. I remember the search boats and the sunset when dusk came. I had never seen a sunset like that: a bright orange flame touching the water's edge and then fanning out, warming the sea.

—Excerpted from *The Joy Luck Club* by Amy Tan, 1989

Answers are on page 222.

EXERCISE 3

Questions 1–3 are based on the following passage.

WHAT DOES ESTELLA REMEMBER?

The garden was too overgrown and rank for walking in with ease, and after we had made the round of it twice or thrice, we came out again into the brewery yard. I
5 showed her to a nicety where I had seen her walking on the casks, that first old day, and she said with a cold and careless look in that direction, "Did I?" I reminded her where she had come out of the house, and
10 given me my meat and drink, and she said, "I don't remember." "Not remember that you made me cry?" said I. "No," said she, and shook her head and looked about her. I verily believe that her not remembering and
15 not minding in the least, made me cry again, inwardly—and that is the sharpest crying of all.

"You must know," said Estella, condescending to me as a brilliant and
20 beautiful woman might, "that I have no heart—if that has anything to do with my memory."

—Excerpted from *Great Expectations*
by Charles Dickens, 1861

1. According to the passage, which of these descriptions best matches the speaker?

   (1) a character in the story who has no part of the action
   (2) the elderly father of Estella
   (3) a speaker who is observing the actions of Estella and the other characters, but not taking part in the action
   (4) a young man who is part of the story
   (5) one of Estella's relatives

2. How does the narrator appear to feel about Estella?

   (1) in love with her
   (2) afraid of her
   (3) angry with her
   (4) apologetic
   (5) excited and motivated

3. Which of the following words best describes the tone of the passage?

   (1) entertaining
   (2) spontaneous
   (3) easy-going
   (4) bitter
   (5) heartbreaking

Answers are on page 223.

Purpose in a Passage

When you read a passage composed of multiple paragraphs, look at the common ideas found in all of the paragraphs to determine the meaning or main idea of the passage. The author's purpose in writing is usually tied to the main idea of the passage. Be sure you consider each paragraph as part of the passage, and don't get distracted by the main idea or theme in one of the paragraphs by itself.

EXERCISE 4

Directions: Read the passage and answer the questions that follow.

Why is a Man Upset?

It was useless. He couldn't read. He couldn't do anything. The wailing of the child pierced the drum of his ear. It was useless, useless! He was a prisoner for life. His arms trembled with anger and suddenly bending to the child's face he shouted:

"Stop!"

The child stopped for an instant, had a spasm of fright and began to scream. He jumped up from his chair and walked hastily up and down the room with the child in his arms. It began to sob piteously, losing its breath for four or five seconds, and then bursting out anew. The thin walls of the room echoed the sound. He tried to soothe it but it sobbed more convulsively. He looked at the contracted and quivering face of the child and began to be alarmed. He counted seven sobs without a break between them and caught the child to his breast in fright. If it died! . . .

The door was burst open and a young woman ran in, panting.

"What is it? What is it?" she cried.

The child, hearing its mother's voice, broke out into a paroxysm of sobbing.

"It's nothing, Annie . . . it's nothing . . . He began to cry . . . "

She flung her parcels on the floor and snatched the child from him.

"What have you done to him?" she cried, glaring into his face.

Little Chandler sustained for one moment the gaze of her eyes and his heart closed together as he met the hatred in them. He began to stammer:

"It's nothing . . . He . . . he began to cry . . . I couldn't . . . I didn't do anything . . . What?"

Giving no heed to him she began to walk up and down the room, clasping the child tightly in her arms and murmuring:

"My little man! My little mannie! Was 'ou frightened, love? . . . There now, love! There now . . . Lambabaun! Mamma's little lamb of the world! . . . There now!"

Little Chandler felt his cheeks suffused with shame and he stood back out of the lamplight. He listened while the paroxysm of the child's sobbing grew less and less; and tears of remorse started to his eyes.

—Excerpted from "A Little Cloud" *(Dubliners)* by James Joyce, 1914

1. What is the relationship between the narrator and Annie?

_____ (1) they are brother and sister

_____ (2) they are husband and wife

_____ (3) they are friends

_____ (4) they are neighbors

_____ (5) they are strangers

2. What word would describe the tone of the passage?

_____ (1) soothing

_____ (2) joyful

_____ (3) regretful

_____ (4) frightening

_____ (5) tense

3. What is the purpose of the passage?

_____ (1) to demonstrate how well the narrator takes care of children

_____ (2) to illustrate the relationship between the narrator and Annie

_____ (3) to explain how to calm a crying child

_____ (4) to show the depths of a mother's love

_____ (5) to reveal the narrator's horrible temper

Answers are on page 223.

Linking the Ideas of a Passage

Nearly every form of writing is composed of paragraphs. For written ideas to flow smoothly, an author must work to connect each paragraph so that their ideas unite and their intentions are clear to the reader.

On the GED Language Arts, Reading Test you may be asked to read a passage, determine the ideas that individual paragraphs express, and then determine the purpose or intention of the entire paragraph. Remember to focus on the main idea of the entire passage rather than the main idea of each paragraph.

EXERCISE 5

Directions: Read this passage from *The Wind in the Willows,* and answer the questions that follow.

Who is Out There?

There was nothing to alarm him at first entry. Twigs crackled under his feet, logs tripped him, funguses on stumps resembled caricatures, and startled him for the moment by their likeness to something familiar and far away; but that was all fun, and exciting. It led him on, and he penetrated to where the light was less, and trees crouched nearer and nearer, and holes made ugly mouths at him on either side.

Everything was very still now. The dusk advanced on him steadily, rapidly, gathering in behind and before; and the light seemed to be draining away like floodwater.

Then the faces began.

It was over his shoulder, and indistinctly, that he first thought he saw a face: a little evil wedge-shaped face, looking out at him from a hole. When he turned and confronted it, the thing had vanished.

He quickened his pace, telling himself cheerfully not to begin imagining things, or there would be simply no end to it. He passed another hole, and another, and another; and then—yes! no!—yes! certainly a little narrow face, with hard eyes, had flashed up for an instant from a hole, and was gone. He hesitated—braced himself up for an effort, and strode on. Then suddenly, and as if it had been so all the time, every hole, far and near, and there were hundreds of them, seemed to possess its face, coming and going rapidly, all fixing on him glances of malice and hatred: all hard-eyed and evil and sharp.

If he could only get away from the holes in the banks, he thought, there would be no more faces. He swung off the pace and plunged into the untrodden places of the wood.

Then the whistling began.

Very faint and shrill it was, and far behind him, when first he heard it; but somehow it made him hurry forward. Then, still very faint and shrill, it sounded far ahead of him, and made him hesitate and want to go back. As he halted in indecision it broke out on either side, and seemed to be caught up and passed on through out the whole length of the woods to its furthest limit. They were up and alert and ready, evidently, whoever they were! And he—he was alone, and unarmed, and far from any help; and the night was closing in.

Then the pattering began.

—Excerpted from *The Wind in the Willows* by Kenneth Grahame, 1908

1. What sort of words or language patterns does the author use to form connections between the paragraphs in this passage?

_____

_____

_____

_____

2. How does the narrator feel in the first two paragraphs?

_____

_____

3. How does the narrator feel in the next four paragraphs?

_____

_____

4. How does the narrator feel in the last three paragraphs?

_____

_____

5. What is the purpose of this passage?

_____ (1) to discuss the sounds the narrator hears

_____ (2) to describe the faces the narrator sees

_____ (3) to demonstrate the narrator's increasing fear

_____ (4) to describe the woods at night

_____ (5) to suggest that the woods are haunted

Answers are on page 223.

Incorporating Outside Information

The GED Language Arts, Reading Test will include questions called *expanded synthesis* questions, in addition to the types of synthesis questions presented earlier in this chapter. Expanded synthesis questions will provide you with additional facts or information not found in the passage. To answer the expanded synthesis questions, you must apply that additional information to the information you have gathered from the passage and draw a conclusion. Read the following passage and the additional information that follows it, and use all of the information to answer the question.

> I really have discovered something at last.
>
> Through watching so much at night, when it changes so, I have finally found out.
>
> The front pattern [of the wall-paper] does move—and no wonder! The woman behind shakes it!
>
> Sometimes I think there are a great many women behind, and sometimes only one, and she crawls around very fast, and her crawling shakes it all over.
>
> Then in the very bright spots she keeps still, and in the very shady spots she just takes hold of the bars and shakes them hard.
>
> And she is all the time trying to climb through. But nobody could climb through that pattern—it strangles so.
>
> —Excerpted from *The Yellow Wallpaper* by Charlotte Perkins Gilman, 1892

Later in the story, we find that the narrator experiences a mental breakdown and begins to hallucinate after spending a great deal of time alone in her room.

Based on this information and the passage you have read, what can you assume about "the woman" described in the passage?

(1) She is trapped in the walls.

(2) She is a ghost that haunts the narrator's room.

(3) She is a figment of the narrator's imagination.

(4) She is trying to scare the narrator by moving around.

(5) She is part of the narrator's family.

The first sentence of this question provides you with information that is not found in the passage you read—it is revealed later in the story. In the passage, the narrator describes the bizarre actions of a woman she sees in her room. When you apply the new information you received (in the question) to the narrator's description of this woman in the passage, you realize that the narrator is imagining the woman due to her declining mental state. Answer (3) is the best answer.

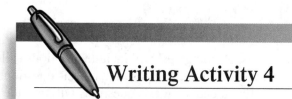

Writing Activity 4

Practice brainstorming the pros and cons of one or more of the following issues:

- year-round school

- the movie rating system

- mandatory school uniforms

- raising the legal driving age

Divide a sheet of paper into two columns. Write PROS at the top of one column, and CONS at the top of the other one. Pick one of the debatable issues from above, and list pros and cons for it on your paper. Then ask a parent or teacher to do the same thing. Compare your lists of pros and cons, and discuss the differences in the ways you approached the issue.

Answers will vary.

Chapter Review

Questions 1–7 are based on the following passage.

WHAT IS PEPE GOING TO DO?

When he was ready and mounted before the door, mounted on his father's saddle that was so old that the oaken frame showed through torn leather in many
5　places, then Mama brought out the round black hat with the tooled leather band, and she reached up and knotted the green silk handkerchief about his neck. Pepé's blue denim coat was much darker than his jeans,
10　for it had been washed much less often.

Mama handed up the big medicine bottle and the silver coins. "That for the medicine," she said, "and that for the salt. That for a candle to burn for papa. That for
15　dulces [candy] for the little ones. Our friend Mrs. Rodriguez will give you dinner and maybe a bed for the night. When you go to the church say only ten Paternosters and only twenty-five Ave Marias. Oh! I know, big
20　coyote. You would sit there flapping your mouth over Aves all day while you looked at the candles and the holy pictures. That is not good devotion to stare at the pretty things."

25　The black hat, covering the high pointed head and black thatched hair of Pepé, gave him dignity and age. He sat the rangy horse well. Mama though how handsome he was, dark and lean and tall. "I
30　would not send thee now alone, thou little one, except for the medicine," she said softly. "It is not good to have no medicine, for who knows when the toothache will come, or the sadness of the stomach. These
35　things are."

"Adios, Mama," Pepé cried. "I will come back soon. You may send me often alone. I am a man."

—Excerpted from "Flight" (*The Long Valley*)
by John Steinbeck, 1938

1. How does Mama feel about sending Pepé on the journey?

   (1) enthusiastic
   (2) reluctant
   (3) confident
   (4) terrified
   (5) calm

2. Which of the following statements best describes Mama's opinion of Pepé?

   (1) He is still her little boy.
   (2) He is mature and trustworthy.
   (3) He is sneaky and deceitful.
   (4) He can look out for himself.
   (5) He is smart and resourceful.

3. When Mama refers to Pepé as "big coyote" in the second paragraph, how would you describe her tone?

   (1) sarcastic
   (2) respectful
   (3) mean
   (4) humiliating
   (5) demanding

4. Why does Pepé tell his mother "I am a man," at the end of the passage?

   (1) He is 18, and legally an adult.
   (2) He wants to assure her that he will be fine.
   (3) He is trying to impress his mother and siblings.
   (4) He wants his friends to respect him.
   (5) He wants his mother to leave him alone.

5. From the references to papa in the passage, what can you conclude about him?

   (1) He does not like his son to travel.
   (2) His family is glad he is gone.
   (3) His family respects and misses him .
   (4) He is gone on an errand and will return soon.
   (5) He cannot read or write.

6. From whose point of view is this passage told?

   (1) from one of Pepé's siblings' point of view
   (2) from an unnamed character in the story's point of view
   (3) from Pepe's point of view
   (4) from an outside observer's point of view
   (5) from Mama's point of view

7. Which choice best represents the author's purpose for this passage?

   (1) to introduce us to Pepé and his family
   (2) to criticize Pepé for his immaturity
   (3) to honor papa
   (4) to describe the place where Pepé lives
   (5) to set the scene for Pepé's journey

Questions 8–11 refer to the following passage.

WHAT DID RICHARD TELL DICKIE?

Joan had sunk into that first deep trough of sleep and was slow to awake. Richard had to repeat, "I told him."

"What did he say?"

5 "Nothing much. Could you go say goodnight to him? Please."

She left their room, without putting on a bathrobe. He sluggishly changed back into his pajamas and walked down the hall. Dickie
10 was already in bed. Joan was sitting beside him, and the boy's bedside clock radio was murmuring music. When she stood, an inexplicable light—the moon?—outlined her body through the nightie. Richard sat on the
15 warm place she had indented on the child's narrow mattress. He asked him, "Do you want the radio on like that?"

"It always is."

"Doesn't it keep you awake? It would me."

20 "No."

"Are you sleepy?"

"Yeah."

"Good. Sure you want to get up and go to work? You've had a big night."

5 "I want to."

Away at school this winter he had learned for the first time that you can go short of sleep and live. As an infant he had slept with an immobile, sweating intensity
10 that had alarmed his babysitters. In adolescence he had often been the first of the four children to go to bed. Even now, he would go slack in the middle of a television show, his sprawled legs hairy
15 and brown. "O.K. Good boy. Dickie, listen. I love you so much, I never knew how much until now. No matter how this works out, I'll always be with you. Really."

Richard bent to kiss an averted face but
20 his son, sinewy, turned and with wet cheeks embraced him and gave him a kiss on the lips, passionate as a woman's. In his father's ear he moaned one word, the crucial, intelligent word: "*Why?*"

25 *Why.* It was a whistle of wind in a crack, a knife thrust, a window thrown open on emptiness. The white face was gone, the darkness was featureless. Richard had forgotten why.

—Excerpted from *Separating* by John Updike, 1979

8. What is the purpose of the narrator's description of Dickie's sleeping habits in lines 6–15?

   (1) to express the narrator's worry over Dickie's lack of sleep
   (2) to reveal that Dickie had been cared for by babysitters
   (3) to help reveal Dickie's age using chronology
   (4) to show a father's love for his son using expressive language
   (5) to add humor to an otherwise dark story

9. Why does the author compare Dickie's single-word question: "Why?" to a "whistle of wind in a crack, a knife thrust, a window thrown open on emptiness" (lines 25–27)?

   Dickie's question
   (1) startles his father and makes him think
   (2) hurts his father deeply
   (3) is insulting and threatening to his father
   (4) makes his father feel lonely
   (5) is something he will apologize for later

10. Based on the information in the passage, who is Joan?

    (1) the narrator's mother
    (2) the narrator's wife
    (3) Dickie's wife
    (4) the narrator's daughter
    (5) Dickie's sister

11. Earlier in the story, Richard tells Dickie that he and Dickie's mother will be separating.

    Based on this information and the passage, how do you think Richard felt about telling his son this news?

    (1) concerned
    (2) excited
    (3) afraid
    (4) satisfied
    (5) hopeful

    Answers are on page 223.

PART II

Understanding Language Arts, Reading

CHAPTER 5

Nonfiction Prose

In this chapter, you will study nonfiction prose. The subjects of nonfiction prose include real people, places, events, and social issues. When you read a newspaper or a magazine, an essay or a speech, a biography or an account of a true experience, or a memo or employee handbook, you are reading nonfiction prose.

Reading Nonfiction Prose

News articles and feature stories are the most common kinds of nonfiction prose. News articles report breaking events—a fire, a robbery, or an election result. They are built around the five Ws: *who, what, when, where,* and *why.* The key information is presented first.

When reading a news story, ask yourself:

- Who or what is the subject of the story?

- What happened?

- When and where did the events take place?

- Why did they occur?

Features are not as limited by time as straight news is. They can examine almost any subject of general interest. Breaking news is often the starting point for feature pieces. But features can also stand perfectly well by themselves.

EXERCISE 1

Directions: Read the nonfiction selection below. Circle *T* for each true statement, or *F* for each false statement.

Covenant House, New York City

Covenant House offers shelter to over 20,000 homeless youths each year who roam 42nd Street. It is a place where the young runaways and delinquents of Times Square can find sanctuary and hope.

Sister Rose McGeady is the director. With a staff of 70 full-time workers and almost 200 part-timers, she keeps Covenant House open 24 hours a day. No child is ever turned away.

In the dangerous world of 42nd Street, sex and drugs are big business. Pimps, drug dealers, and pornography hustlers lure young people into crime with cruel promises of money and security.

The children who turn up at Covenant House tell horror stories of life on the street. An 11-year-old explains how he was given a new video game for spending a night as a male prostitute. A 14-year-old says her first job was acting in a pornographic movie. A friend of hers was stabbed to death after refusing to shoot heroin with a customer.

Covenant House offers help to young victims of crime and indifference. Runaways receive food, clothing, shelter, medical care, counseling, and job training. "It's a fresh start," says one 16-year-old who, a month ago, was running away from neighborhood gangs. "A fresh start in a safe place."

T F **1.** Covenant House is located in Times Square.

T F **2.** Criminals lure teenage runaways with offers of money.

T F **3.** Covenant House is one of 70 shelters for homeless children in the 42nd Street area.

T F **4.** The purpose of the article is to present a profile of the director.

T F **5.** The youngest child mentioned in the article was 9 years old.

T F **6.** The child who was knifed to death had once been turned away from Covenant House.

T F **7.** The full-time staff at Covenant House numbers almost 200.

T F **8.** In the street world of drugs and sex for sale, teenage delinquents all too often find sanctuary.

Answers are on page 223.

EXERCISE 2

Directions: Read the selection below, which combines science and history, to report new findings about the death of the emperor Napoleon. Then answer the questions that follow.

The French emperor Napoleon died in 1821, in the prime of his life. One of the most powerful European leaders of all time, he ended his days in exile, a tragic figure. History tells us that the cause of his death was stomach cancer. But recent evidence suggests that he was murdered.

In the book *The Murder of Napoleon,* Sten Forshufvud, a Swedish author, makes a strong case that Napoleon was poisoned by his longtime rival and fellow officer, Count Charles Tristan de Montholon.

The evidence points to arsenic poisoning over a period of five or six years. The autopsy revealed an enlarged liver, a telltale sign of arsenic overdose. Records indicate that, while in exile on the island of St. Helena, Napoleon showed symptoms of chronic arsenic poisoning. Family members reported that he complained of sleepiness, insomnia, swollen feet, and excessive weight gain.

Dr. Forshufvud chemically analyzed strands of Napoleon's hair that relatives had saved. The analysis showed abnormally high traces of arsenic.

The most startling evidence of murder actually came to light in 1840. Napoleon's body was moved to Paris. When the coffin was opened, observers were shocked to see a well-preserved body instead of bones and dust. One of the most unusual effects of arsenic is that it greatly slows the decay of living tissue.

1. According to Dr. Forshufvud, what was the cause of Napoleon's death?

   _____

2. What symptoms of arsenic poisoning did Napoleon have?

   _____

3. How did the autopsy results support Dr. Forshufvud's theory?

   _____

4. What is the strongest evidence that Napoleon died of arsenic poisoning?

   _____

5. What chemical analysis did Dr. Forshufvud perform?

   _____

6. Where did Napoleon spend the last years of his life? Why?

   _____

Answers are on page 223.

EXERCISE 3

Directions: Read the passage below. Circle *T* for each true statement, or *F* for each false statement.

For centuries, venereal diseases (VD) have afflicted king and commoner alike and may even have changed the course of history. Henry VIII and Ivan the Terrible are only two of the rulers now believed to have had syphilis and to have suffered from its complications.

When antibiotics were discovered, many thought that the problem of venereal diseases had been solved.

Such has not been the case. Recent VD increases around the world have indicated that the traditional methods of control—treatment with drugs and tracing an infected person's sexual contacts for treatment—have not been completely effective. Some organisms that cause VD have become increasingly drug resistant and, like other infections, venereal diseases are often transmitted before symptoms occur and treatment is begun.

The National Institute of Allergy and Infectious Diseases (NIAID) several years ago began a program in research on sexually transmitted diseases—primarily syphilis and gonorrhea. These studies are carried out by grant- and contract-supported investigators at institutions around the country.

The NIAID program is based on the opinion of experts who believe that a better basic understanding of all sexually transmitted diseases and of the organisms causing them must be developed before there can be improvement in methods of prevention or therapy.

T F 1. According to the passage, improvement in the treatment of venereal diseases lies in greater use of drug therapy.

T F 2. NIAID's position is that, before there can be substantial improvement in the treatment of venereal diseases, there must be more effective tracing of the sexual contacts of infected persons.

T F 3. NIAID is calling for a better basic understanding of sexually transmitted diseases and their causes.

T F 4. The word *complications* at the end of the first paragraph most likely refers to negative effects.

T F 5. It can be inferred from the passage that some venereal diseases are becoming more difficult to treat.

Answers are on pages 223–224

Facts and Opinions

The ability to distinguish fact from opinion is an important skill. A *fact* can be proved by observation or research. An *opinion* is a personal judgment or belief. Look at the following statements.

Fact: The first American president to resign from office was Richard Nixon.

Opinion: Politicians are all dishonest.

Fact: The United States and Russia possess more nuclear weapons than any other nation.

Opinion: Nuclear weapons will eventually destroy all life on Earth.

Opinions can be introduced with such phrases as *I feel, I think, I believe, in my opinion,* and *from my viewpoint.*

Read the paragraph below and answer the questions that follow in the space provided.

(1) Yesterday, I went to Thrifty's Food Store. **(2)** It seems to me that Thrifty's is the cheapest supermarket in town. **(3)** I noticed that Cluck's Chicken Soup is ten cents less there than at Buy Right. **(4)** Fancy Farms Whole Wheat Bread is two cents a loaf cheaper than at Buy Right. **(5)** Thrifty's offers the best value.

1. Which sentences in the passage are facts? Write the numbers.

    _____

2. Which sentences in the passage are opinions? Write the numbers.

    _____

Sentences (1), (3), and (4) are facts. They name the stores and give specific prices. Sentences (2) and (5) are the personal opinions of the shopper. The words *cheapest* and *best* signal that personal opinions are being stated.

EXERCISE 4

Directions: Read the passage below and then put a check in front of the correct answer to the questions that follow.

A high school diploma or a high school equivalency diploma is vital for success in today's society. One manager at a large company says that he won't hire a person without a diploma. The military wants enlistees to have completed formal education before beginning active duty. Training schools and colleges require applicants to have a high school diploma.

Adults 18 and older can earn a high school diploma through home study or at adult education centers. More than one million adults do so each year. Of these, more than two-thirds pass the five tests required for a high school equivalency diploma, more commonly known as the GED.

I believe one student put it best when he said that the GED offered him a second chance at life. Another explained that a terrible burden had been lifted from her shoulders.

"No doubt about it. My GED made all the difference," declared a recently promoted office worker.

1. Which of the following statements is based on information in the passage?

_____ (1) You can't get a job without a high school diploma.

_____ (2) A high school diploma increases a person's chances for success.

_____ (3) The military will not accept dropouts.

2. According to the selection, which of the following is a fact?

_____ (1) More than one million adults try to complete their high school education each year.

_____ (2) Most employers require at least a high school education.

_____ (3) Most people earn a GED to feel better about themselves.

3. Which of the following is the author's opinion?

_____ (1) Training schools and colleges cater to high school graduates.

_____ (2) A GED certificate offers a second chance for many adults.

_____ (3) Employers place too much emphasis on qualifications.

4. Which of the following describes the graduate who was quoted?

_____ (1) He or she had recently been promoted.

_____ (2) He or she served in the military.

_____ (3) He or she had no opinion.

Answers are on page 224.

Detecting an Author's Bias

Authors' personal opinions can give their writing a positive or negative slant, called a *bias*. Biased writing stresses certain facts and omits others. It makes assertions that are unsupported by facts. Its purpose is to influence the reader toward a particular point of view. Writing that is intended to influence people without their being aware of it is called *propaganda*.

Read each selection below. Write *balanced* if it appears to be truthful and fair. Write *biased* if it distorts or slants information.

1. Buy Wonder Vitamin C today. It's better for you than oranges. Just pop a tablet into your mouth and enjoy the refreshing taste.

    _____

2. The City Council meeting broke up after a lengthy debate. The woman's supporters argued that she was the duly elected representative of the people and should be allowed to take her seat on the council. Her opponents disputed this, saying that her previous disruptions of council activities disqualified her from holding public office.

    _____

3. There is still controversy about the future of the space program. While critics say it diverts much-needed funds away from social programs, supporters point to the great scientific advances that have resulted from the exploration of space. The widespread use of microprocessors is one major result of space-related research.

    _____

4. Do you want the federal government to tax your savings income? Senior citizens will be hurt by this proposed legislation. Don't let greedy Uncle Sam pocket more of your hard-earned money. Write to your representative and senators today.

    _____

Statement 1 is *biased*. The ad is slanted in favor of a commercial product. It claims the vitamin C tablet is superior to oranges. Statement 2 is *balanced*. The author describes what happened and sticks to the facts, offering no personal opinions about either position. Statement 3 is *balanced*. This is a factual explanation of two opposing views of the space program. The author discusses others' opinions but does so in a balanced manner. Statement 4 is *biased*. The author says that the government is greedy and will pocket taxes from the savings of senior citizens. No facts are given to support this.

EXERCISE 5

Directions: As you read the selection below, look for the author's biases. Then put a check in front of the correct answer to the questions that follow.

Do you enjoy your diet when you are trying to lose weight fast? On a low-carbohydrate diet, you give up bread, spaghetti, cake—all the good things in life. On a low-protein diet, you're anemic without steak and homesick for ham. A low-fat diet means turning away from cheddar cheese and chocolate ice cream.

With the Easy Diet Program, you can enjoy life while you peel off the pounds. You simply mix half a cup of Easy Diet Formula in a glass of water, put the mixture into the blender, and sip away your worries. Enjoy the sweet, rich flavor of a milk shake while getting all your daily nutritional requirements. Drink the formula three times a day and lose weight the Easy Diet way!

1. Why does the writer mention the low-carbohydrate, low-protein, and low-fat diets?

_____ (1) to present their good points

_____ (2) to inform the reader about them

_____ (3) to emphasize the advantages of the Easy Diet Program

2. Which of the following best illustrates the use of biased language?

_____ (1) "You're anemic without steak and homesick for ham."

_____ (2) "You give up bread, spaghetti, cake."

_____ (3) "Mix half a cup of Easy Diet Formula in a glass of water."

Answers are on page 224.

Informational Nonfiction

Informational nonfiction includes newspapers, magazines, speeches, research reports, and business documents—sources of factual information. Remember, the topics of nonfiction prose include real people, places, events, and social issues.

Newspapers provide up-to-date information about news in local areas and around the world. They inform people about a wide variety of topics, such as politics, sports, human interest stories, and entertainment. Millions of people read a daily or weekly newspaper so they can stay informed about current events.

Editorials are the opinions of newspapers. One newspaper's stand on an issue can be the opposite of another's. A paper's opinion usually appears on the editorial page so that readers do not confuse it with straight news.

A straight news story about an election, for example, would report the positions that the candidates represent. But an editorial might urge readers to vote for one candidate instead of another.

Periodicals (magazines) are usually published by the week or month. Unlike newspapers, they tend to specialize in a certain topic. You might find a column on hunting or fishing in your local paper, but for an in-depth look at these subjects, you would turn to a magazine such as *Outdoor Life* or *Field and Stream*.

EXERCISE 6

Directions: Read the passage below and answer the questions that follow.

Ever since Israel became independent in 1948, it has had unusual educational needs. Two factors account for this.

First, Israel's topography [land] is inhospitable [harsh]. Much of the country is desert or mountainous. Second, Israel is always in a state of military alert because of border disputes with neighboring countries.

Though this nation of four million has regular primary and secondary schools, the *Nahal* has evolved as a unique educational unit for the special needs of border settlements. The *Nahal* is a branch of the military. Unlike traditional schools, it offers a curriculum composed of military training and cooperative agriculture. It stresses loyalty and social responsibility to the state. In addition to required courses, students can also take dancing, Hebrew, and folksinging.

The basic structural unit of the *Nahal* is the *garin,* a group of young people serving in the army together. Their education begins with basic infantry training. After they learn soldiering, they join a *kibbutz,* a collective farm, to work as farmers on the frontier.

A *garin's* military training never ends. Settlements are always in danger of attack. After months of army training, the members of the *garin* return to civilian life as soldier-farmers.

Match the terms listed on the left with their definitions on the right. Write the correct letter on the line.

_____ 1. topography   (a) the courses that make up a program of study

_____ 2. inhospitable   (b) a place's physical landscape

_____ 3. Nahal   (c) barren and rough

_____ 4. curriculum   (d) an educational unit of the Israeli military

_____ 5. garin   (e) a group of young soldiers who are trained and educated together

_____ 6. kibbutz   (f) a collective farm

_____ 7. civilian   (g) someone who is not in the military

Answers are on page 224.

EXERCISE 7

Directions: Read the editorial below and then put a check in front of the correct answer to the questions that follow.

The city council is debating a ban on the ownership of handguns by private citizens. Supporters argue that one out of every two homicides here is committed with a handgun. A ban on handguns, they say, would drastically reduce the rate of violent crime.

5   We believe that banning handguns won't solve our crime problem. Anyone with an ounce of common sense can see why.

Our Bill of Rights guarantees "the right of the people to keep and bear arms." Government cannot and must not violate this basic freedom under the law. Most of our citizens keep firearms for protection against
10 the small but dangerous minority of armed criminals among us.

If we banned handguns, the illegal buying and selling of firearms would become big business overnight on the black market.

Thousands of us already own handguns. A ban would be impractical, if not impossible, to enforce.

15   And what about the tax increase that would be needed for enforcement? Our city budget is already strained. A new tax would break it.

If someone wants to commit a crime, he will. If he has no handgun, he'll pick up a knife, a pipe, or a bottle. Thieves and murderers are
20 lawbreakers by definition. If they want handguns, no ban is going to stop them. They'll get them on the black market. Or they'll steal them.

When only the bad guys have guns, how will the rest of us defend ourselves against assault or robbery? Law-abiding citizens of all ages will be defenseless.

25   If the city takes away our handguns, it will be robbing us of our rights. We will be unable to meet our responsibilities to protect ourselves and our loved ones. We emphatically oppose any misguided attempts by the city to compromise our safety and jeopardize our lives.

1. What is the purpose of the editorial?

   _____ (1) to inform

   _____ (2) to describe

   _____ (3) to persuade

2. Why does the third paragraph say banning handguns is unacceptable?

   _____ (1) Other weapons are less effective against crime.

   _____ (2) Handgun ownership is guaranteed under the Bill of Rights.

   _____ (3) People will commit crimes regardless of the laws.

3. Which of the following does the editorial NOT imply would happen if handguns were banned?

   _____ (1) Handguns would be bought and sold illegally.

   _____ (2) Taxes would go up.

   _____ (3) The murder rate would drop by half.

4. What does the editorial imply about banning handguns?

   _____ (1) It would make it impossible for ordinary people to protect themselves.

   _____ (2) It would drastically reduce the rate of violent crime.

   _____ (3) It would solve the crime problem once and for all.

Answers are on page 224.

EXERCISE 8

Directions: Now read a second editorial about handguns that has a very different point of view from the last editorial you read. Then put a check in front of the correct answer to the questions that follow.

Three days ago, Lisa Park was murdered. A masked gunman walked into her flower shop and ended her life with a bullet. Less than two weeks before, Officer Donald Smith responded to a domestic disturbance. In a scuffle with an angry husband wielding a handgun,
5 the 31-year-old policeman and father of two was shot dead.

Handguns were involved in 22 of the 38 murders here this year. The time has come to ban these weapons.

Americans today are an angry, quick-tempered people in a society that glorifies crime and criminals. A ban on handguns would help
10 redirect our increasingly violent impulses in less lethal directions.

More than half of all murders and suicides are committed with handguns. And accidental shootings occur routinely because people who do not know how to use handguns have easy access to them. Firearms training, while certainly recommended, is at best only a partial answer.

15 Handguns are more lethal than other weapons. There is no defense against them. It doesn't matter how strong you are or how fast. When crimes are committed with knives or other weapons, injury is more common than death. But when crimes are committed with handguns, victims are more likely to die. It's over in an instant. A handgun is small
20 enough to conceal until the last moment, and then it is too late for all the Lisa Parks and Donald Smiths of this world.

Handguns have no real value for sport, either. Nobody needs handguns except the police and the armed forces.

What would be the result of a handgun ban? Since Great Britain
25 outlawed handguns in the 1920s, its rate of violent crime has dropped dramatically. Despite the fact that even the British police are unarmed, peace and moderation are the rule in English cities and towns.

We, too, need to ban handguns to make our community a safer place to live and work.

1. What is the main point of the editorial?

_____ (1) Handguns are a major cause of violence in the community.

_____ (2) Great Britain is an example of effective handgun control.

_____ (3) The murder rate in the community is far too high.

2. What does the word *scuffle* (line 4) mean?

_____ (1) fight

_____ (2) race

_____ (3) dispute

3. According to the editorial, what would happen if a handgun ban went into effect?

_____ (1) Criminals would find it easier to prey on defenseless citizens.

_____ (2) Violent crime would decrease.

_____ (3) Criminals would have all the guns.

4. Both editorials about handguns agree that better protection is urgently needed for whom?

_____ (1) shop owners

_____ (2) handgun owners

_____ (3) potential victims of crime

Answers are on page 224.

Writing Activity 5

In 1994, an American teenager living in Singapore was arrested on vandalism charges for spray-painting cars. Under Singapore law, vandalism is punishable by caning. The American youth received four painful lashes with a rattan cane. The caning provoked a huge controversy in the United States. Are you for or against such punishment? Write a two- or three-paragraph editorial defending your opinion. In each paragraph, discuss one reason for your position.

Answers will vary.

EXERCISE 9

Questions 1–3 refer to the following passage.

IS NUCLEAR POWER SAFE?

The Dwight Nuclear Power Station opened yesterday in Yerba Valley. The dedication ceremonies were attended by a mixed crowd, including a group of
5 antinuclear protesters.

Owned and operated by Consolidated Electric Company, the Dwight Station is the first of three nuclear plants to be built in the Yerba Valley. The station will serve more
10 than one million customers and at full capacity will generate almost three million kilowatts of electricity.

Situated on 500 acres, the station consists of two reactors, two cooling towers,
15 and two turbine generators. The cost of the entire project has been estimated at more than one billion dollars.

Stanley Novak, president of Consolidated Electric, started the festivities
20 promptly at 9:00 A.M. Standing in the control room, he activated the reactors. He then made his way to the entrance, where he addressed the crowd. He told them that the station will save customers money
25 because nuclear power requires less energy than fossil fuel. He said that the Nuclear Regulatory Commission had certified plant operations as safe.

Novak's remarks were interrupted
30 several times by shouts of protest but drew general applause at the end.

Citizens for a Safe Society (CSS), a protest group, displayed signs against nuclear power. CSS spokesman Bill Kerby
35 demanded written assurances from Consolidated Electric that it would follow all recommended safeguards in disposing of nuclear wastes. He also called for a meeting with Novak to discuss radiation hazards.

1. What is the best expanded title for this selection?

   (1) Stanley Novak Speaks About Energy
   (2) Nuclear Plant Opens to Mixed Reaction
   (3) The Dangers of Nuclear Waste
   (4) Nuclear Station to Cut Costs of Electricity
   (5) New Construction in Yerba Valley

2. Where did this passage most likely appear?

   (1) in a scientific journal
   (2) in an encyclopedia
   (3) in a periodical
   (4) in a news story
   (5) in an editorial

3. What is the main concern of CSS?

   (1) the acreage of Dwight Station
   (2) the dollar cost of electricity
   (3) the disposal of nuclear waste
   (4) design flaws in the reactors
   (5) the economy of Yerba Valley

Questions 4–7 refer to the following passage.

The medium, or process, of our time— electric technology—is reshaping and restructuring patterns of social interdependence and every aspect of our
5 personal life. It is forcing us to reconsider and reevaluate practically every thought, every action, and every institution formerly taken for granted. Everything is changing— you, your family, your neighborhood, your
10 education, your job, your government, your relation to "the others." And they're changing dramatically.

Societies have always been shaped more by the nature of the media by which men
15 communicate than by the content of the communication. The alphabet, for instance, is a technology that is absorbed by the very young child in a completely unconscious manner, or by osmosis...Words and the
20 meaning of words predispose [incline] the child to think and act automatically in certain ways. The alphabet and print technology fostered and encouraged a fragmenting process, a process of specialism and of
25 detachment. Electric technology fosters and encourages unification and involvement. It is impossible to understand social and cultural changes without a knowledge of the workings of media.

30 The older training of observation has become quite irrelevant in this new time, because it is based on psychological responses and concepts conditioned by the former technology—mechanization.

—Excerpted from *The Medium Is the Message,*
by Marshall McLuhan and Quentin Fiore

4. What is the main idea of this passage?

   (1) Technology causes division in society.
   (2) Technology changes our social relationships and personal lives.
   (3) Society today is confused by technology.
   (4) The alphabet is a technology absorbed by young children.
   (5) People are unaware how technology is shaping the future.

5. To what do the words *by osmosis* (line 19) refer?

   (1) thought
   (2) imagination
   (3) studying hard
   (4) unconscious learning
   (5) a technological event

6. Which of the following best illustrates electric technology?

   (1) newspapers
   (2) conversation
   (3) television
   (4) books
   (5) the alphabet

7. What can you infer from the last paragraph?

   (1) People cannot adjust to new technology.
   (2) Our past training will help us learn today's skills.
   (3) Technology will bring people together.
   (4) New technology will anger and confuse many people.
   (5) We must learn new ways of relating to modern technology.

Questions 8–10 refer to the following passage.

Skilled miners from Cornwall, England, began arriving in southwest Wisconsin by the mid-1830s. They brought with them a specialized knowledge of mining gleaned
5 from centuries of deep copper and tin mining in Cornwall.

The new arrivals noticed that the Wisconsin miners worked mainly surface deposits in shallow pits. The Cornish men
10 showed them some better methods. As a result, not only were abandoned mines reopened and expanded, but new ones were discovered. By 1840, Wisconsin was producing more than half of the nation's
15 lead. More settlers poured into the territory. But when the California gold rush began in 1848, the lure of striking it rich became a stronger drawing card.

Many forty-niners who lit out to
20 California in search of gold eventually returned to Wisconsin. Transient miners traveled the state, taking work in the mines wherever they could find it.

Although the mining industry in
25 southwest Wisconsin has a long history, the work was never steady. Whenever market prices dropped, mines shut down, leaving hundreds of men out of work and unsure when or if they would be called back. Some
30 of them managed to survive during these shutdowns by relying on a second occupation—farming.

—Excerpted from "Mining Part of Early History," *Uplands*

8. Which of the following statements describe the Cornish miners?

   (1) They helped improve mining methods in Wisconsin.
   (2) They came from Cornwall, California.
   (3) They helped bring down the price of lead.
   (4) They worked mainly surface deposits in shallow pits .
   (5) They were more interested in gold than in lead.

9. Which of the following would be the best title for this passage?

   (1) A Short History of Mining in Southwest Wisconsin
   (2) Cornish Miners Settle in Wisconsin
   (3) The California Gold Rush
   (4) Unemployment in the Lead-Mining Industry
   (5) Farming and Mining in Southwest Wisconsin

10. What caused the loss of mining jobs in Wisconsin?

    (1) the California gold rush
    (2) new iron and copper mines opening in Upper Michigan
    (3) market prices dropping
    (4) the arrival of Cornish miners
    (5) settlers pouring into the state

Questions 11–13 refer to the following passage.

Today, as a community, we pause to remember two of our own. Lavinia Phelps and Walter Kinski will not soon be forgotten.

It was just one year ago today that
5 Lavinia and Walter presided at the official opening of the Y.E.S. (Youth Encounter Seniors) Center here. It was their dream, a place where young and old could share their lives. We are glad that they lived to see it
10 come true and grateful that it lives on, so vibrant, after them.

As many of you know, Lavinia hardly fit the stereotype of the frail old lady in a rocking chair. Dynamic and determined, she
15 worked tirelessly for our needy youth and senior citizens. We remember with admiration and gratitude how she pried investment dollars out of our businesses, churches, public agencies, and even
20 newspapers for the revitalization [bringing to life] of our now-beautiful downtown.

It was while working on her downtown project that Lavinia met Walter, a retired engineer. Something clicked. They fell in
25 love—with an idea. They decided to help the two neediest groups downtown— aimless youth and lonely (and sometimes frightened) senior citizens. Their radical plan was to help these two groups help each
30 other.

Every day at the Y.E.S. Center you can see young and old doing just that. You'd be surprised how much they have in common and how much each group has to offer the
35 other. Retired nurses show teenage mothers how to take care of their babies. Computer-wise teens show retirees that high tech is nothing to be afraid of and can even be a lot of fun. Troubled and confused youth have
40 sympathetic seniors to turn to for advice. Seniors have strong, healthy new friends whose energy is contagious and whose mere presence reassures them.

You can see them all at the center
45 every day, talking, walking, playing cards, strumming guitars, building furniture, and generally carrying on together across the generations. What a sight! What good news! Walter and Lavinia, thank you.

11. What is the purpose of this passage?

   (1) to persuade
   (2) to inform
   (3) to honor
   (4) to criticize
   (5) to define

12. How were Lavinia and Walter alike?

   (1) they were wealthy
   (2) they lived in the same neighborhood
   (3) they were outgoing and talkative
   (4) they had engineering backgrounds
   (5) they shared the same vision

13. What does the word *stereotype* (line 13) mean?

   (1) common image
   (2) best example
   (3) opposite
   (4) personality
   (5) temperament

Questions 14–19 refer to the following passage.

To kick off her campaign for re-election, Representative Margaret Palmer took a whirlwind tour of the Southern farming region today.

5 Her first stop was the Spring Agriculture Convention in Torrence, where she spoke briefly to a crowd of about a thousand farmers and agribusinessmen.

In her bright pink Chanel suit, jangling
10 bangle bracelets, and broad-brimmed hat festooned with ribbons, Palmer was at the center of attention wherever she went. She was wooing the farm vote in a district where it is hard to find a farmer who has not had to
15 borrow heavily just to hold on to his land.

Palmer worked the crowd with her trademark energy. She laughed easily with conventiongoers who crowded around her. When asked what she intended to do about
20 the farm problem here, she airily promised to seek more federal aid for agriculture.

Later in the day, Palmer toured the 4,000-acre Powell farm. Tramping gamely through the cow barns in her high heels, she
25 stopped frequently to pose for photographers.

"We did not get to talk to her or even to meet her," said Ed Powell, whose grandfather started the farm with just 40
30 acres more than half a century ago.

The last stop on Palmer's tour was Green Corners, where the political representative urged a gathering of surprised picnickers to remember the importance of homegrown
35 food to the economy. Then she got into her black limousine. Waving from the window, she promised to return again soon.

14. What is the passage biased against?

   (1) Congress
   (2) Representative Palmer
   (3) designer clothing
   (4) farmers
   (5) agribusiness interests

15. How is the writer's attitude toward the farmers best described?

   (1) indifferent
   (2) sympathetic
   (3) impatient
   (4) disdainful
   (5) fearful

16. Based on Representative Palmer's conduct throughout her tour, what is her main concern?

   (1) high fashion
   (2) farmers' problems
   (3) the Powell family
   (4) federal aid to agriculture
   (5) re-election

17. What dos the term *festooned* (line 11) mean?

   (1) carved
   (2) molded
   (3) decorated
   (4) obtained
   (5) enjoyed

18. What was Palmer's first stop on the tour?

   (1) a large farm
   (2) a convention
   (3) a cow barn
   (4) a picnic
   (5) a clothing store

19. Which of the following did Palmer promise to the people on her tour?

   (1) more frequent conventions
   (2) better loan programs
   (3) more funding for agriculture
   (4) more contact with voters
   (5) improvements in the economy

Answers are on pages 224–225.

Business-Related Documents

In the job market today, companies seek employees who can understand company policies and rules, forms, and training information. The GED Language Arts, Reading Test may include examples of business documents, including mission statements, employee handbooks, training manuals, and legal documents for you to interpret.

Mission statements explain why a company exists and what its function is in society. It is obviously important for employees to understand the purpose their company serves in order to perform their duties.

Employee handbooks are often given to new employees as a source of information about company policies and procedures. Handbooks often contain guidelines for employee behavior, including dress and attendance, as well as information about wages, benefits, and promotions.

Training manuals are intended to help employees do their jobs by providing detailed instructions for them to follow.

Legal documents make employees aware of workplace-related laws and policies that could affect them or be helpful to them.

EXERCISE 10

Directions: Read the following mission statement and answer the questions below.

GZ Mattress Company Mission Statement

Our Goals: To be the top manufacturer of mattresses in the world. In order to meet this goal, we must constantly seek innovations and new designs to ensure that our products are superior to all others.

Our Pledge: We will provide cost-effective, high-quality mattresses internationally, in order to improve the quality of our customers' sleep. This pledge exemplifies our reason for being in business in the mattress industry, and represents the way we will go about realizing our goals.

Our Professionalism: Our standards for professionalism are reflected in the way we do business. They include a commitment to: courtesy, pride, superiority, innovation, determination, honor, and philanthropy. We expect all of our employees to adhere to these standards when working with each other and with people outside of our company.

1. According to this mission statement, what type of mattresses does this company plan to sell to improve the sleep of its customers?

   _____

   _____

   _____

2. What is the GZ Mattress Company's main goal?

   _____

   _____

   _____

3. What sort of behavior does this employer expect from its employees, according to its standards of professionalism?

   _____

   _____

   _____

Answers are on page 225.

EXERCISE 11

Directions: Review the following employee disciplinary action form, and answer the following questions.

Disciplinary Action Form

Please complete this form and place it in the Human Resources in-box. Managers submitting forms may sign their own submissions. Other employees must obtain a manager's signature before submitting this form. The information on this form will remain confidential unless appropriate authorization is received.

Submitting Employee's Name: _____ Date_____

requests disciplinary action against:

Employee's Name:_____

Department:_____

Supervisor:_____ Hire Date:_____

Today's Date:_____ Date of Incident (if applicable):_____

Reasons for disciplinary action request (check all that apply):

_____ repeated tardiness   _____ harassment of workers

_____ repeated absence   _____ suspected theft

_____ suspected substance abuse   _____ insubordination

_____ violation of smoking policy   _____ abuse of company machinery

_____ violation of dress code

_____ other (please explain) _____

Please describe the incident(s) in detail below, including date, time, and context of incident, witnesses, and prior attempts at resolution.

_____

_____

_____

_____

Submitting employee's signature:_____

Manager's signature:_____

1. What is the purpose of the Disciplinary Action Form?

    _____ (1) to allow managers to punish their employees

    _____ (2) to assess an employee's job performance

    _____ (3) to inform a manager of his or her employee's behavior

    _____ (4) to request a review of an employee's behavior

    _____ (5) to request that an employee be removed from the company

2. Under what circumstances would only one signature be required at the bottom of the form?

    _____ (1) an employee submits the form himself or herself

    _____ (2) a manager submits the form himself or herself

    _____ (3) the violation of company policy is minor

    _____ (4) the violation of company policy is major

    _____ (5) an employee submits the form confidentially

3. Which type of company policy violation is not specifically listed on this form?

    _____ (1) possibly abusing drugs or alcohol

    _____ (2) wearing inappropriate clothing

    _____ (3) revealing confidential information to others

    _____ (4) using the telephone to make personal calls

    _____ (5) taking office supplies home

Answers are on page 225.

EXERCISE 12

Directions: Read the following excerpt from an employee handbook. Then answer the questions.

Medical Leave of Absence

The Metropolitan Zoo prides itself on accommodating the needs of its employees and their families. If a serious medical condition, such as a scheduled surgery or the delivery of a child, prevents you from working for more than ten consecutive workdays, you may take a medical leave of absence from your job. This leave of absence may be extended for up to one year, and is available to full-time employees after six months of employment.

Employees who take a medical leave of absence may be asked to do the following:

- obtain a medical evaluation from a zoo-designated physician

- complete the forms required by the Human Resources department

- join a rehabilitation program, if necessary (see section 5A on Substance Abuse)

- obtain a certified physician's release note upon returning to work

If a sudden and serious medical condition develops and will require an extended absence (for example, appendicitis) you (or a family member) must notify your supervisor quickly and maintain contact with him or her during the duration of your absence. If your absence will exceed ten consecutive days (a medical leave of absence) your supervisor may need to arrange for temporary coverage of your job duties. Therefore, your cooperation with and advance notice (when possible) of such absences is greatly appreciated.

If your medical leave of absence does not exceed four months in length, you will return to your former position if it is still available, or a similar position. If your medical leave of absence exceeds four months in length, you may return to your former position if it is still available, or apply for other available positions at the Metropolitan Zoo.

1. How long must an employee work at the Metropolitan Zoo in order to qualify for the extended medical leave policy?

_____ (1) one year

_____ (2) one month

_____ (3) six months

_____ (4) six weeks

_____ (5) four months

2. Which of the following is not something a zoo employee might be asked to do during his or her extended medical leave?

_____ (1) have a physical exam by a doctor

_____ (2) attend physical therapy sessions

_____ (3) fill out paperwork

_____ (4) get a doctor's permission to return to work

_____ (5) attend substance abuse support group sessions

3. Circle true or false for each of the following statements:

T F An employee is always guaranteed his or her former job back after an extended medical leave of absence.

T F After ten or more days of absence in a row, an employee may take an extended medical leave of absence.

T F A heart attack is an example of a sudden and serious medical condition.

T F Information about substance abuse can be found elsewhere in this employee handbook.

T F According to this employee handbook, a medical leave of absence can be extended for longer than one year, if necessary.

Answers are on page 225.

Writing Activity 6

Select an element of this employee handbook section that you consider to be unfair. Explain what you have selected, and why you feel it is unreasonable. Provide specific examples or situations.

Answers will vary.

EXERCISE 13

Directions: Read the following business memo and answer the questions that follow.

Memorandum

To: Employees of Peyton Discount Stores
From: Samantha Peyton, Owner of Peyton Discount Stores
Date: January 30, 2002
re: shoplifting reminders

In the wake of the shoplifting attempt in the hardware department of our Louisville store last month, I would like to take this opportunity to remind you of the proper procedures for handling a suspected shoplifter in one of our stores. The quick and calm actions of cashier James McGuire during that potentially costly theft attempt serve as a reminder to us all that a few moments of forethought are well worth the time and effort.

Please be advised that in a situation in which a suspected shoplifter is still present in the store, all efforts should be made to delay his or her departure from the store to allow time for the proper authorities to arrive at the scene. However, at no time should human safety be compromised. The shoplifter should no be confronted, accused, or physically prevented form leaving the store. If possible, the store manager should also be informed of the situation, as he or she has received additional training in loss-prevention.

In a situation in which a suspected shoplifter leaves the store, employees should remain inside the store and follow the explicit instructions of the store manager. These instructions may include noting the make, model, and license plate number of any vehicle the suspect uses to leave the store, and attempting to assess the physical appearance of the suspect, including height, weight, hair color, and distinguishing physical features. Employees should remain calmly in the store until authorities arrive.

To make our store "unfriendly" to shoplifters, remain visible and attentive to your customers at all times. I also encourage employees to greet each customer warmly, and offer your assistance. This simple behavior is perceived as friendly and helpful by most customers, and can effectively deter potential shoplifters, who usually prefer to remain unnoticed by store employees.

Your cooperation with these safety procedures is greatly appreciated, and I believe it will help to reduce inventory-loss in our stores safely.

1. What is the subject of the memo?

_____ (1) Peyton Discount Stores

_____ (2) shoplifting reminders

_____ (3) recent shoplifting criminals

_____ (4) emergency situations

_____ (5) inventory concerns

2. During which month did the "potentially costly shoplifting attempt" occur?

_____ (1) April

_____ (2) May

_____ (3) March

_____ (4) October

_____ (5) December

3. In a situation where a suspected shoplifter has left the store, which of the following things are Peyton Discount Store employees *not* advised to do?

_____ (1) remain inside the store

_____ (2) write down the suspect's license plate number

_____ (3) note the suspect's appearance

_____ (4) follow the suspect to his or her vehicle

_____ (5) follow their manager's instructions

4. What is Samantha Walker's job at Peyton Discount Stores?

_____ (1) She is a security guard.

_____ (2) She is a cashier.

_____ (3) She is the head of the human resources department.

_____ (4) She is the owner of the stores.

_____ (5) She is the store owner's secretary.

Answers are on page 225.

Literary Nonfiction

The passages that appear on the GED Language Arts, Reading Test may include selections from biographies, diaries, letters, essays, and memoirs. Read the following passages to become familiar with some examples of literary nonfiction.

EXERCISE 14

Directions: Read the following letter from John Adams to his wife Abigail. Then answer the questions that follow.

August 3, 1776

The Post was later than usual today, so that I had not yours of July 24 till this Evening. You have made me very happy, by the particular and favorable Account you give me of all the Family. But I don't understand how there are so many who have no Eruptions, and no Symptoms. The
5 Inflammation in the Arm might do, but without that, there is no small Pox.

I will lay a Wager, that your whole Hospital have not had so much small Pox, as Mrs. Katy Quincy. Upon my Word she has had an Abundance of it, but is finely recovered, looks as fresh as a Rose, but
10 pitted all over, as thick as ever you saw any one. I this Evening presented your Compliments and Thanks to Mr. Hancock for his polite offer of his House, and likewise your compliments to his Lady and Mrs. Katy.

—Excerpted from *My Countrymen Want Art and Address,*
John Adams to Abigail Adams by John Adams, 1776

1. What can you infer that the word *Post* in line 1 means?

    _____ (1) post office

    _____ (2) fence post

    _____ (3) mail

    _____ (4) delivery truck

    _____ (5) postcard

2. What made John Adams very happy (lines 2–3)?

    _____ (1) his wife's letter

    _____ (2) his wife's updates on their family

    _____ (3) his visit with Mr. Hancock

    _____ (4) his wife's good health

    _____ (5) his lack of smallpox symptoms

3. What does the author mean when he says Mrs. Katy Quincy "looks fresh as a Rose" in line 9?

    _____ (1) she smells nice

    _____ (2) she has rosy cheeks

    _____ (3) she has a rose in her hair

    _____ (4) she looks wide-awake

    _____ (5) she looks healthy

Answers are on page 225.

EXERCISE 15

Directions: Read the following diary entry, written by 14-year-old Lithuanian Yitskhok Rudashevski in 1942, and answer the questions.

Sunday the 1st of November

This is a beautiful day. Every day it has been cloudy and rainy. Today, as though suddenly, a spring day broke through between the autumn days. The sky is blue, the sun warms affectionately. And so indeed the ghetto people burst forth over the little streets to catch
5   what are probably the very last sunbeams. Our police dressed up in their new hats. Here one of them is passing—my blood boils—in a new leather overcoat, with an insolent air, his officer's hat askew. Its peak shines in the sun. The cord of his hat dropped over his chin, he clicks his shiny little boots. Satiated, gorged with food, he struts proudly like an
10   officer, delights—the snake—in such a life, and plays his comedy. This is the source of all my anger against them, that they are playing a comedy with their own tragedy.

—From *Children in the Holocaust and World War II: their secret diaries,*
compiled by Laurel Holliday, 1995

1. When does the author seem to be writing this diary entry?

_____ (1) hours after he watched the events unfold before him

_____ (2) as he watches the events unfold before him

_____ (3) as he reflects on the events of the past

_____ (4) as he wistfully thinks about how things could have been

_____ (5) two days after the events occurred

2. Why does the author provide so many details about the police officer's uniform?

_____ (1) to reveal his admiration for the bravery of the police

_____ (2) to show how handsome the officer looks

_____ (3) to demonstrate his knowledge about uniforms

_____ (4) to express his disgust with the arrogance and pride of the police

_____ (5) to make it clear how important it is to have well-dressed police officers

3. What does the author mean when he says his "blood boils" (line 6)?

_____ (1) He is outraged.

_____ (2) He has a violent temper.

_____ (3) He is extremely hot.

_____ (4) He is ill with a fever.

_____ (5) He is excited.

Answers are on page 225.

EXERCISE 16

Directions: Read the following passage and answer the questions.

What News did the Author Receive?

I was still standing in the doorway, looking across the living room toward our bedroom and the crib where Joe slept. Our place on Sanford Street rented for ninety dollars a month and this man I'd only met once face-to-face was telling me I'd just won the lottery. The strength ran out of my legs. I didn't fall, exactly, but I kind of whooshed down to a sitting position there in the doorway.

"Are you sure?" I asked Bill.

He said he was. I asked him to say the number again, very slowly and very clearly, so I could be sure I hadn't misunderstood. He said the number was a four followed by five zeros. "After that a decimal point with two more zeros," he added.

We talked for another half an hour, but I don't remember a single word of what we said. When the conversation was over, I tried to call Tabby at her mother's. Her youngest sister, Marcella, said Tab had already left. I walked back and forth through the apartment in my stocking feet, exploding with good news and without an ear to hear it. I was shaking all over. At last, I pulled on my shoes and walked downtown. The only store that was open on Bangor's Main Street was the LaVerdiere's Drug. I suddenly felt that I had to buy Tabby a Mother's Day present, something wild and extravagant. I tried, but here's one of life's true facts: there's nothing really wild and extravagant for sale at LaVerdiere's. I did the best I could. I got her a hair-dryer.

When I got back home she was in the kitchen, unpacking the baby bags and singing along with the radio. I gave her the hair-dryer. She looked at it as if she'd never seen one before. "What's this for?" she asked.

I took her by the shoulders. I told her about the paperback sale. She didn't appear to understand. I told her again.

—Excerpted from *On Writing—A Memoir of the Craft*, by Stephen King

1. Based on information in the excerpt, what can you infer?

_____ (1) Before the sale of this book, Stephen King was wealthy.

_____ (2) Stephen King's wife was upset by the sale of his book.

_____ (3) This was the first major book Stephen King had sold to a publisher.

_____ (4) Stephen King's sister-in-law was the first to hear his news.

_____ (5) Bill is Stephen King's brother.

2. What was King's initial reaction when he heard Bill's news?

_____ (1) horror

_____ (2) smugness

_____ (3) fear

_____ (4) disappointment

_____ (5) shock

3. Why did King buy his wife a hair-dryer on Mother's Day?

_____ (1) to replace her old broken one

_____ (2) to celebrate the sale of his book

_____ (3) because he wanted to borrow it

_____ (4) because she was a good mother to their children

_____ (5) because she had hinted that she needed one

4. How much money did Stephen King's book sell for?

_____ (1) $400.00

_____ (2) $4,000.00

_____ (3) $40,000.00

_____ (4) $400,000.00

_____ (5) $4,000,000.00

Answers are on pages 225–226.

Visual Communication

You are probably already familiar with movie and television reviews. If you have ever read reviews of fiction, nonfiction, poetry, or drama, then you are also acquainted with commentaries on literature. Most ***commentaries*** on the arts take the form of reviews and essays about popular culture. The performing arts—music, dance, and theater—are often covered in magazines and big-city newspapers. So are the visual arts of painting, architecture, sculpture, and photography.

Newspapers and magazines regularly feature ***reviews*** of movies, books, television, and radio. Reviews are *subjective* because the reviewers give their opinions and defend them. A review can help you decide whether you would enjoy a particular book, program, or film.

While reviews are specific to a single work, ***essays*** are about categories. If the subject of a movie review is *My Fair Lady,* a related essay might be about one aspect of movie musicals in general.

An ***informative essay*** is written for readers with no special background. Informative essays are written to teach. They inform without judging. A ***critical essay*** is written for readers who are familiar with a subject. Because they are aimed at readers who already have the basics, critical essays tend to be at a more advanced level. Like reviews, critical essays are subjective because the writers give their own interpretation, analysis, and personal opinions.

The best way to read reviews and essays is to keep in mind the reading skills you have already learned. Start by scanning. This will help you find the main idea. Keep the main idea in mind as you read.

- If the commentary is a review or a critical essay, remember that it is an *opinion piece*. Look for the opinions. How does the author back them up?

- Does the commentary include a plot summary, a description of artwork, or biographical information about an artist? If so, study such material carefully.

- Think about the commentary's writing style and structure. Notice the author's choice of words and the order in which details are presented.

- Form your own opinion. What do you think about the work being discussed? Is it something you would like to experience for yourself? Why? How did the main idea and supporting details influence your opinion?

The commentaries you are about to read cover a great many art forms. They will require you to use all of the reading skills you have learned so far. Since reviewers and critics rely heavily on fact, opinion, and descriptive language, this section also provides additional work on these elements.

Directions: All of the statements below refer to the long-running television soap opera *All My Children*. Some of the statements are facts. Others express opinion. Even if you have never seen the show, you should have no difficulty recognizing which is which.

Write *F* for each statement that is a fact or *O* for each statement that expresses an opinion.

_____ 1. *All My Children* is set in the fictional town of Pine Valley.

_____ 2. With so many characters added in recent years, it has become impossible to keep track of the plot's bizarre twists and turns.

_____ 3. The characters of Erica Kane, Dr. Joe Martin, and Ruth Martin have been part of the show since it premiered as a half-hour drama on January 5, 1970.

_____ 4. The show was created by Agnes Nixon.

_____ 5. Erica has more romantic chemistry with Jack than with Dimitri.

_____ 6. Nobody could possibly replace Michael E. Knight in the role of Tad Martin.

_____ 7. For his portrayal of twin brothers Adam and Stuart Chandler, David Canary has won the Daytime Emmy award for best actor.

_____ 8. It must be frustrating to play a character as simple and naive as Dixie.

_____ 9. Dixie should never have had her hair cut.

_____ 10. Brooke English had a daughter who was killed in an accident.

Statements 1, 3, 4, 7, and 10 are facts. Statements 2, 5, 6, 8, and 9 are opinions. Did you identify all of them correctly? Research can verify the accuracy of the factual statements. The opinion statements should have been easy to spot. Elements such as whether a plot is bizarre or impossible to follow, romantic chemistry between actors, if a character seems naive or simple, and the best length for someone's hair are all matters of opinion.

EXERCISE 17

Part A

Directions: Read the four reviews below. Then write *F* for each statement that is a fact or *O* for each statement that expresses an opinion.

1. *Carousel*—"A wildly acclaimed revival of the 1945 Rodgers & Hammerstein musical about a carnival barker whose romance leads to violence and finally redemption. As contemporary as anything on Broadway. Winner of five 1994 Tony awards, including Best Musical Revival, and deserving of even more."

—Excerpted from *New York* magazine, September 5, 1994

_____ (1) *Carousel* is a revival of a 1945 musical by Rodgers and Hammerstein.

_____ (2) It deserved more than the five Tony awards it won.

_____ (3) It won the 1994 Tony award for Best Musical Revival.

2. *Nunsense*—An "entertaining musical comedy, now in its ninth year, of five sensible motivated nuns who mount a talent show to raise money for what they personally and firmly consider to be a good and noble cause."

—Excerpted from *New York* magazine, September 5, 1994

_____ (1) *Nunsense* is an entertaining musical comedy.

_____ (2) The main characters are five nuns who put together a talent show.

_____ (3) The show has been running for nine years.

3. *Damn Yankees*—"A revival of the 1956 Tony-award-winning musical comedy, about a baseball fan who sells his soul to the Devil so that his favorite team can win. Director Jack O'Brien has deftly updated the book, and his visual touches are as quotably witty as his additions to the dialogue."

—Excerpted from *New York* magazine, September 5, 1994

_____ (1) *Damn Yankees* is a revival of a musical comedy first presented in 1956.

_____ (2) The title of the play refers to a baseball team.

_____ (3) Director Jack O'Brien has added witty new elements to the dialogue and the action.

4. *Jackie Mason: Politically Incorrect*—"Oy, is he ever! A new one-man show written and performed by Mason, who jokes ruthlessly and effectively about every touchy social issue and racial minority imaginable. He might enjoy some heckling; it would give him a chance to harangue even more."

—Excerpted from *New York* magazine, September 5, 1994

_____ (1) *Jackie Mason: Politically Incorrect* is a new one-man show.

_____ (2) Mason's jokes are ruthless and effective.

_____ (3) The jokes target minorities and controversial issues.

Part B

Directions: Reread the preceding four commentaries. Then, for each question below, write the number of the correct commentary.

_____ 1. Which commentary praises the work of a musical comedy director?

_____ 2. Which commentary is about a musical that is not a comedy?

_____ 3. Which commentary jokingly recommends that members of the audience heckle a performer?

_____ 4. Which commentary implies some unfairness in the awards process?

Answers are on page 226.

EXERCISE 18

Directions: Commentaries on the arts are filled with descriptive language, both positive and negative. Read the following review. Then list five words or phrases that convey the reviewer's negative opinion of the show in the space provided.

"Comedy strikes out! This simpy sitcom about life on a major-league baseball team was launched just weeks after the actual baseball fraternity went on strike. But this show has worse problems than bad timing. Take, for instance, bad writing, cardboard characters and witless plots."

—Excerpted from *People* magazine, October 10, 1994

1. _____

2. _____

3. _____

4. _____

5. _____

Answers are on page 226.

EXERCISE 19

Directions: Read the following reviews about the Chicago production of the play *Angels in America*. Then, in the space provided, find and write the positive adjectives and adverbs that praise the play.

"A remarkable, richly imagined odyssey"

—Richard Christiansen, *Chicago Tribune*

"Daring, bold, ruthlessly comical and intellectually stimulating"

—Roy Leonard, WGN Radio/TV

"The finest ensemble performance on any Chicago stage in years"

—Sherman Kaplan, WBBM Radio

"Every bit as effective as the Broadway production"

—Tom Valeo, *Daily Herald*

1. _____

2. _____

3. _____

4. _____

5. _____

6. _____

7. _____

8. _____

Answers are on page 226.

EXERCISE 20

Directions: Read the following five short excerpts from reviews of the movie *The River Wild*. Then answer the questions that follow in the space provided.

The River Wild is a thrilling movie. A personal triumph for Meryl Streep. I wouldn't be surprised if she is nominated for a raft of honors."

—Gene Shalit, NBC-TV, *Today* show

"A superior thriller in every way, with brilliant performances by Meryl Streep and Kevin Bacon"

—Michael Medved, *Sneak Previews*

"A smart, spunky Meryl Streep triumphs."

—*Time* magazine

"A heart-pounding adventure, if ever there was one! Meryl Streep reveals a new depth of her acting dynamic. An excellent performance."

—David Sheehan, KCBS-TV

"Tense, satisfying entertainment. The fun and the power come from Meryl Streep's newly robust heart . . . a fiercely convincing matriarchal action hero."

—David Ansen, *Newsweek* magazine

1. What two words does the *Time* review use to describe Streep?

   _____

2. What two words does David Sheehan use to describe the type of adventure found in the film?

   _____

3. Which play on words does Gene Shalit use to say what he thinks Streep deserves for her performance in the film?

   _____

4. Which two positive phrases does Michael Medved use to describe the film and Streep's and Bacon's acting in the film?

   _____

Answers are on page 226.

EXERCISE 21

Questions 1–7 are based on the passage below.

I learned, first of all, that if you're going to do a television show you should keep it to yourself. The minute your plans are known, all your friends generously dedicate themselves
5 to giving you the benefit of their experience. I made the mistake of announcing my entrance into television several weeks ahead of time. They were all ready for me. When I arrived in New York to start rehearsals, who
10 should be at Grand Central [train station] to meet me but Eddie Cantor. Being my friend and having already absorbed the vast experience of two appearances before video cameras, he felt it was his moral obligation to
15 be the first to explain to me the facts of life in television. All the way through the station, he kept jumping up and down, telling me what to do and what to avoid.

When we got into the cab, Milton Berle [a
20 well-known comedian] was sitting there waiting for us. He said he'd left his rehearsal just to come down and give me some technical advice. And then, in a few thousand well-chosen words, he briefed me on the art
25 of how to close your eyes when getting hit with a pie. Unfortunately, as Miltie was tapering off, the cab had to stop for a red light on Forty-fifth Street. It was just long enough for Jimmy Durante [another well-
30 known comedian] to jump in with the warning that, "When youse is in television, youse is gotta speak distinkly." By this time the taxi was so crowded I could hardly hear the meter. Fortunately, the three of them were so
35 busy expounding their theories that I was able to slip out unnoticed at Forty-ninth and Broadway. But that was only the beginning of a siege of helpful advice that didn't let up until the curtain rose on my show. The only
40 ones who didn't have suggestions for my first television program were my writers.

Another thing I discovered about television is that there are far too many distractions for the studio audience. On radio
45 comedy shows, we learned a long time ago that the laughter of the studio audience has a direct effect on the home listeners' appreciation of the program. Consequently, everything humanly possible is done to direct
50 the attention of those in the audience to the person who is delivering the lines. On a TV comedy program, the reaction of the studio audience is equally important to its success. But with television, there is not only the
55 frequent distraction of stagehands moving and sometimes dropping props as they get ready for the next scene, but the sets are so constructed that those in the studio inevitably miss half of what is going on. What little they
60 might otherwise see is often obscured by the three cameramen, usually hefty, whose bulk hovers between the studio audience and the performers on stage. Fortunately I had been warned about this condition, and when the
65 time came for me to select a cameraman for my show, my first question was not "How good is he?" but "How much does he weigh?"

The things I have just mentioned are a few of the discouraging aspects of the present
70 television scene. But, on the whole, I was amazed at the phenomenal progress that this infant industry has already made. I found that the technicians not only have a high degree of competence, but that they face the problems
75 that are constantly cropping up with speed, skill, and imagination. Some of the sets that I saw constructed in a few hours would do credit to a $3 million movie production. The directors, despite a lack of time, space, and
80 facilities, are staging scenes day after day that it would take Hollywood weeks to duplicate.

And the cameramen do more than get in the way of the studio audience. On a live television show, there is no such thing as a
85 retake. It has to be right the first time. And yet, with a very few hours of rehearsal for their benefit, these cameramen somehow manage to shoot even hour-long dramatic shows without noticeable mistakes. If it is

90 true that TV has borrowed from the techniques of movie making, it is also true that the movie industry would do well, even at this early stage, to adapt many of the streamlined methods of television.

—Excerpted from *Jack Benny: The Radio and Television Work,* by the Museum of Television and Radio

1. To what was Jack Benny referring when he said, "If you're going to do a television show you should keep it to yourself." (lines 1–3)?

   (1) the fear of performing on television
   (2) the need to come up with his own ideas
   (3) a lot of unnecessary advice he got from friends
   (4) a preference for working on radio instead of television
   (5) a mistrust of writers' ideas

2. What is Benny's opinion of television technicians?

   (1) They interfered with the home audience's enjoyment of a show.
   (2) They would benefit from exercise since they were overweight.
   (3) They showed great creativity in dealing with problems as they arose.
   (4) They designed sets better suited to movies.
   (5) They did not know about moviemaking techniques.

3. What opinion of the movie industry does Benny express?

   (1) It spends too much money on producing sets.
   (2) It should be more careful in its selection of cameramen.
   (3) It lacks creative directors.
   (4) It needs more imaginative writers.
   (5) It could learn a lot from the television industry.

4. How would you best describe the tone of Benny's article?

   (1) insincere and joking
   (2) humorous and informative
   (3) distant and serious
   (4) forced and rehearsed
   (5) discouraged and regretful

5. What does the term *duplicate* (line 81) mean?

   (1) trick
   (2) copy
   (3) send
   (4) admire
   (5) imagine

6. What does the term *phenomenal* (line 71) mean?

   (1) fortunate
   (2) laughable
   (3) slow
   (4) remarkable
   (5) problematic

7. What does the following quote exemplify? "And then, in a few thousand well-chosen words, he [Milton Berle] briefed me on the art of how to close your eyes when getting hit with a pie."

   (1) literal language
   (2) figurative language
   (3) comedic expression
   (4) technical advice
   (5) rehearsal directions

Answers are on page 226.

EXERCISE 22

Directions: Read the passage below about the career of Paul Robeson, one of the finest actors of his day. Then answer the questions that follow.

[His starring role in the play *All God's Chillun Got Wings*] made Robeson famous. Critics exclaimed over his movements, his expressive features, his resonant voice. He was soon giving concerts of spirituals and black work songs at the Provincetown Playhouse, and he quickly became nearly as famous for his singing as he was for his acting. In fact, [playwright Eugene O'Neill] and the Provincetown director, James Light, added a black spiritual to one of the jungle scenes in *The Emperor Jones*. When that play began its second run, Robeson's importance as an actor was increased. In 1925, he went to London with the production, thus becoming the first black American dramatic actor to play on the English stage since Ira Aldridge had played Othello there over a half century earlier.

But here the comparison between Robeson and Aldridge ended. Robeson hadn't had enough stage experience to be considered a trained actor, as he was the first to admit. His real skill was singing, a discipline he preferred. When white critics pronounced him a "natural actor," neither he nor blacks who knew anything about acting were pleased. It was like saying that blacks had natural rhythm or were natural athletes. Whites seemed unable to admit that blacks could work and train hard to be good at what they did.

Paul Robeson's next role was that of a black prizefighter in *Black Boy*, a play by two white writers. He then toured in the musical play *Show Boat*. Although neither play did much for his acting reputation, the stage experience he gained made him better prepared to play Othello in London. The play opened in 1930. Robeson now had six years of stage experience. He was also older. He brought a tremendous sensitivity to the role, and London critics raved about his "dignity, simplicity and true passion." Although Robeson would forever after be identified with the character of Brutus Jones even more so than Gilpin because Robeson also appeared in the film version of the play, his favorite role and the one he felt he played best was that of Othello.

The next time Robeson performed as Shakespeare's tragic hero was thirteen years later. He was now forty-five years old and very experienced. He'd appeared in several motion pictures, a few more plays, and had spent nearly ten years giving concerts all over Europe. Mature and dignified, he brought these qualities to that demanding role in an unforgettable way. His portrayal of Othello in the American Theatre Guild production of the play was not only a high point in his career but also a high point in the history of the American theater. *Othello* opened at the Shubert Theater on October 19, 1943, and ran until July 1, 1944, playing to packed houses for 296 consecutive performances, a record run for Shakespeare in New York.

—Excerpted from *Black Theater in America*, by James Haskins

Put a check in front of the correct answer to questions 1–3.

1. What is the subject of this passage?

_____ (1) Paul Robeson's development as an actor

_____ (2) Paul Robeson's singing career

_____ (3) the history of black theater

2. Which of the following can be inferred about Brutus Jones?

_____ (1) He is a historical figure.

_____ (2) He is the title character in Eugene O'Neill's *The Emperor Jones.*

_____ (3) He is a character in *Othello.*

3. What was the high point of Paul Robeson's dramatic career?

_____ (1) starring in *All God's Chillun Got Wings*

_____ (2) playing Othello in the American Theatre Guild production

_____ (3) being called "a natural actor"

4. Put the following events in order by numbering them from 1 to 5.

_____ Paul Robeson starred as Othello in London.

_____ Robeson became the first black American actor to appear on the English stage in half a century.

_____ The American Theatre Guild production of *Othello* opened in New York.

_____ Robeson toured in *Show Boat.*

_____ Robeson began performing concerts of spirituals and work songs.

5. List five words or phrases used to describe the acting genius of Paul Robeson.

_____

_____

_____

Answers are on pages 226–227.

EXERCISE 23

Directions: Read the passage below and answer the questions that follow in the space provided.

From 1888–1889, the artist Vincent Van Gogh lived in the south of France, in the little town of Arles. Here, despite illness, he worked with great energy, producing paintings and drawings at an astonishing rate. He experimented with new ways of using color, and with different styles and subjects. This period has been described as both the height of his career and a turning point in the history of Western art.

In letters from Arles to his family and friends, Van Gogh described his ideas, his health, and his work. While painting what has become a very famous picture of his bedroom, Van Gogh wrote:

"I have been and still am nearly half-dead from the past week's work. So I am forced to be quiet. I have just slept sixteen hours at a stretch, and it has restored me considerably. . . ."

"Today I am all right again. My eyes are still tired, but then I had a new idea in my head and here is the sketch of it. This time it's just simply my bedroom, only here color is to do everything. The finished picture should suggest rest or sleep in general. In a word, looking at the picture ought to rest the brain, or rather the imagination. The walls are pale violet. The floor is of red tiles. The wood of the bed and chairs is the yellow of fresh butter, the sheets and pillows very light greenish citron [yellow]. The bedspread scarlet. The window green. The dressing table orange, the basin blue. The doors lilac. And that is all—there is nothing in this room with its closed shutters. The broad lines of the furniture again must express completed and undisturbed rest. Portraits on the walls, and a mirror and a towel and some clothes. The frame—as there is no white in the picture—will be white. I shall work on it again all day, but you see how simple the conception [idea] is. By means of all these diverse tones I have wanted to express an *absolute restfulness.*"

—Excerpted from *The Complete Letters of Vincent Van Gogh* by Vincent Van Gogh, in *Van Gogh in Arles,* by Ronald Pickvance

1. In which town and country did Van Gogh paint the bedroom described in the passage?

   _____

2. Who wrote the description of the painting?

   _____

3. Write two phrases from Van Gogh's own words that tell something about the state of his health.

   _____

4. What did Van Gogh want the painting of his bedroom to express?

   _____

5. Van Gogh chose many bright colors to express his image. Which colors would you have used? Explain why.

   _____

   _____

   _____

   _____

6. With which three elements did Van Gogh experiment in his paintings during this period?

   _____

7. Which color is NOT used in Van Gogh's painting of his bedroom?

   _____

8. For which two reasons does Van Gogh describe himself as "nearly half-dead"?

   _____

   _____

Answers are on page 227.

EXERCISE 24

Questions 1–4 refer to the following passage about poetry.

WHAT IS POETRY?

Poetry should be a deep delight, which you would enjoy as you enjoy a day in Spring, when the sun is rising, the birds are singing, and the first flowers of the year are
5 discovered along the edge of the woods. You must not think of it as a school subject about which you will be questioned one day; you must not even think of it as "literature" which is an ugly word invented by
10 schoolmasters. Poetry is like the bird's song, but since it is sung by a human being, it has meaning, and that meaning is given in words.

But the words which the poet finds—
15 and he finds them like flowers in his path: he does not look for them—these words are special words. Some of them are sweetly musical, words that are thrilling to the tongue as we utter them; others are magical
20 words that fill the mind with wonder. Music and magic are both present in the best poems, and together they give us the particular delight of poetry.

But that delight is not always simple
25 delight—some poems make us sad, because they are about sorrow or death; others make us thoughtful, because they tell us what the poet thinks about life or about the many things that happen in life. Such
30 subjects are not forbidden, but just as a clear stream will break into cloudy froth when it meets rough rocks, so thought dims brightness of pure poetry. Poetry is not made by taking thought about a subject;
35 rather it forms in the mind like a crystal; its words are like snowflakes that fall on a green leaf. Such an event is rare, and the perfect poems in any language are so few that they could all be included in a book
40 much smaller than the Bible.

—Excerpted from *This Way, Delight* by Herbert Read

1. What simile is used in the first paragraph?

    (1) "an ugly word invented by schoolmasters"
    (2) "poetry is like the bird's song"
    (3) "the first flowers of the year are discovered"
    (4) "poetry should be a deep delight"
    (5) "a day in Spring, when the sun is rising"

2. According to the author, what do the best poems have in common?

    (1) music and magic
    (2) birdsong and music
    (3) music and literature
    (4) thought and emotion
    (5) magic and deep thought

3. What is the main idea of this selection?

    (1) The best poetry is characterized by clear thinking.
    (2) The wrong word can spoil a poem.
    (3) Poetry needs images of nature.
    (4) Some poems are sad and thoughtful.
    (5) Reading poetry should be a joyful experience.

4. What can you infer as the reason the author advises against thinking of poetry as a school subject?

    (1) Poetry is too hard to understand.
    (2) Poetry is so easy it doesn't need to be studied.
    (3) Schools already have too many other subjects to teach.
    (4) The delight of poetry will be lost.
    (5) Children are too young to understand poetry.

Answers are on page 227.

Chapter Review

Questions 1–6 refer to the following excerpt from a review of an art exhibition.

The liveliness and color of Latino culture, its music, food, art and style, lend a layer of richness to Chicago culture we often take for granted in a city already thick with ethnic
5 diversity. So the excitement generated by "Images and Objects of the Spirit," the new show at the Aldo Castillo Gallery, offers a welcome opportunity to focus clearly on the best of Latino art.

10 An eclectic [varied] presentation of contemporary [current] Latin American fine art mixed together with furniture, textiles and religious artifacts from Colombia, Guatemala, Mexico and Peru, the show offers
15 a concentrated look into a culture steeped in religion, political conflict and passion...

Aldo Castillo describes his labor of love as a gallery with a social mission. An established Nicaraguan sculptor, Castillo left
20 his homeland to escape civil war and received political asylum in the United States where he continued his studies at the Art Institute of Chicago. Originally intending to create a sculpture studio, he decided instead to turn
25 his beautiful rehabbed space in Lakeview into a gallery where he could showcase his own work and that of fellow Latino artists.

The result is a glorious crash course in Latino visual arts. Contemporary work by
30 painters Antonio Bou and Luis Fernando Uribe hang over rough-hewn cabinets. Ceremonial garments woven in bright hot colors are laid about among religious objects...

Some of the most stunning pieces in
35 the show are the humblest. Simple retablos, small carved wooden niches designed to hold images of saints, are both rough and powerful.

—Excerpted from the *Chicago Sun-Times*,
October 21, 1994

1. What type of exhibition is "Images and Objects of the Spirit"?

(1) a sculpture collection
(2) a collection of *retablos*
(3) an exhibition featuring Chicago artists
(4) an exhibition featuring Latino artists
(5) a one-man show

2. Which of the following statements about Aldo Castillo is *not* true?

(1) He is a sculptor born in Nicaragua.
(2) His studio is devoted to ancient art.
(3) His gallery presents the work of Latino artists.
(4) He studied at the Art Institute of Chicago.
(5) He considers religious objects a form of art.

3. How does the reviewer describe the *retablos* in the show?

(1) complicated
(2) political and passionate
(3) ethnically diverse
(4) rough and powerful
(5) brightly colored

4. Who are Antonio Bou and Luis Fernando Uribe?

(1) contemporary painters
(2) contemporary sculptors
(3) contemporary cabinetmakers
(4) contemporary Peruvian weavers
(5) contemporary gallery owners

5. What can you infer about the reviewer?

(1) He or she enthusiastically recommends this exhibition.
(2) He or she is not familiar with Castillo's work.
(3) He or she prefers ceremonial garments to paintings and sculpture.
(4) He or she found the exhibit disappointing.
(5) He or she is reluctant to give a personal opinion.

6. The exhibit does NOT present works of art from which of the following places?

(1) Colombia
(2) Honduras
(3) Peru
(4) Guatemala
(5) Mexico

Questions 7–11 refer to the following review of Andrew Chaikin's book A Man on the Moon: The Voyages of the Apollo Astronauts.

The Apollo program sent twenty-four men to the moon, among them Neil A. Armstrong, who, twenty-five years ago this month, accomplished his famed "giant leap
5 for mankind" by taking the first human step on lunar soil. Twelve of the astronauts walked on the moon—the rest flew around it—and their tasks progressed from the demonstration that a lunar visit could be
10 safely concluded to far-ranging scientific explorations of the moon's surface. Chaikin's narrative of the Apollo voyages, based on extensive interviews with the astronauts, is riveting—especially his account of Apollo
15 13, the mission that turned into a cliff-hanger when an oxygen tank exploded, crippling the spaceship on its way to the moon. He brings the astronauts to life, stripping away the gray cloak of all-
20 American squareness in which NASA dressed them, and revealing the bright colors of their personalities and the fears and exhilaration [excitement] of their remarkable journeys. They brought high
25 competence and courage to a feat that rested on a vast political and technological enterprise. After the first couple of moon walks, public interest plummeted [fell], and, once it became evident that the Soviet
30 Union had opted out of the moon race, support for Apollo dissolved. Chaikin calls the Apollo program "the last great act this country has undertaken out of a sense of optimism," whereas in truth it was one of
35 the greatest acts America undertook—and would sustain—only in response to the goad [pressure] of Cold War competition.

—Excerpted from *The New Yorker*, August 1, 1994

7. What does the word *riveting* (line 14) mean?

(1) exciting
(2) mechanical
(3) boring
(4) technical
(5) advanced

8. From what did the writer obtain much information?

(1) personal experience
(2) extensive interviews with the *Apollo* astronauts
(3) NASA
(4) Cold War documents
(5) classified information

9. Which of the following expresses the reviewer's opinion?

(1) The *Apollo* program sent 24 men to the moon.
(2) Neil Armstrong took the first human step on lunar soil.
(3) The *Apollo* program was kept going only in response to the pressure of Cold War competition.
(4) The astronauts demonstrated great competence.
(5) Public interest in the *Apollo* program fell after the Soviet Union dropped out of the moon race.

10. For what does the reviewer praise the writer?

(1) revealing the astronauts' true personalities
(2) revealing an act of American optimism
(3) criticizing NASA
(4) explaining complex experiments
(5) rekindling the public's interest in America's space program

11. Why is the *Apollo 13* mission described as a "cliff-hanger"?

    (1) The ship landed on a rocky ledge on the moon's surface.
    (2) An oxygen tank exploded in flight.
    (3) It carried 24 astronauts.
    (4) The astronauts aboard had strong personalities.
    (5) It almost collided with a Soviet ship in deep space.

Questions 12–16 refer to the following excerpt from Roger Ebert's review of the movie Hoop Dreams.

    A film like *Hoop Dreams* is what the movies are for. It takes us, shakes us, and makes us think in new ways about the world around us. It gives us the impression of
5 having touched life itself.

    Hoop Dreams is, on one level, a documentary about two African-American kids named William Gates and Arthur Agee, from Chicago's inner city, who are gifted
10 basketball players and dream of someday starring in the NBA. On another level, it is about much larger subjects: about ambition, competition, race and class in our society. About our value structures. And about the
15 daily lives of people like the Agee and Gates families, who are usually invisible in the mass media, but have a determination and resiliency [staying power] that is a cause for hope.

20   The movie spans six years in the lives of William and Arthur, starting when they are in the eighth grade, and continuing through the first year of college. It was intended originally to be a 30-minute short, but as the
25 filmmakers followed their two subjects, they realized this was a much larger, and longer story. And so we are allowed to watch the subjects grow up during the movie, and this palpable [almost physical] sense of the
30 passage of time is like walking for a time in their shoes.

    They're spotted during playground games by a scout for St. Joseph's High School in west suburban Westchester, a
35 basketball powerhouse. Attending classes there will mean a long daily commute to a school with few other black faces, but there's never an instant when William or Arthur, or their families, doubt the wisdom
40 of this opportunity: St. Joseph's, we hear time and again, is the school where another inner-city kid, Isiah Thomas, started his climb to NBA stardom.

—Excerpted from the *Chicago Sun-Times*,
October 21, 1994

12. Which rating would the reviewer give this film (one star being the lowest rating and four stars the highest)?

    (1) one
    (2) two
    (3) two and a half
    (4) three
    (5) four

13. According to the reviewer, what is this film about?

    (1) ambition and competition
    (2) race and class
    (3) value structures
    (4) the lives of ordinary people
    (5) all of the above

14. Who are the main characters in the movie?

    (1) college athletes
    (2) NBA stars
    (3) invisible families
    (4) fictional teenagers
    (5) real kids

15. You can infer that the reviewer is recommending this film for what type of viewers?

(1) all audiences
(2) professional athletes only
(3) urban audiences only
(4) sports fans only
(5) high school students only

16. What does the last paragraph imply about Arthur and William?

(1) They will adjust easily to St. Joseph's.
(2) They will reach the NBA just as Isiah Thomas did.
(3) They will face problems at their new school.
(4) They will abandon their dreams when they are older.
(5) They will find many friends at St. Joseph's.

Answers are on page 227.

READING EFFICIENCY A

Directions: This activity will help you to improve your reading efficiency. Before you start to read, write the present time at the top of the page. When you have completed the reading and all 5 questions, write your finishing time. Subtract to find how long you took. Score your answers. Then turn to page 234 to find your E-Factor and graph your progress.

Finishing Time

Starting Time −

Reading Time =

Number of Answers Correct

AN AMAZING EVENT

Meriwether Lewis and William Clark led the first American expedition west of the Mississippi River. The group had about 45 men and one woman. That was Sacagawea. She was a Shoshone Indian and the wife of a
5 French fur trader. Sacagawea joined the expedition in the winter of 1804–1805. The group was camped in what is now North Dakota. Sacagawea could guide the group. She could also speak Indian languages. One
10 time she saved the day for Lewis and Clark. This was because of an amazing event.

Lewis and Clark wanted to follow the Missouri River west to the Pacific Ocean. In August 1805 they came to the end of the
15 Missouri. Now they had to cross the rocky Mountains. They needed horses. They met a band of Shoshone Indians. Their chief was Cameahwait. Lewis needed the chief's help and friendship. He began talking with the
20 chief. It was hard. Lewis's men had to translate two Indian languages into French. Then they had to translate French into English. Sacagawea arrived. She looked closely at Cameahwait. Then she ran to him.
25 She was crying happily. He was her long-lost brother! Lewis and Clark got horses and help from Cameahwait and his people. As one historian said, "The stars had danced for Lewis and Clark."
30

1. What event is the main subject of the passage?

   (1) Lewis meeting Cameahwait
   (2) Sacagawea and her husband joining the Lewis and Clark expedition
   (3) Lewis and Clark reaching the end of the Missouri river
   (4) Lewis's men being able to translate the Indian languages
   (5) Sacagawea meeting her long-lost brother

2. In general, why was Sacagawea helpful to the Lewis and Clark expedition?

   (1) As a woman, she handled situations differently than Lewis and Clark did.
   (2) As an Indian, she knew things about the land and people that Lewis and Clark did not.
   (3) She was an excellent horse handler.
   (4) She knew many Indian chiefs.
   (5) She knew the best ways to travel down the Missouri River.

3. What would have happened if Sacagawea had not recognized Cameahwait?

   (1) The Lewis and Clark expedition would have failed.
   (2) The Shoshone Indians would have attacked the American expedition.
   (3) Sacagawea would have had to leave the expedition.
   (4) The expedition would have had more difficulty getting over the mountains.
   (5) Cameahwait would have recognized Sacagawea.

4. How does the author prove the passage's main idea?

   (1) with a series of examples
   (2) with descriptive details
   (3) with a list of facts
   (4) with a detailed story
   (5) with deductive reasoning

5. What can you conclude about the relationship between Indians and Americans when Americans first began moving westward?

   (1) The Indians and Americans did not have to interact.
   (2) It was difficult because they couldn't communicate
   (3) It was filled with hatred and mistrust.
   (4) It was very friendly.
   (5) There was none.

Answers are on page 228.

READING EFFICIENCY B

Directions: This activity will help you to improve your reading efficiency. Before you start to read, write the present time at the top of the page. When you have completed the reading and all 5 questions, write your finishing time. Subtract to find how long you took. Score your answers. Then turn to page 234 to find your E-Factor and graph your progress.

Finishing Time [ ]

Starting Time − [ ]

Reading Time = [ ]

Number of Answers Correct [ ]

THE FIRST SNOWBOARD

Many inventions have changed our lives. Airplanes, televisions, and computers are some of the most important inventions of the twentieth century. The snowboard
5 should be added to this list. It took several people to perfect this amazing board. It cleverly combines surfing, skiing, and skateboarding.

A creative 13-year-old made the first
10 snowboard in 1963. He was Tom Sims. Tom liked to both ski and surf. He made a plywood model and later a fiberglass one. But he did not patent them. In 1966, Sherman Poppen of Muskegon, Michigan, patented a snowboard.
15 He called this fun piece of sporting equipment a Snurfer. It was invented to be used to ride on the snowy sand dunes near Lake Michigan. It was a uniform width. It had a rope for riders to hold onto.

20 In 1973, Robert Weber made a snowboard with many improvements. It was thinner in the middle to help riders turn. It included foot straps for the rider. Meanwhile, Sherman Poppen held popular Snurfer competitions on
25 the Michigan sand dunes. One competitor, Jake Buton Carpenter, injured himself on his Snurfer. He decided to improve it. He made it wider. He added bindings to make riders more secure. Carpenter started a snowboard
30 company in Vermont. Today it is the leading snowboard maker. All these clever people helped create a great piece of sporting equipment, the snowboard.

1. What was the purpose of inventing a snowboard?

   (1) to offer a new form of transportation
   (2) to provide exercise for its rider
   (3) to create a new way to have fun in the snow
   (4) to create a new kind of sporting competition
   (5) to prove that several existing sports could be combined

2. What do all the people mentioned in the passage have in common?

   (1) They are professional inventors.
   (2) They applied for patents.
   (3) They are all kids.
   (4) They wanted to make a lot of money.
   (5) They liked to have fun in the snow.

3. The author says the snowboard should be added to the list of great inventions such as airplanes and computers. What is the best way to describe this statement?

   (1) humorous exaggeration
   (2) literal opinion
   (3) valid fact
   (4) supporting detail
   (5) false statement

4. What is the author's attitude toward the snowboard and the people who invented it?

    (1) neutral
    (2) admiring
    (3) unimpressed
    (4) puzzled
    (5) joking

5. What conclusion can you draw from the passage?

    (1) People are always willing to spend money for unusual inventions.
    (2) Few inventions change much after they are first created.
    (3) People are inspired to invent things through their own interests and experiences.
    (4) Patenting an invention is a difficult process.
    (5) Most patents are issued for inventions that make people's lives easier.

    Answers are on page 228.

READING EFFICIENCY C

Directions: This activity will help you to improve your reading efficiency. Before you start to read, write the present time at the top of the page. When you have completed the reading and all 5 questions, write your finishing time. Subtract to find how long you took. Score your answers. Then turn to page 234 to find your E-Factor and graph your progress.

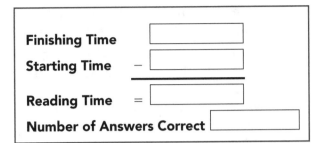

Finishing Time [ ]

Starting Time − [ ]
_____

Reading Time = [ ]

Number of Answers Correct [ ]

MEDICAL INSURANCE
Dear Mr. Stone:

Thank-you for your recent application for medical insurance. We are happy to serve your insurance needs.

5 Enclosed is your medical insurance registration form. It includes the information you gave us. Please note that it shows the doctors you have visited in the last ten years. It shows your hospital stays. It shows the inoculations you have received. It also shows the medications you
10 currently take. Please check the facts you provided about your doctor in Canada. I could not reach her at the address you gave.

Please review the information on the form. If it is correct, you do not need to
15 make any changes. If you need to make changes, make them in the spaces provided. In addition, please add your e-mail address in the space provided. We did not ask for this information previously.
20

I have enclosed a return envelope for your use. Please return the form within three weeks. This will ensure that your medical coverage is not interrupted. If you have questions, feel free to call me.
25

Very Truly Yours,

Vivian Fowler

Vivian Fowler
New Customer Relations
Modern Medical Insurance
30

1. Why has Mr. Stone received this letter?

   (1) because he recently stayed in the hospital
   (2) because Modern Medical Insurance wants him as a customer
   (3) because he recently sent the company a claim
   (4) because he recently applied for insurance
   (5) because his insurance has expired

2. Where did the company get the information on the form they are sending?

   (1) from the Internet
   (2) from Mr. Stone's doctors
   (3) from Mr. Stone's previous insurance company
   (4) from Mr. Stone
   (5) from a doctor in Canada

3. What is the best description of the letter?

   (1) junk mail
   (2) an unimportant form letter
   (3) a personalized letter that needs to be responded to immediately
   (4) business mail that can be laid aside indefinitely
   (5) a letter that requires an immediate phone call

4. Suppose Mr. Stone has no changes to make. What should he do with the form?

   (1) throw it away
   (2) file it with other important documents
   (3) send it back with no additions
   (4) write his e-mail address and send it back
   (5) call Vivian Fowler and ask what he should do

5. What will probably happen if Mr. Stone does not return the form within three weeks?

   (1) Vivian Fowler will call him on the phone.
   (2) His medical coverage will be suspended.
   (3) Nothing will happen.
   (4) The company will keep waiting for his form.
   (5) He will be fined.

Answers are on page 228.

READING EFFICIENCY D

Directions: This activity will help you to improve your reading efficiency. Before you start to read, write the present time at the top of the page. When you have completed the reading and all 5 questions, write your finishing time. Subtract to find how long you took. Score your answers. Then turn to page 234 to find your E-Factor and graph your progress.

Finishing Time	
Starting Time	−
Reading Time	=
Number of Answers Correct	

TERMS OF EMPLOYMENT

This certifies that Phoebe's Fitness Gym will employ Janice Gonzalez as a teacher. Ms. Gonzalez will work for three seasons this year. She will work for the fall, winter,

5 and spring seasons. She will teach at least two basic courses each season. Enrollment at the Fitness Gym may be higher than usual. If so, the employee will have the opportunity to teach additional courses with

10 appropriate course pay. The courses may include aerobic dancing, step aerobics, weight lifting, or swimming. Ms. Gonzalez will receive $1,000 per course per season.

In addition, Ms. Gonzalez will serve as a

15 personal trainer. The employee's personal training duties will vary. They will depend on the number of clients who request a personal trainer. She will receive $20 for each hour of personal training. Following are

20 the employee's personal training duties:

- identify a client's fitness needs with various fitness tests
- outline and suggest a fitness program
- teach fitness methods

25 - supervise the client's fitness program
- check the client's fitness progress

The employee may be dismissed by Phoebe's Fitness Gym for any of the following reasons:

30 - more than a few absences
- any repeated tardiness
- any unprofessional behavior

If there are any complaints by clients about the employee, they will be discussed

35 with the employee.

1. This document could best be described as which of the following?

   (1) offer of employment
   (2) resumé
   (3) employment contract
   (4) legal agreement
   (5) memo

2. According to the document, what is the maximum number of courses Ms. Gonzalez can teach per season?

   (1) one
   (2) two
   (3) three
   (4) four
   (5) The document does not say.

3. What choices about her work load can Ms. Gonzalez make, according to the document?

   (1) She can teach only one class.
   (2) She can teach only courses and do no personal training.
   (3) She can work for twenty hours per week as a personal trainer.
   (4) She can teach more than two courses if they are offered.
   (5) She has no choices.

4. In choosing a style for the document, what was the author's most important consideration?

   (1) entertaining the audience
   (2) being clear and thorough
   (3) adding interesting details
   (4) being polite
   (5) sounding important

5. How does the document help Ms. Gonzalez?

   (1) It guarantees that she will not be laid off.
   (2) It ensures that she will make at least $10,000 per year.
   (3) It gives her medical insurance.
   (4) It tells exactly what her responsibilities and wages are.
   (5) It promises many years of employment.

   Answers are on page 228.

CHAPTER 6

Prose Fiction

Novels and short stories are two types of *prose fiction*. They both deal with imaginary characters and events. In this section, you will study seven basic elements of fiction: setting, plot, conflict, character, point of view, literal and figurative language, and theme.

Setting

The *setting* of a story is a combination of place, time, and atmosphere. It tells where and when a story takes place. A story may be set in a real or an imaginary place. It may be also set in the past, present, or future.

Place

Place refers to physical setting. A turn-of-the-century castle, a high-rise apartment building, an ocean liner, somebody's living room—these are all examples of place.

The action of a story can be confined to one place, or it can move around from one place to the next. *Jaws* takes place in a small resort community on Long Island. In *The Adventures of Huckleberry Finn,* the action follows the Mississippi River through three states—Missouri, Illinois, and Mississippi. Occasionally, you must infer the physical setting of a story from details the author provides.

As you read the following paragraph, try to picture the place the author is describing. Then put a check in front of the correct answer to the questions that follow.

> The bright sun overhead warmed the crowds scurrying across the streets and sidewalks. Office workers poured out of modern skyscrapers in unending streams. Cars, cabs, and buses honked and bellowed at each other like angry bulls. Near every street corner, red tulips nodded under budding trees. People scurried in and out of busy restaurants.

1. Where does this scene take place?

_____ (1) company's headquarters

_____ (2) major urban business district

_____ (3) restaurant

2. Where does most of the action in this passage take place?

_____ (1) in cars, cabs, and buses

_____ (2) on city streets and sidewalks

_____ (3) in restaurants

For the first question, choice (2), a *major urban business district,* is correct. You can tell from the references to skyscrapers, cars, cabs, buses, and the large numbers of people. For the second question, choice (2), *on city streets and sidewalks,* is correct. Crowds fill the sidewalks and traffic jams the streets.

Time

The second element of setting is ***time***. Every story takes place in time—in the past, the present, or the future.

Some stories are set in a particular time period. Herman Wouk's *The Winds of War* takes place at the start of World War II. Charles Dickens' *Oliver Twist* is set in mid-19th-century London.

How long a period can a story cover? James Joyce's *Ulysses,* which runs hundreds of pages, covers only one day in 1904. *Roots,* the popular historical novel about slavery by Alex Haley (made into a very moving television miniseries in 1977), plays out over centuries.

Based on the passage on page 132, put a check in front of the correct answer to the questions that follow.

1. When does the scene occur?

_____ (1) early morning

_____ (2) noon

_____ (3) late afternoon

_____ (4) evening

2. In which month does the scene most probably take place?

_____ (1) May

_____ (2) July

_____ (3) September

_____ (4) December

For the first question, the correct answer is choice (2), *noon.* You can figure this out from the references to the overhead sun and to what is obviously the lunchtime crowd. The correct answer to the second question is choice (1), *May.* You can infer the spring season from the tulips and budding trees. May is the only spring month given in the choices.

Atmosphere

Atmosphere refers to the nonphysical environment of a story, the mood or general feeling in which a story is rooted.

The atmosphere of *The Wizard of Oz,* like the land of Oz itself and the yellow brick road, is bright, colorful, and happy. If you have read Stephen King's *Carrie,* you know that the atmosphere in that high school gym is unbearably tense. The dark, barren, and lonely landscape of Transylvania adds to the already gloomy atmosphere of *Dracula.*

Whenever you read fiction, pay attention to the atmosphere. Notice how it affects the characters and how the characters react to it.

Pay particular attention to the setting and atmosphere in the passage below. Then put a check in front of the correct answers.

The deserted road suddenly gave way to a long, wide boulevard. On either side stood a single row of stately oak trees. The overarching branches formed a protective canopy. From the lower limbs, strands of Spanish moss seemed to wave a gray salute.

Tyrone's heart beat faster as the wagon wheels rolled nearer Brentwood. Before the sun dipped beneath the horizon, he had been able to catch a glimpse of the plantation house with its white pillars and the wrought-iron balcony. By some miracle, it was still standing. Four years of civil war had not changed the beautiful old place.

But where was Julia? It wouldn't be homecoming until, from the balcony railing, her voice rang out, calling his name. He walked faster, heading hopefully toward the sound of home.

1. What type of atmosphere does this passage contain?

_____ (1) fear

_____ (2) hope

_____ (3) sadness

2. When he sees that his old home still stands, what does Tyrone feel?

_____ (1) doubt

_____ (2) disappointment

_____ (3) anticipation

3. Where does this scene most likely take place?

_____ (1) Oregon

_____ (2) Hawaii

_____ (3) Louisiana

4. When does the action take place?

_____ (1) just before sunrise

_____ (2) in the morning

_____ (3) late afternoon

For the first question, choice (2), *hope,* is the correct answer. With every step he draws nearer home, Tyrone feels encouraged. The tall trees protect him. The moss seems to salute him. His old home still stands. For the second question, choice (3), *anticipation,* is the correct answer. Tyrone anticipates his reunion with Julia. For the third question, choice (3), *Louisiana,* is the correct answer. The references to Spanish moss, the plantation house, and a recent civil war suggest a Southern setting such as Louisiana. For the fourth question, choice (3), *late afternoon,* is the correct answer. Tyrone catches a glimpse of the house before the sun sets.

EXERCISE 1

Directions: Read the following passage and then put a check in front of the correct answer to the questions that follow.

Knowing that there would be ample food, if he could but catch it, Pentaquod pulled his canoe farther inland, hiding it among the oaks and maples which lined the shore, for he knew that he must explore this island quickly. And as he moved among the trees and came to a
5 meadow, he heard the comforting cry so familiar in his days along the great river: "Bob-white! Bob-white!" Now the call came from his left, then from a clump of grass to his right, and sometimes from a spot almost under his feet, but always it was as clear and distinct as if an uncle who could whistle had been standing at his side.

10 "Bob-white!" It was the call of the quail, that sly bird with the brown-and-white head. Of all the birds that flew, this was the best eating, and if this island held a multitude, Pentaquod could not only survive on his fish but eat like a chieftain with his quail.

With extreme caution he started inland, noticing everything, aware
15 that his life might depend upon the carefulness of his observation. With every step he found only reassurance and never a sight of danger: nut trees laden with midsummer shells not yet ripe; droppings of rabbits, and the signs that foxes lived here, and the location of brambled berry bushes, and the woody nests of eagles, and the honeysuckle twisting
20 among the lower branches of the cedar trees.

—Excerpted from *Chesapeake,* by James A. Michener

1. What is Pentaquod exploring?

_____ (1) a forest

_____ (2) a river

_____ (3) an island

2. During what month does the passage most likely take place?

_____ (1) March

_____ (2) May

_____ (3) July

3. What can you infer about Pentaquod?

_____ (1) He is an Indian.

_____ (2) He is a bob-white.

_____ (3) He is running from someone.

4. How would you best describe the atmosphere conveyed by the passage?

_____ (1) hopeful

_____ (2) tropical

_____ (3) lonely

5. What does the word *ample* (line 1) mean?

_____ (1) cooked

_____ (2) more than enough

_____ (3) not nearly sufficient

Answers are on page 228.

Plot

Plot consists of the action or series of events around which a story is built. Plot tells what happens. An effective plot keeps the reader eager to find out what happens next.

As you read the following story, pay particular attention to the series of events that contribute to the plot. Then answer the questions that follow.

Early Autumn

When Bill was very young, they had been in love. Many nights they had spent walking, talking together. Then something not very important had come between them, and they didn't speak. Impulsively [without much thought], she had married a man she
5 thought she loved. Bill went away, bitter about women.

Yesterday, walking across Washington Square [a park in New York City], she saw him for the first time in years.

"Bill Walker," she said.

He stopped. At first he did not recognize her, to him she looked
10 so old.

"Mary! Where did you come from?"

Unconsciously [without thinking], she lifted her face as though wanting a kiss, but he held out his hand. She took it.

"I live in New York now," she said.

15   "Oh"—smiling politely. Then a little frown came quickly between his eyes.

"Always wondered what happened to you, Bill."

"I'm a lawyer. Nice firm, way downtown."

"Married yet?"

20   "Sure. Two kids."

"Oh," she said.

A great many people went past them through the park. People they didn't know. It was late afternoon. Nearly sunset. Cold.

"And your husband?" he asked her.

25   "We have three children. I work in the bursar's [treasurer's] office at Columbia [University]."

"You're looking very . . ." (he wanted to say old) ". . . well," he said.

She understood. Under the trees in Washington Square, she found herself desperately reaching back into the past. She had been older 30   than he in Ohio. Now she was not young at all. Bill was still young.

"We live on Central Park West," she said. "Come and see us sometime."

"Sure," he replied. "You and your husband must have dinner with my family some night. Any night. Lucille and I'd love to have you."

35   The leaves fell slowly from the trees in the square. Fell without wind. Autumn dusk. She felt a little sick.

"We'd love it," she answered.

"You ought to see my kids." He grinned.

Suddenly the lights came on up the whole length of Fifth Avenue, 40   chains of misty brilliance in the blue air.

"There's my bus," she said.

He held out his hand, "Good-bye."

"When . . ." she wanted to say, but the bus was ready to pull off. The lights on the avenue blurred, twinkled, blurred. And she was afraid to open her mouth as she entered the bus. Afraid it would be impossible to utter a word.

Suddenly she shrieked very loudly, "Good-bye!" But the bus door had closed.

The bus started. People came between them outside, people crossing the street, people they didn't know. Space and people. She lost sight of Bill. Then she remembered she had forgotten to give him her address—or to ask him for his—or tell him that her youngest boy was named Bill, too.

—Excerpted from "Early Autumn" by Langston Hughes

1. Why did Bill and Mary break up?

_____ (1) They had very different interests.

_____ (2) They didn't really love each other.

_____ (3) They had a fight about something unimportant.

2. After her breakup with Bill, who did Mary marry?

_____ (1) a nice man and had four children

_____ (2) a man she thought she loved and had three children

_____ (3) a lawyer like Bill and named her son after Bill

3. Why did Bill stop in midsentence when he started to tell Mary how she looked?

_____ (1) because he thought she looked more beautiful

_____ (2) because he thought she looked older

_____ (3) because he thought she looked much heavier

The answer to the first question is choice (3), *had a fight about something unimportant.* You learn this fact in the first paragraph of the story. The answer to the second question is choice (2), *a man she thought she loved and had three children.* In the first paragraph, you learn that "impulsively, she [Mary] had married a man she thought she loved." Line 25 tells you that Mary has three children. The answer to the third question is choice (2), *older.* You learn this in lines 9–10 and again in an aside at the story's midpoint (line 27). The information is set off in parentheses.

Conflict

Every event in a story is essential to the plot. Each development advances the action of the story. *Conflict* is the struggle between opposing forces. The points of tension in a story are part of the conflict. There is almost no limit to the forms conflict can take. The conflict can take place within a person, with others, against nations, or against nature. Another common conflict pits good against evil. A single character often wrestles with a difficult decision or struggles to carry on in spite of great pain or intense emotion. Note the chart shown below.

FOUR MAJOR TYPES OF CONFLICT

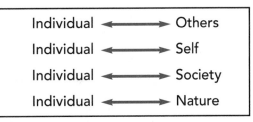

Individual ⟷ Others
Individual ⟷ Self
Individual ⟷ Society
Individual ⟷ Nature

In "Early Autumn," several events precede the *climax,* or turning point, in the story. Bill and Mary had been in love years before. Bill is younger than Mary. They broke up over something unimportant. Mary married another man she thought she loved. Bill became bitter about women. Then, unexpectedly, they meet on a cold afternoon in a park in New York City. Mary is surprised to see Bill. He is amazed at how much older she looks. Mary expects a kiss, but Bill just shakes her hand. They realize they both now live in New York City and that each is married and has children.

At the turning point (climax) of the story, Bill says to Mary, "You're looking very . . ." and his voice trails off. He wants to say "old," and Mary understands what he is thinking. She wants desperately to reach back into the past and make a connection with Bill once again, but with his unfinished sentence she realizes that this isn't possible. Bill invites Mary to bring her family for dinner sometime. She agrees but feels sick inside. Suddenly she sees her bus coming. Bill holds out his hand and says good-bye. Mary is so filled with emotion that she can't speak. She is not able to say good-bye until after the bus door closes, and then she does so in a loud shriek. It dawns on her that they forgot to exchange addresses and that she didn't tell Bill that she has named her son after him.

You can visualize the plot of a story in the general shape of a hill or ocean wave. One or usually several events lead upward toward the climax, or turning point. Once the climax is reached, the plot heads downward toward a *resolution,* or ending.

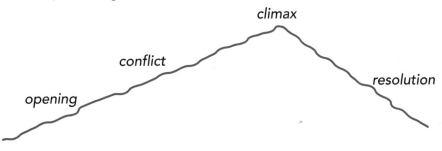

In "Early Autumn," the climax occurs when Bill begins to tell Mary how she looks but doesn't complete the sentence. Mary knows at that point that there is no further connection between her and Bill. From its opening, the story builds toward this moment. Once it is over, the tension is broken and the story ends.

EXERCISE 2

Directions: Read the selection below and then put a check in front of the correct answer to the questions that follow.

"Well, which is it, son?"

"I told you I don't have nothin' to say to you, man. And I ain't your son."

"You're either an Overlord or an East King," Detective Mack said, for about the tenth time. "We know you're one or the other."

"Brilliant," I said. The Overlords and the East Kings were the only two gangs in the whole East End.

He ignored the sarcasm, deciding instead to pretend like he already knew everything else there was to know about me. "You're Mary Lucy's boy, Johnny. You live in the Roberts Homes, Building 7, second floor, with your mom and two little sisters. They depend on you. So do yourself a big favor now and level with me. Which of these guys can you identify?" He spread the photographs out on the table.

I didn't like him talking about Mom and the girls. I didn't like being pushed.

Just then, two cops came to the door. They said something to Mack. By the looks on their faces, I knew Eddie was dead. I listened as hard as I could.

"Multiple stab wounds," somebody said.

Eddie was my best friend in the world.

Mack walked back over to me. He threw a beefy arm around my shoulder. "We got us a murder case, Johnny," he said. "So you can talk to me now or you can talk to the judge and jury later. Up to you."

At that moment, I hated myself. Hated that I wasn't home where Mom and the girls needed me, where I could have been if I'd just stayed away from the whole thing. I could have stayed away. I could have. Easy. But I didn't. So now I was stuck here with this fat Mack. And he wouldn't stop pushing till I talked. But I couldn't talk. And I couldn't let him see I was scared.

The two cops had left the door wide open. I knew the steps were right outside. Mack was too fat to run. My heart was pounding. My mouth was dry as paper. Nobody'd ever catch me again.

I made a run for the door, turned, and flew down the steps. Next thing I knew, a plainclothesman had me in a headlock. I was gasping for breath, but I kicked and yelled with all my might.

"Quiet," somebody thundered, and it wasn't the guy who had me. It was somebody new in the stairwell, somebody with the biggest, meanest voice I ever heard. She wore a badge and was tapping a nightstick across her palm.

"Quiet," she said again. "And I mean this minute. Next minute'll be too late."

1. How does Johnny feel about Detective Mack?

_____ (1) scared

_____ (2) indifferent

_____ (3) hostile

2. The conflict in the paragraph beginning "At that moment . . ." is happening between Johnny and who?

_____ (1) himself

_____ (2) the police

_____ (3) Eddie

3. When does the turning point of the action occur?

_____ (1) when Johnny encounters the plainclothesman

_____ (2) when Johnny learns that Eddie is dead

_____ (3) when the policewoman silences Johnny

4. What can be inferred about the location of this scene?

_____ (1) it occurs in a police station

_____ (2) it occurs in a housing project

_____ (3) it occurs in a prison

5. Why was Detective Mack questioning Johnny?

_____ (1) Johnny was suspected of stabbing Eddie.

_____ (2) Johnny had witnessed a stabbing.

_____ (3) Mary Lucy had turned her son in to the authorities.

Answers are on page 228.

EXERCISE 3

Directions: Read the selection below and then put a check in front of the correct answer to the questions that follow.

Someone thrust a mask at the young man near Gwen, who had been wounded. Though swaying, and scarcely aware of what was happening, he managed to hold it to his face.

Even so, barely half the passengers were on oxygen at the end of fifteen seconds—the critical time. By then, those not breathing oxygen were lapsing into drowsy stupor; in another fifteen seconds, most were unconscious.

Gwen Meighen received no oxygen, nor immediate help. The unconsciousness, caused by her injuries, deepened.

Then, on the flight deck, Anson Harris, accepting the risk of further structural damage and possible total destruction of the aircraft, made his decision for a high-speed dive, saving Gwen and others from asphyxiation [unconsciousness].

The dive began at twenty-eight thousand feet altitude; it ended, two and a half minutes later, at ten thousand feet.

A human being can survive without oxygen for three to four minutes without damage to the brain.

For the first half of the dive—for a minute and a quarter, down to nineteen thousand feet—the air continued to be rarefied and insufficient to support life. Below that point, increasing amounts of oxygen were present and breathable.

At twelve thousand feet regular breathing was possible. By ten— with little time to spare, but enough—consciousness returned to all aboard Flight Two who had lost it, excepting Gwen. Many were unaware of having been unconscious at all.

—Excerpted from *Airport,* by Arthur Hailey

1. Around what does the action in this passage center?

_____ (1) restoring oxygen in the cabin

_____ (2) assisting critically injured passengers

_____ (3) repairing a damaged aircraft

2. What does Anson Harris think about a high-speed dive?

_____ (1) It is too dangerous to try.

_____ (2) It is worth a gamble.

_____ (3) It is technically impossible.

3. When did the passengers regain consciousness?

_____ (1) when the plane dived to 12,000 feet

_____ (2) when the plane equalized pressure

_____ (3) when the plane reached 10,000 feet

4. What can be inferred about the loss of much oxygen?

_____ (1) It was a result of damage to the aircraft.

_____ (2) It was a result of engine malfunction.

_____ (3) It was a result of human error.

5. When did the turning point in the action occur?

_____ (1) when the passengers regained consciousness

_____ (2) when the pilot decided to dive

_____ (3) when the plane was damaged

Answers are on pages 228–229.

Character

Character is an essential element of fiction. Writers strive to create characters who are believable and who stir our sympathy. To do this, they often draw upon their own everyday experiences.

Some fictional characters strike us as quite familiar. In Charles Dickens' *A Christmas Carol,* Ebenezer Scrooge reminds us of stingy people we have met in real life. We also recognize Bob Cratchit from our own experiences with people who are good-natured and easygoing.

As you read about fictional characters, think about these three questions:

1. What details does the writer use to describe the characters?

2. What do the characters say and do as they react to others and to different situations?

3. What do the characters' thoughts and feelings reveal about them?

When you study character, it may help you to think of the three questions as sides of a triangle. Each side represents one general category of information about a particular character.

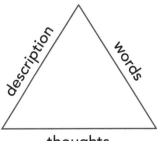

Now let's look at how one distinguished American writer described one of her fictional characters. Read the passage below and then put a check in front of the correct answer to each question.

It was December—a bright frozen day in the early morning. Far out in the country there was an old Negro woman with her head tied in a red rag, coming along a path through the pinewoods. Her name was Phoenix Jackson. She was very old and small and she walked slowly in the dark pine shadows, moving a little from side to side in her steps, with the balanced heaviness and lightness of a pendulum in a grandfather clock. She carried a thin, small cane made from an umbrella, and with this she kept tapping the frozen earth in front of her. This made a grave and persistent noise in the still air that seemed meditative [reflective] like the chirping of a solitary little bird.

She wore a dark striped dress reaching down to her shoe tops, and an equally long apron of bleached sugar sacks, with a full pocket: all neat and tidy, but every time she took a step she might have fallen over her shoelaces, which dragged from her unlaced shoes. She looked straight ahead. Her eyes were blue with age. Her skin had a pattern all its own of numberless branching wrinkles and as though a whole little tree stood in the middle of her forehead, but a golden color ran underneath, and the two knobs of her cheeks were illuminated [lit] by a yellow burning under the dark. Under the red rag her hair came down on her neck in the frailest of ringlets, still black, and with an odor like copper.

—Excerpted from "A Worn Path," by Eudora Welty

1. How does this passage portray Phoenix Jackson?

_____ (1) old

_____ (2) happy

_____ (3) confused

2. How can you best describe Phoenix Jackson's clothes?

_____ (1) very messy

_____ (2) unusual but neat

_____ (3) dirty

3. How does the passage paint Phoenix Jackson?

_____ (1) unfriendly

_____ (2) stylish

_____ (3) odd

The answer to the first question is choice (1), *old.* The passage emphasizes her great age. The writer describes her deep wrinkles and likens her movements to those of a pendulum in a grandfather clock. For question 2, choice (2), *unusual but neat,* is correct. She is described as neat and tidy. Her clothing is simple and a little strange. The answer to the third question is choice (3), *odd.* The old woman's appearance is curious and odd, but in a pleasant sort of way.

Notice how the description of Phoenix Jackson helps reveal her character. We can see her almost perfectly with her red rag turban, tiny stature, slow, rocking gait, aged eyes, many wrinkles, and frail ringlets. Her cane, dress, and dragging shoelaces suggest that she is somewhat odd, or unusual.

EXERCISE 4

Directions: The passage below reveals character through speech and action. As you read it, take note of what the character says and does. Then answer the questions that follow in the space provided.

After a while the fish stopped beating at the wire and started circling slowly again. The old man was gaining line steadily now. But he felt faint again. He lifted some sea water with his left hand and put it on his head. Then he put more on and rubbed the back of his neck.

"I have no cramps," he said. "He'll be up soon and I can last. You have to last. Don't even speak of it."

He kneeled against the bow [forward part of a boat] and, for a moment, slipped the line over his back again. I'll rest now while he goes out on the circle and then stand up and work on him when he comes in, he decided.

It was a great temptation to rest in the bow and let the fish make one circle by himself without recovering any line. But when the strain showed the fish had turned to come toward the boat, the old man rose to his feet and started the pivoting [turning] and the weaving pulling that brought in all the line he gained.

—Excerpted from *The Old Man and the Sea,* by Ernest Hemingway

1. Why did the old man pour seawater on his head?

2. What do the actions of the old man reveal about his character?

3. To whom is the old man speaking?

4. In this story, what is a *bow*?

Point of View

Character can also be revealed from the first-person point of view. *Point of view* refers to how a particular series of events looks to a specific individual. When two people describe an event that both have witnessed, the descriptions differ because each person speaks from his or her perspective, or viewpoint. Point of view is unique for each person.

When a story is told in the first person, the writer and main character appear to be one and the same. The words *I* and *me* are used frequently as the main character reveals deeply personal thoughts and feelings. The reader has a sense of being able to read the character's mind from the inside.

In the following selection, the writer uses the first-person point of view to help the reader get to know the main character.

EXERCISE 5

Directions: Read the passage below. For each statement that follows, write *A* if the narrator would agree. Write *D* if the narrator would disagree.

The night was not so pleasant as the evening, for it got chilly; and being put between two gentlemen (the rough-faced one and another) to prevent my tumbling off the coach, I was nearly smothered by their falling asleep, and completely blocking me up. They squeezed me so hard sometimes, that I could not help crying out, "Oh, if you please!" which they didn't like at all, because it woke them. Opposite me was an elderly lady in a great fur cloak, who looked in the dark more like a haystack than a lady, she was wrapped up to such a degree. This lady had a basket with her, and she hadn't known what to do with it, for a long time, until she found that, on account of my legs being short, it could go underneath me. It cramped and hurt me so, that it made me perfectly miserable; but if I moved in the least, and made a glass that was in the basket rattle against something else (as it was sure to do), she gave me the cruelest poke with her foot, and said, "Come, don't you fidget. Your bones are young enough, I'm sure!"

—Excerpted from *David Copperfield*, by Charles Dickens

_____ 1. My ride in the coach was generally comfortable.

_____ 2. My companions in the coach were friendly.

_____ 3. I am still growing.

_____ 4. I am tall for my age.

_____ 5. The lady treated me in a kindly, reassuring way.

Answers are on page 229.

EXERCISE 6

Questions 1–7 are based on the passage below, which is written in a Southern dialect.

He was drunk, and weaving about in his saddle; he was over fifty years old, and had a very red face. Everybody yelled at him, and laughed at him, and sassed him, and he sassed
5 back, and said he'd attend to them and lay them out in their regular turns, but he couldn't wait now, because he'd come to town to kill old Colonel Sherburn, and his motto was, "meat first, and spoon vittles to top off on."

10 He see me, and rode up and says—

"Whar'd you come f'm, boy? You prepared to die?"

Then he rode on. I was scared; but a man says—

15 "He don't mean nothing; he's always a carryin' on like that, when he's drunk. He's the best-naturedest old fool in Arkansaw— never hurt nobody, drunk nor sober."

Boggs rode up before the biggest store in
20 town and bent his head down so he could see under the curtain of the awning, and yells—

"Come out here, Sherburn! Come out and meet the man you've swindled. You're the houn' I'm after, and I'm a gwyne to have you, too!"

25 And so he went on, calling Sherburn everything he could lay his tongue to, and the whole street packed with people listening and laughing and going on. By-and-by a proud-looking man about fifty-five—and he was a
30 heap the best dressed man in that town, too— steps out of the store, and the crowd drops back on each side to let him come. He says to Boggs, mighty ca'm and slow—he says:

"I'm tired of this; but I'll endure it till one
35 o'clock. Till one o'clock, mind—no longer. If you open your mouth against me only once, after that time, you can't travel so far but I will find you."

—Excerpted from *The Adventures of Huckleberry Finn,*
by Mark Twain

1. From whose point of view is the story told?

    (1) Boggs'
    (2) Colonel Sherburn's
    (3) the narrator's
    (4) the townspeople's
    (5) a store owner's

2. Why does Boggs want to kill Colonel Sherburn?

    (1) He is jealous of the colonel's wealth.
    (2) He thinks Sherburn has cheated him.
    (3) Colonel Sherburn insulted Mrs. Boggs.
    (4) He is offended by Sherburn's drunken behavior.
    (5) Colonel Sherburn started a fight inside a store.

3. How does the narrator describe Colonel Sherburn?

    (1) well dressed
    (2) humble
    (3) grandfatherly
    (4) nervous
    (5) hated by the townspeople

4. How does the narrator feel when Boggs asks him if he is prepared to die (lines 11–12)?

    (1) singled out
    (2) afraid
    (3) amused
    (4) surprised
    (5) angry

5. How would you describe Colonel Sherburn's final response to Boggs?

    (1) military
    (2) threatening
    (3) drunken
    (4) tolerant
    (5) amused

6. How do the townspeople feel about Boggs?

   (1) They prefer to keep their distance from him.
   (2) They fear him when he's drunk.
   (3) They consider him harmless.
   (4) They think he rides his horse well.
   (5) They are upset by his outbursts.

7. "Whar'd you come f'm, boy?" is an example of what?

   (1) character
   (2) dialect
   (3) prejudice
   (4) point of view
   (5) setting

Answers are on page 229.

Literal and Figurative Language

In the conversation below, a group of students talk about taking an important test. Joe, Tony, and Sasha use *figurative language* to express their feelings. A figurative expression does not mean exactly what it says. It conveys the speaker's message with words chosen for effect, not literal truth.

JOE: I'm on pins and needles about this test. Aren't you worried, Martha?

MARTHA: Of course not. I've been studying.

TONY: Martha, you're always as cool as a cucumber. But not me. I'm shaking like a leaf. What about you, Sasha?

SASHA: Pins, needles, cucumbers, leaves. I'll tell you one thing—I'm shooting for the stars.

In the example above, Joe is not sitting "on pins and needles." Martha's temperature is not really "as cool as a cucumber." Nor is Sasha really "shooting for the stars."

Now read the same conversation, but written with literal language. With *literal language*, writers say exactly what they mean.

JOE: I'm really nervous about this test. Aren't you worried, Martha?

MARTHA: Not at all. I've been studying.

TONY: You're always calm, Martha. Not me. I'm worried. What about you, Sasha?

SASHA: All I know is I'm aiming for the best grade I can get.

Fiction writers rely on figurative language to express meanings in fresh and surprising ways. Figurative speech, used carefully, catches our attention and holds our interest. Sometimes, it is the most powerful way to show emotion.

Literal: The star burned brightly in the dark sky.

Figurative: The star was a diamond in the black velvet of the sky.

Do you see how the figurative statement is stronger and more expressive? Sometimes an author uses exaggeration for greater effect.

Literal: The old car was sounding worse and worse.

Figurative: The old car coughed and belched. Then it gave a terrible sigh.

The literal meaning, of course, is that the car broke down. But notice how figurative speech can give human qualities to the old machine. A vehicle can't really cough, belch, or sigh, but such language can be much more vivid, or lively.

EXERCISE 7

Directions: Match each figurative expression listed on the left with its literal meaning on the right. Write the correct letter on the line.

Figurative Expressions

_____ 1. raining cats and dogs

_____ 2. make hay while the sun shines

_____ 3. head in the clouds

_____ 4. with hair standing on end

_____ 5. eat crow

_____ 6. like death warmed over

_____ 7. hit the jackpot

_____ 8. like two peas in a pod

_____ 9. beat around the bush

_____ 10. keep your shirt on

Literal Meanings

(a) visibly afraid

(b) sickly in appearance

(c) alike in every way

(d) downpour

(e) give unclear answers

(f) win a lot of money

(g) take advantage of opportunity

(h) not practical

(i) stay calm

(j) admit publicly that you were wrong

Answers are on page 229.

EXERCISE 8

Directions: Write *L* in front of each statement that is used literally. Write *F* in front of each statement that is meant figuratively.

_____ 1. From the plane, we could see white, fluffy clouds below us.

_____ 2. To eat the nuts, first crack the shells.

_____ 3. They'll be jumping for joy when they get the good news.

_____ 4. Watch your step on the stairway.

_____ 5. That bucket won't hold water.

_____ 6. Dogs can be trained to walk on their hind feet.

_____ 7. The whole world smiled at me.

_____ 8. It's a marriage made in heaven.

_____ 9. She was walking on air.

_____ 10. The children were beside themselves with anticipation.

Answers are on page 229.

EXERCISE 9

Directions: As you read the passage below, notice how figurative language is used. Then put a check in front of the correct answer to the questions that follow.

The tractors came over the roads and into the fields, great crawlers moving like insects, having the incredible strength of insects. They crawled over the ground, laying the track and rolling on it and picking it up. Diesel tractors, puttering while they stood idle; they thundered
5 when they moved, and then settled down to a droning roar. Snubnosed monsters, raising the dust and sticking their snouts into it, straight down the country, across the country, through fences, through dooryards, in and out of gullies [valleys] in straight lines. They did not run on the ground, but on their own roadbeds. They ignored hills and
10 gulches, water courses, fences, houses.

The man sitting in the iron seat did not look like a man; gloved, goggled, rubber dust mask over nose and mouth, he was a part of the monster, a robot in the seat. The thunder of the cylinder sounded through the country, became one with the air and the earth, so that
15 earth and air muttered in sympathetic [shared] vibration. The driver could not control it—straight across country it went, cutting through a dozen farms and straight back.

—Excerpted from *The Grapes of Wrath,* by John Steinbeck

1. What does the entire first paragraph describe?

_____ (1) monsters

_____ (2) tractors

_____ (3) insects

2. In the first sentence, what does the phrase "moving like insects" indicate about the machines?

_____ (1) They flew over the ground.

_____ (2) They kicked up dust.

_____ (3) They crawled across the ground.

3. What does the passage imply about the farms?

_____ (1) They were being destroyed.

_____ (2) Spring planting was in progress.

_____ (3) Machinery was being used to increase production.

4. What is the description of the tractors "raising the dust and sticking their snouts into it" (line 6) intended to suggest?

_____ (1) pigs

_____ (2) monsters

_____ (3) machines

5. The man on the tractor is described as looking like which of the following?

_____ (1) monster

_____ (2) robot

_____ (3) insect

Answers are on page 230.

EXERCISE 10

Directions: Read the passage below and then put a check in front of the correct answer to the questions that follow.

One night, a moth flew into the candle, was caught, burnt dry, and held. I must have been staring at the candle, or maybe I looked up when a shadow crossed my page; at any rate, I saw it all. A golden female moth, a biggish one with a two-inch wingspan, flapped into the fire,
5 dropped her abdomen into the wet wax, stuck, flamed, frazzled and fried in a second. Her moving wings ignited like tissue paper, enlarging the circle of light in the clearing and creating out of the darkness the sudden blue sleeves of my sweater, the green leaves of jewelweed by my side, the ragged red trunk of a pine. At once the light contracted
10 again and the moth's wings vanished in a fine, foul smoke. At the same time, her six legs clawed, curled, blackened, and ceased, disappearing utterly. And her head jerked in spasms, making a spattering noise; her antennae crisped and burned away and her heaving mouth parts crackled like pistol fire. When it was all over, her head was, so far as
15 I could determine, gone, gone the long way of her wings and legs. Had she been new, or old? Had she made and laid her eggs, had she done her work? All that was left was the glowing horn shell of her abdomen and thorax [throat]—a fraying, partially collapsed gold tube jammed upright in the candle's round pool.

—Excerpted from *Holy the Firm*, by Annie Dillard

1. What does the action in this passage center around?

_____ (1) the author

_____ (2) a fire

_____ (3) a moth and a candle

2. "Her moving wings ignited like tissue paper" (line 6) means what about the moth's wings?

_____ (1) they were made of tissue paper

_____ (2) they burned quickly

_____ (3) they were beautiful

3. To what does the phrase "crackled like pistol fire" (line 14) refer?

_____ (1) sights

_____ (2) sounds

_____ (3) feelings

4. The action in this passage most likely takes place in which location?

_____ (1) in a forest clearing

_____ (2) at a kitchen table

_____ (3) on a windowsill

Answers are on page 230.

Theme

The theme is the basic idea that underlies a work of fiction and gives it meaning. Rarely, if ever, is it directly stated. You should be able to infer it from the setting, plot, characters, and language. Certain themes appear over and over in literature. Here are some of the most common.

Story	Theme
Huckleberry Finn	The journey from innocence to experience
Robinson Crusoe	Facing and overcoming the unknown
The Wizard of Oz	Good overcomes evil
The Lord of the Flies	Evil overcomes good

There are, of course, many other themes as well. Writers sometimes combine several themes in a single novel or short story. After you read the story below, write its theme on the line provided.

Estara walked carefully between the yawning craters of Novos. Moments before, her bubble rocket had crash-landed on a ridge of soft volcanic sand. Little was left of the vast meteor shower that had carried her off course, hurling the rocket into this strange place.

She stared into the black void of space. Somewhere out there was a burning cinder or perhaps a swirl of smoky debris. That was all one would find of the planet Earth. Because of the Great A-War, she and thousands like her had sought a way out of the annihilation [sudden death]. The famous bubble rockets were the answer, but only a few people had been able to secure them. She was sure the rest had perished.

Where were the others, she wondered? Did they reach the earthlike planet Geos, or did they too lose their way?

Ahead of her, Estara saw rocks of many colors, and they glowed. She heard an odd sound like water rushing over rocks. She listened more closely for other sounds. Suddenly, there was a noise like a squeal, perhaps human but possibly an animal. She was not sure. She pulled out her laser gun, stopped, and listened again. Was she safe or was she about to confront an alien? Estara did not know, but she was not going to take any chances.

THEME: _____

_____

Which of the themes listed on the previous page is also the theme of this passage? You are right if you said that the theme is *facing and overcoming the unknown*. You cannot tell if Estara will overcome whatever awaits her.

EXERCISE 11

Directions: As you read the passage below, note the setting, the plot, and the characters. These will help you identify the theme. Then put a check in front of the correct answer to the questions that follow.

He could just see himself in a new home with a nice back yard, nice trees and lawn, a patio with a barbecue—these things he'd never had, never missed. But why not? A nice garage with a little workshop, like the gringo magazines show all the time. It would be fun.

The more he thought about it, the more he liked the idea. What he enjoyed most was the ability he now had—the freedom due to his financial success—that allowed him to make a decision to move where he wanted. This was a luxury little known in his environment. And on the way home from his various out-of-town jobs he began dropping in to look at houses in new tract developments.

It was an old story, but new to Pete. The ghetto protects as well as imprisons. As he drove along in the burgeoning [growing] suburbs, he saw tract after tract, with signs advertising the homes for miles in all directions.

Pete almost believed it when the salesman at the first office where he stopped told him there were no homes available. He didn't want to argue. But a few days later, when he'd stopped at the fifth or sixth tract office, he was a little better prepared. Not much, but a little.

"No, I'm sorry, Mr. Sandoval. The houses are all taken."

"Well, that one on the corner, it has a for sale sign on it. I want that one."

"It's taken. We haven't had a chance to take the sign down yet."

"I don't believe you. Show me the name of the guy that bought it."

"Just a minute," and the salesman went to consult a more experienced man. The other man came back to Pete.

"All our homes are taken," he said simply.

"Then why . . . "

"Make what you want of it, sir, but we have none to sell you."

—Excerpted from *Chicano*, by Richard Vasquez

1. What is Pete doing?

_____ (1) mowing his lawn

_____ (2) looking for a house

_____ (3) shopping for a low-interest mortgage

2. At first, Pete expects which of the following things?

_____ (1) The good houses will be all gone.

_____ (2) The salesmen will try to sell him anything.

_____ (3) His money will buy him whatever he wants.

3. What is the salesmen's attitude toward Pete?

_____ (1) avoidance

_____ (2) indifference

_____ (3) helpfulness

4. Which of the following statements best expresses the theme of this passage?

_____ (1) Everyone dreams about a better life.

_____ (2) People do not give up their prejudices without a fight.

_____ (3) Financial success is no guarantee against discrimination.

Answers are on page 230.

Writing Activity 7

Write three paragraphs about your favorite work of fiction, or choose one you have read in this chapter. In the first paragraph, describe the setting. In the second, summarize the plot. In the third, identify the theme. Refer to the themes listed on page 153 to help you. Be sure to give at least one specific example of how your book's or story's setting, plot, or characterization helps convey the theme.

Answers will vary.

Chapter Review

Questions 1–4 refer to the following passage.

Presently he proceeded again on his forward way. The battle was like the grinding of an immense and terrible machine to him. Its complexities and powers, its grim
5 processes, fascinated him. He must go close and see it produce corpses.

He came to a fence and clambered over it. On the far side, the ground was littered with clothes and guns. A newspaper, folded
10 up, lay in the dirt. A dead soldier was stretched with face hidden in his arm. Farther off there was a group of four or five corpses keeping mournful company. A hot sun had blazed upon the spot.

15 In this place the youth felt that he was an invader. This forgotten part of the battle ground was owned by the dead men, and he hurried, in the vague apprehension [fear] that one of the swollen forms would rise and
20 tell him to begone.

He came finally to a road from which he could see in the distance dark and agitated bodies of troops, smoke-fringed. In the lane was a blood-stained crowd streaming to the rear.
25 The wounded men were cursing, groaning, and wailing. In the air, always, was a mighty swell of sound that it seemed could sway the earth. With the courageous words of the artillery and the spiteful sentences of the musketry mingled
30 red cheers. And from this region of noises came the steady current of the maimed [wounded].

One of the wounded men had a shoeful of blood. He hopped like a schoolboy in a game. He was laughing hysterically.

35 One was swearing that he had been shot in the arm through the commanding general's mismanagement of the army. One was marching with an air imitative of some sublime drum major. Upon his features was
40 an unholy mixture of merriment and agony.

—Excerpted from *The Red Badge of Courage,*
by Stephen Crane

1. How is the youth walking among the wounded portrayed as feeling?

   (1) immortal
   (2) optimistic
   (3) neutral
   (4) worried
   (5) like an invader

2. Where does the scene take place?

   (1) in a hospital
   (2) on a battlefield
   (3) in an army camp
   (4) on a troopship
   (5) at a retirement facility

3. When the author says that "the battle was like the grinding of an immense and terrible machine" (lines 2–3), what does he mean?

   (1) Machines are terrible.
   (2) The war was being fought with many tanks.
   (3) Soldiers were fighting in large formations.
   (4) War is inhuman.
   (5) The battle seemed endless.

4. Which of the following best states the theme of this passage?

   (1) If you are not prepared for battle, you'll be gravely injured.
   (2) Victory brings honor and glory.
   (3) War brings pain and misery.
   (4) One victory doesn't decide a war.
   (5) Generals are responsible for the lives of their men.

Questions 5–7 refer to the following passage.

"I have had so many hardships in this life," said Simple, "that it is a wonder I'll live until I die. I was born young, black, voteless, poor, and hungry, in a state where white
5 folks did not even put Negroes on the census. My daddy said he were never counted in his life by the United States government. And nobody could find a birth certificate for me nowhere. It were not until I
10 come to Harlem that one day a census taker dropped around to my house and asked where were I born and why, also my age and if I was still living. I said, 'Yes, I am here, in spite of all.' "

15 " 'All of what?' asked the census taker. 'Give me the data.' "

" 'All of my corns and bunions, for one,' I said. 'I were borned with corns. Most colored peoples get corns so young, they
20 must be inherited. As for bunions, they seem to come natural, we stands on our feet so much. These feet of mine have stood in everything from soup lines to the draft board. They have supported everything
25 from a packing trunk to a hongry woman. My feet have walked ten thousand miles running errands for white folks and another ten thousand trying to keep up with colored. My feet have stood before altars, at crap
30 tables, bars, graves, kitchen doors, welfare windows, and social security railings. Be sure and include my feet on that census you are taking," I told that man.

"Then I went on to tell him how my feet have helped to keep the American shoe
35 industry going, due to the money I have spent on my feet. 'I have wore out seven hundred pairs of shoes, eighty-nine tennis shoes, forty-four summer sandals, and two hundred and two loafers. The socks my feet
40 have bought could build a knitting mill. The razor blades I have used cutting away corns could pay for a razor plant. Oh, my feet have

helped to make America rich, and I am still standing on them.' "

—Excerpted from "Census" in *Simple's Uncle Sam*, by Langston Hughes

5. How can the tone of Simple's speech best described?

(1) objective
(2) patient
(3) long-suffering
(4) hopeful
(5) arrogant

6. With which of the following does Simple regard his country?

(1) resentment and bitterness
(2) optimism
(3) hatred
(4) affection
(5) loyalty and pride

7. What is the best title for this passage?

(1) The Census Taker
(2) Making a Living on Your Feet
(3) Simple's Corns
(4) The Hardships of Being Black
(5) Wealth and Poverty in America

Questions 8–11 refer to the following passage.

On Sunday, at breakfast, his grandmother asks, "What time did you get in?"

He knows that she knows. The light was on in their bedroom when he pulled into the
5 drive; off, as he came up the stairs.

"I don't know. Twelve? Twelve-thirty?"

"One-thirty," she says.

"One-thirty, then." He nods amiably [cheerfully], helping himself to the toast she
10 has kept warm for him in the oven. The small breakfast nook is washed in sunlight. Sun glints off the jar of honey sitting on the table, filtering through the pale yellow curtains at the window. His head sings with an intricate,
15 melodic line—Telemann? Marais? John Bull? He cannot remember, but he loves those fresh and unfamiliar instruments, the recorder, the harpsichord; their simple statements of truth. He wonders what the weather is like in
20 Dallas. Sunny, he hopes. Warm.

"How can you expect to get a decent night's sleep, coming in at that hour?" She is frowning across the table at him.

"I give up. How can I?"

25 She sighs. "Everything's a joke with you, isn't it?"

"Grandmother, you know something, I'm nuts about you," he says cheerfully. "You're always agitating. I think it's great. You
30 oughta run for President. No kidding."

He gets to his feet, pushing the chair back.

"Where are you going?"

"Outside to wash my car."

35 "Well, don't get chilled. It's not summer, you know."

"I know, I know!"

—Excerpted from *Ordinary People,* by Judith Guest

8. Around what does the action of this passage center?

   (1) a breakfast conversation
   (2) a shared interest in music
   (3) an election
   (4) washing a car
   (5) health

9. How does the young man behave toward his grandmother?

   (1) rudely
   (2) angrily
   (3) sarcastically
   (4) affectionately
   (5) disrespectfully

10. Why does the woman fuss about her grandson?

   (1) because she is a nag
   (2) because she is concerned about his health
   (3) because she is in a bad mood
   (4) because she is lonely
   (5) because she is feeling ill

11. What does the grandson plan to do after breakfast?

   (1) go to a party
   (2) listen to Telemann and Marais
   (3) drive to Dallas
   (4) wash the dishes
   (5) wash the car

Questions 12–14 refer to the following passage.

Yossarian walked out of the office and down the stairs into the dark, tomblike street, passing in the hall the stout woman with warts and two chins, who was already
5 on her way back in. There was no sign of Milo outside. There were no lights in any of the windows. The deserted sidewalk rose steeply and continuously for several blocks. He could see the glare of a broad avenue at
10 the top of the long cobblestone incline. The police station was almost at the bottom; the yellow bulbs at the entrance sizzled in the dampness like wet torches. A frigid, fine rain was falling. He began walking slowly,
15 pushing uphill. Soon he came to a quiet, cozy, inviting restaurant with red velvet drapes in the windows and a blue neon sign near the door that said: TONY'S RESTAURANT, FINE FOOD AND DRINK.
20 KEEP OUT. The words on the blue neon sign surprised him mildly for only an instant. Nothing warped seemed bizarre anymore in his strange, distorted surroundings. The tops of the sheer buildings slanted in weird,
25 surrealistic [unnatural] perspective, and the street seemed tilted. He raised the collar of his warm woolen coat and hugged it around him. The night was raw. A boy in a thin shirt and thin tattered trousers walked out of the
30 darkness on bare feet. The boy had black hair and needed a haircut and shoes and socks. His sickly face was pale and sad. His feet made grisly, soft, sucking sounds in the rain puddles on the wet pavement as he
35 passed, and Yossarian was moved by such intense pity for his poverty that he wanted to smash his pale, sad, sickly face with his fist and knock him out of existence because he brought to mind all the pale, sad, sickly
40 children in Italy that same night who needed haircuts and needed shoes and socks. He made Yossarian think of cripples and of cold and hungry men and women, and of all the dumb, passive, devout mothers with
45 catatonic [expressionless] eyes nursing

infants outdoors that same night with chilled animal udders bared insensibly to that same raw rain. Cows. Almost on cue, a nursing mother padded past holding an infant in
50 black rags, and Yossarian wanted to smash her too, because she reminded him of the barefoot boy in the thin shirt and thin, tattered trousers and of all the shivering, stupefying misery in a world that never yet
55 had provided enough heat and food and justice for all but an ingenious [clever] and unscrupulous [immoral] handful. What a lousy earth!

—Excerpted from *Catch-22*, by Joseph Heller

12. Why does Heller use the words "frigid, fine rain" (line 13)?

(1) to stand for spiritual cleansing
(2) to suggest the coming of spring
(3) to create a gloomy atmosphere
(4) to show the freshening power of water
(5) to emphasize Yossarian's disagreeable nature

13. The central conflict in this passage is between Yossarian and what/whom?

(1) an unjust world
(2) the restaurant
(3) the weather
(4) the boy
(5) himself

14. What is the tone of the passage?

(1) flowery
(2) informal
(3) passive
(4) pessimistic
(5) violent

Answers are on page 230.

READING EFFICIENCY E

Directions: This activity will help you to improve your reading efficiency. Before you start to read, write the present time at the top of the page. When you have completed the reading and all 5 questions, write your finishing time. Subtract to find how long you took. Score your answers. Then turn to page 234 to find your E-Factor and graph your progress.

Finishing Time	
Starting Time –	
Reading Time =	
Number of Answers Correct	

from Pride and Prejudice

Jane Austen

Jane and Elizabeth were alone. Jane, who had been cautious in her praise of Mr. Bingley before, expressed to her sister how very much she admired him.

5   "He is just what a young man ought to be," said she. "He is sensible, good-humoured, lively; and I never saw such happy manners! He is so much at ease, with such perfect good breeding!"

10   "He is also handsome," replied Elizabeth, "which a young man ought likewise to be, if he possibly can. His character is thereby complete."

    "I was very much flattered by his asking 15 me to dance a second time. I did not expect such a compliment."

    "Did not you? *I* did for you. But that is one great difference between us. Compliments always take you by surprise, 20 and *me* never. What could be more natural than his asking you again? He could not help seeing that you were about five times as pretty as every other woman in the room. No thanks to his gallantry for that. Well, he 25 certainly is very agreeable, and I give you leave to like him. You have liked many a stupider person."

    "Dear Lizzy!"

    "Oh! You are a great deal too apt, you 30 know, to like people in general. You never

see a fault in anybody. All the world are good and agreeable in your eyes. I never heard you speak ill of a human being in my life."

    "I would wish not to be hasty in censuring 35 anyone. But I always speak what I think."

1. When is the conversation taking place?

(1) right before Jane's wedding
(2) early in the morning
(3) after a dance
(4) during a family dinner
(5) before a dance

2. What kind of relationship do Jane and Elizabeth have?

(1) close and loving
(2) distant
(3) friendly but wary
(4) distrustful
(5) casual

3. Which is a valid character description of Elizabeth?

(1) self-centered
(2) overly critical
(3) generous and outspoken
(4) timid and shy
(5) demanding

4. How does the author illustrate the differences between Jane and Elizabeth?

   (1) by having them talk in very different styles
   (2) by describing each one in detail
   (3) by contrasting their opinions of Mr. Bingley
   (4) by showing each girl's personality in her dialogue
   (5) by telling how others see them

5. What does the passage show about the author?

   (1) She is shallow.
   (2) She is interested in human relationships.
   (3) She likes dances.
   (4) She never had a sister.
   (5) She doesn't have insight into people's characters.

Answers are on page 231.

READING EFFICIENCY F

Directions: This activity will help you to improve your reading efficiency. Before you start to read, write the present time at the top of the page. When you have completed the reading and all 5 questions, write your finishing time. Subtract to find how long you took. Score your answers. Then turn to page 234 to find your E-Factor and graph your progress.

Finishing Time

Starting Time −

Reading Time =

Number of Answers Correct

from "To Build a Fire"

Jack London

He plunged in among the big spruce trees. The trail was faint. A foot of snow had fallen since the last sled had passed over, and he was glad he was without a sled,
5 travelling light. In fact, he carried nothing but the lunch wrapped in the handkerchief. He was surprised, however, at the cold. It certainly was cold, he concluded, as he rubbed his numb nose and cheekbones with
10 his mittened hand. He was a warm-whiskered man. But the hair on his face did not protect the high cheekbones and the eager nose that thrust itself aggressively into the frosty air.

15 At the man's heels trotted a dog, a big native husky, the proper wolf dog. It was gray-coated and without any visible or temperamental difference from its brother, the wild wolf. The animal was depressed by
20 the tremendous cold. It knew that it was no time for travelling. Its instinct told it a truer tale than was told to the man by the man's judgment. In reality, it was not merely colder than fifty below zero; it
25 was colder than sixty below, than seventy below. It was seventy-five below zero. The dog did not know anything about thermometers. Possibly in its brain there was no sharp consciousness of a condition
30 of very cold such as was in the man's brain. But the brute had its instinct.

1. What is the most probable setting of the story?

   (1) a city in Russia
   (2) a New England farm
   (3) the Alaskan wilderness
   (4) Mt. Everest
   (5) Antarctica

2. What is the main action of the passage?

   (1) A man is trying to get rid of a dog.
   (2) A man is taking his dog for a walk.
   (3) A winter storm is brewing.
   (4) A man and a dog are on a journey in the wilderness.
   (5) A man and a dog are trying to figure out how cold it is.

3. Which is the most accurate characterization of the man?

   (1) bold
   (2) overly cautious
   (3) stupid
   (4) cowardly
   (5) cruel

4. What is the conflict of the passage?

   (1) the disagreement about the cold between the dog and the man
   (2) the man's trying to escape from society
   (3) the inability to know how cold it is
   (4) the man's lack of respect for the dog's instincts
   (5) the man's and dog's struggle against the cold

5. What is the author's purpose in describing what is going on in the dog's head?

    (1) to show that the animal will protect the man
    (2) to show that sometimes animals' instincts work better than men's intellects
    (3) to emphasize how dumb animals are
    (4) to show that the cold is nothing to worry about
    (5) to appeal to readers who love dogs

Answers are on page 231.

CHAPTER 7

Poetry

In this chapter, you will learn what poetry is. You will look at the differences between prose and poetry. You will study a poem's rhyme and rhythm. You will determine the meaning of various poems. And you will look at poetic elements such as imagery, figurative language, and symbolism.

What is Poetry?

Poetry is an art form that communicates feelings or ideas by use of stanzas, or verses, instead of paragraphs; it uses figurative language; and it has rhythm and, sometimes, rhyme.

Poetry has a distinct form of its own—or the way it looks on a page. The words in a poem are written in lines. Some are short; some are long. Some lines are complete sentences, and others are not. Some lines are indented for special emphasis, or to give the poem visual appeal.

The best way to become acquainted with poetry is to compare it with prose.

In his poem "The Eagle," Alfred, Lord Tennyson depicts the great bird in its natural surroundings.

First read a prose translation of the poem. Then look at the original poem on the next page. What difference do you see between the two?

Prose Translation

The eagle clings to a rocky ledge high in the blue sky. It studies the small waves in the sea below. Suddenly, it dives to the surface of the water.

Now read the original poem as written by Tennyson.

The Eagle

He clasps the crag with crooked hands
Close to the sun in lonely lands,
Ringed with the azure world, he stands.

The wrinkled sea beneath him crawls;
He watches from his mountain walls
And like a thunderbolt he falls.

Which version captures your interest more—the prose version or the original poem? Notice the familiar structure of the prose translation. It is written in sentences that form a paragraph.

Rhythm

By contrast, the poem is written in two stanzas of three lines each. Notice the rhythm of the poem's stanzas. The rhythm is the sound and the beat of each line and verse. One change in the order or selection of the words would ruin the rhythmic unity of the poem as a whole.

Figurative Language

Poetry stirs our senses. Its figurative language speaks to the imagination. "The wrinkled sea beneath him crawls" is a beautiful example of figurative speech that conveys a physical reality more effectively than literal language could. The sea is not wrinkled; it does not crawl. But those words enable us to see it from where the eagle sits.

In the last line of the poem, the poet has chosen exactly the right words and not one more. You can see the dive, hear the wings, and sense the speed. You can almost hear the splash. The words are stunning and hard to forget. This is poetry.

Rhyme

Rhyme heightens a poem's effect. In traditional poetry, sounds are repeated at the ends of lines. Rhyme makes poetry easier to remember. Because poetry is meant to be read aloud, rhyme also adds to the enjoyment of it. Rhyming sounds emphasize what the poet wants us to understand. Reread Tennyson's poem "The Eagle." Which words rhyme in each stanza?

You were correct if you identified the rhyming words hands, lands, and stands in the first stanza and the rhyming words crawls, walls, and falls in the second stanza.

EXERCISE 1

Directions: Read the poem below and then answer the questions that follow.

A Sad Song
About Greenwich Village

She lives in a garret
Up a haunted stair,
And even when she's frightened
There's nobody to care.

She cooks so small a dinner
She dines on the smell,
And even if she's hungry
There's nobody to tell.

She sweeps her musty lodging
As the dawn steals near,
And even when she's crying
There's nobody to hear.

I haven't seen my neighbor
Since a long time ago,
And even if she's dead
There's nobody to know.

—Frances Park

1. Which words rhyme in each stanza?

   Stanza 1: _____ _____

   Stanza 2: _____ _____

   Stanza 3: _____ _____

   Stanza 4: _____ _____

2. What is this poem about?

   _____ (1) a run-down neighborhood

   _____ (2) a haunted house in the city

   _____ (3) a lonely older woman who lives alone

Answers are on page 231.

How to Read Poetry

Before you read a poem, look at its title. Keep it in mind as you read. How does the title relate to the body of the poem?

Remember that, much like a paragraph, each stanza of a poem represents a different thought. Stanzas are also separated by space breaks, much as paragraphs are set off by indents.

Look carefully at how the poem is written. Look at the lines of each stanza. Notice that the first word of a line may be capitalized even if it does not begin a sentence. Don't let this confuse you. Sentences in poetry are indicated by periods. Capital letters don't necessarily mean the start of a new sentence; sometimes they just emphasize the start of a line. If a capital is preceded by a period, you know that it begins a new sentence. If there is no period, the old sentence has not ended.

Study the end of each line. Are there any punctuation marks? There may not be. But if there are, remember that punctuation works the same way in poetry as in prose. If there is no punctuation at the end of a line, simply continue reading without a pause. Let the punctuation tell you when to pause; do not automatically pause at the end of a line.

Look at the following poem by William Carlos Williams.

The Term

A rumpled sheet
of brown paper
about the length

and apparent bulk
of a man was
rolling with the

wind slowly over
and over in
the street as

a car drove down
upon it and
crushed it to

the ground. Unlike
a man it rose
again rolling

with the wind over
and over to be as
it was before.

In this poem, the first sentence does not end until the word *ground* in the fifth stanza.

The second sentence, beginning with "Unlike a man," is read straight through to the end of the poem. In the entire poem, only the first letters of each sentence are capitalized. After the first line, which begins a sentence, every line begins with a lowercase letter.

The Meaning of Poetry

Now let's look again at the poem and see what Williams is saying. The title says that this poem is about a term. But if you read it carefully, you will see that a specified length of time is not what is being discussed.

Look at the two statements in the poem. They refer to the term—the span of existence—of a man and of a large crumpled sheet of brown paper roughly the same size and shape (but not weight) of a man. The term of the paper is endless. It is unaffected even after an automobile drives over it. The term of a man would be cut short by such an event.

Even though the poem is short, it provides much to visualize and think about. You can see that huge sheet of paper rolling down the street where the wind is blowing it. You can see the car roll over it and drive on. You can see that the paper keeps right on going, basically unchanged by what just happened to it.

Contrast this with something the approximate shape and size (but not weight) of the paper—a man. A man could never emerge from beneath the wheels of a moving car the same as he was before.

Why does Williams make this comparison? Why has he drawn this simple but serious picture? What do we learn from it? "The Term" has a message about the fragility of life. It compares a living human being to an old ball of paper. The paper has no real value and nothing to fear. Even a moving automobile cannot hurt it. But the living man, whose value is beyond calculation, has much to fear. Life for him is as dangerous as it is precious.

Poetry, like prose, consists of a main idea and the details that enrich it. You can draw inferences from these elements. Beginning with the title, read a new poem straight through. See if you can find the main idea. What does the title tell you? You may need to read a poem several times to figure it out.

EXERCISE 2

Directions: Read the poem below and then put a check in front of the correct answer to the questions that follow.

Taught Me Purple

My mother taught me purple
Although she never wore it.
Wash-grey was her circle,
The tenement her orbit.

5 My mother taught me golden
And held me up to see it,
Above the broken molding,
Beyond the filthy street.

My mother reached for beauty
10 And for its lack she died,
Who knew so much of duty
She could not teach me pride.

—Evelyn Tooley Hunt

1. What type of feelings is the poet expressing?

_____ (1) love and sadness

_____ (2) bitterness and self-hatred

_____ (3) pride and fearlessness

2. What does the poet say about her mother?

_____ (1) She reached for beauty and found it.

_____ (2) She died for want of beauty.

_____ (3) She inhabited a beautiful world of colors.

3. Why was the mother's "circle" "wash-grey"?

_____ (1) because she was a laundress

_____ (2) because she was a poor woman living in a gloomy environment

_____ (3) because she had too difficult a life to think about beautiful things

4. To what do the terms *purple* and *golden* refer?

_____ (1) colorful clothes the mother wore

_____ (2) the brighter side of life

_____ (3) beautiful sunsets the mother showed the daughter

5. Explain what the poet meant when she said that her mother "knew so much of duty she could not teach me pride."

   _____

   _____

   _____

6. Which two sets of words rhyme in the third stanza?

   _____   _____

   _____   _____

Answers are on page 231.

Imagery

The word poet comes from the Greek word poesis, meaning "to make." To create new and exciting language, a poet needs imagination.

Poets use carefully chosen words to create images and figures of speech. The language of a poem enables us to understand the poet's vision almost as if we could experience it with our own senses. Just as an artist uses colors to make a painting, so a poet chooses words to convey thoughts and feelings. Images and figurative language make poetry come alive.

Poets use *imagery* to share their way of seeing the world. Images are what the words of a poem enable you to see. They are the pictures that come into your mind as you read the poet's words. They are your link to the poet's imagination.

Read the poem below carefully. Then describe in your own words the images the poem enables you to see.

Cat's World

The white cat steps carefully
almost mechanical
along the crumbling stone wall
then sits still
and sergeant straight.

—Ed Beatty

Lines 1 and 2

_____

_____

Line 3

_____

_____

Line 4

_____

_____

Line 5

_____

_____

Lines 1 and 2 give the image of a white cat walking along so precisely that it resembles a mechanical device, perhaps a windup toy. Line 3 shows that the cat is balancing on an old, broken cement wall. In line 4 the cat stops walking and sits down. Line 5 describes the cat's posture in terms of military straightness, "sergeant straight."

Figurative Language

As you have already learned, figurative language goes beyond the literal meaning of words. Poets use figurative language to heighten the visual and emotional power of their words. In this section, you will study three specific types of figurative language:

- simile and metaphor

- personification

- symbolism

Simile and Metaphor

A *simile* uses the words *like, as,* or *than* to make a comparison. If you say that someone is as "light as a feather," you mean that the person has a very slight figure, not that he or she weighs literally no more than a feather.

A man who says to the woman he loves, "Your eyes are *like* diamonds," is not saying that the woman's eyes look like jewelry but that they shine with brilliance like diamonds do.

The legendary Paul Bunyan is described as being "taller than a mountain." This expression is not meant to give his actual height but to convey Bunyan's giantlike appearance. You can recognize these similes by the use of the words *as*, *like*, or *than*.

A **metaphor** is a comparison without the use of the words *like*, *as*, or *than*.

Tate University played with feet of lead in its loss to Kemper.

The feet of the Tate players are compared to lead, which is heavy and lifeless. So the metaphor means that the Tate team played without energy or speed.

EXERCISE 3

Directions: Write *S* in front of the statements that are similes. Write *M* in front of the statements that are metaphors.

_____ 1. "She walks in beauty, like the night."

_____ 2. ". . . time flows on and on,
That narrow noiseless river. . . ."

_____ 3. She had the strength of a lioness and the cunning of a fox.

_____ 4. Superman is "faster than a speeding bullet and more powerful than a locomotive."

_____ 5. "The moon is a balloon."

Answers are on page 231.

Personification

Personification is another type of figurative language. When writers use this technique, they give an object the characteristics of living things or use human qualities to describe something that is not human. Personification helps reveal a poet's vision.

Tennyson's poem "The Eagle" begins with the line "He clasps the crag with crooked hands." Ralph Waldo Emerson once observed, "The wings of time are black and white." What do these lines by Tennyson and Emerson have in common?

Tennyson's eagle has hands; eagles do not really have hands. Emerson describes time as having wings; literally speaking, wings belong only to birds and certain other creatures. Eagles cannot have hands any more than time can have wings, except by means of personification.

EXERCISE 4

Directions: Read the poem below and then answer the questions that follow.

Night

Night gathers itself into a ball of dark yarn.
Night loosens the ball and it spreads.
The lookouts from the shores of Lake Michigan
    find night follows day,
5   and ping! ping! across the sheet gray
    the boat lights put their signals.
Night lets the dark yarn unravel,
Night speaks and the yarns change
    to fog and blue strands.

—Carl Sandburg

1. What is Night described as in line 1?

_____

2. In lines 1–7, which four action words are used to personify night?

_____ _____

_____ _____

3. In lines 8 and 9, after night speaks, what two things do the yarns change into?

_____ _____

Answers are on page 231.

Symbolism

A symbol is anything that represents something else. McDonald's yellow arches symbolize the fast-food chain. A wave of the hand is a gesture symbolizing hello or good-bye.

The following poem relies heavily on romantic *symbolism*. Even the title is symbolic. Since valentines symbolize the heart, they are used to express love. In addition to the valentine and the heart, this poem also uses a third symbol to express the depths of the poet's feelings. What is this third symbol?

Valentines

Forgive me if I have not sent you
a valentine
but I thought you knew
that you already have my heart
Here take the space where my
heart goes
I give that to you too

—Henry Dumas

The heart in the poem symbolizes the poet's feelings of love. But he also says that his beloved already has his heart. Since he cannot give what he has already given, he offers the space that encloses his heart.

That space around the poet's heart is the third symbol in this poem. Here, Dumas uses it to symbolize a greater love than his heart alone represents.

EXERCISE 5

Questions 1–4 are based on the poem below.

Apartment House

A filing-cabinet of human lives

Where people swarm like bees in tunneled
 hives,

Each to his own cell in the towered comb,

Identical and cramped—we call it home.

—Gerald Raftery

1. What is the main image of this poem?

 (1) bees swarming in a hive
 (2) people happy in their bustling
  environment
 (3) people locked in a metal file drawer
 (4) a comb constructed of cells
 (5) impersonal, dehumanizing housing

2. The second line in the poem is an example of
 which literary device?

 (1) personification
 (2) exaggeration
 (3) simile
 (4) metaphor
 (5) symbolism

3. Which two words rhyme in the poem?

 (1) swarm and bees
 (2) cabinet and cramped
 (3) tunneled and towered
 (4) comb and home
 (5) bees and each

4. How does the poet describe people's living
 spaces?

 (1) spacious and airy
 (2) well lit and in good order
 (3) comfortable and inviting
 (4) crowded and similar
 (5) busy and square-shaped

Answers are on page 231.

EXERCISE 6

Questions 1–4 are based on the poem below.

Harlem Night Song

Come,
Let us roam the night together
Singing

I love you

5 Across
The Harlem rooftops
Moon is shining.
Night sky is blue
Stars are great drops
10 Of golden dew.

Down the street
A band is playing.

I love you

Come,
15 Let us roam the night together
Singing

—Langston Hughes

1. To what does the poet compare stars?

   (1) golden dewdrops
   (2) a band playing
   (3) the shining moon
   (4) Harlem
   (5) the blue night sky

2. What do lines 9 and 10 illustrate?

   (1) personification
   (2) simile
   (3) metaphor
   (4) symbolism
   (5) internal rhyme

3. According to the poem what is a vital part of Harlem life at night?

   (1) its crowded streets
   (2) its honking horns
   (3) its music
   (4) its warm weather
   (5) its moonlight

4. What type of feelings is the poet expressing?

   (1) anger
   (2) sadness
   (3) disappointment
   (4) confusion
   (5) happiness

Answers are on pages 231–232.

Understanding Poetry

A poem's rhythm, images, and figurative language will help you understand it. If you already know something about the background of the poet, this will help you, too. If not, you can expect to discover something about the poet as you unlock the meaning of a poem.

EXERCISE 7

Directions: Read the poem below and then put a check in front of the correct answer to the questions that follow.

Crows

Hear them speak like men
to one another. Their gravel voices
are thunder breaking the sky,
a gun cracking air,
5 the bad air
filled with birds whose wings
tip indigo [blue] in the light.

Beneath them, men with blue guns
turn up the whites of their eyes.
10 The feathers,
the feathers come apart, falling
specks of dust.

My ears want to hear them
begin to speak,
15 to hear the dark berries
uncoil through flesh.
They are quiet,
so still
I wait for a breath
20 to escape the warm feathers.

—Linda Hogan

1. Which of the following is an example of metaphor?

    _____ (1) "their gravel voices are thunder"

    _____ (2) "men with blue guns turn up the whites of their eyes"

    _____ (3) "I wait for a breath to escape the warm feathers"

2. Lines 1 and 2 are examples of which literary device?

    _____ (1) metaphor

    _____ (2) internal rhyme

    _____ (3) simile

Answers are on page 232.

Writing Activity 8

Choose one poem from this chapter that you enjoyed and read it aloud. Try to follow it word by word and line by line. Pause where the punctuation tells you to do so. Look up any words that are unfamiliar to you. Notice if ordinary words are used figuratively. Rewrite the poem in your own words. Use ordinary words in place of any figurative or difficult language.

Answers will vary.

Chapter Review

Questions 1–6 refer to the poem below.

The Bus

I was the last passenger of the day,
I was alone on the bus,
I was glad they were spending all that
    money
5 just getting me up Eighth Avenue.
Driver! I shouted, it's you and me tonight,
let's run away from this big city
to a smaller city more suitable to the heart,
let's drive past the swimming pools of Miami
10   Beach,
you in the driver's seat, me several seats
    back,
but in the racial cities we'll change places
so as to show how well you've done up
15   North,
and let us find ourselves some tiny American
    fishing village
in unknown Florida
and park right at the edge of the sand,
20 a huge bus pointing out,
metallic, painted, solitary,
with New York plates.

               —Leonard Cohen

1. Where is the bus from?

   (1) Miami Beach
   (2) New York City
   (3) Tampa Bay
   (4) a small city
   (5) Chicago

2. The mood of this poem can best be described as which of the following?

   (1) sadness
   (2) confusion
   (3) escapism
   (4) cheerfulness
   (5) boastfulness

3. Why will the passenger and the driver change places "in the racial cities"?

   The driver is
   (1) prejudiced
   (2) friendly
   (3) black
   (4) white
   (5) fearful

4. Why does the passenger want to trade places with the driver?

   (1) because he has always wanted to drive a bus
   (2) because he wants to drive up Eighth Avenue
   (3) because he wants to collect fares from boarding passengers
   (4) because he would like to show others that the bus driver has done well
   (5) because he wants to go swimming in Miami Beach

5. Where does the passenger want to go?

   (1) up North
   (2) to New York
   (3) to Miami Beach
   (4) up Eighth Avenue
   (5) to a small city in Florida

6. What is the main idea of this poem?

   (1) escaping from big city life
   (2) the American landscape
   (3) the loneliness of riding the bus at night
   (4) the great wealth of Miami Beach
   (5) integrating public transportation

Questions 7–10 refer to the poem below.

Voice

At school my voice is a plain
the soil of northern terrain
a great field of monotone days
flatland from October to May.

5 At home it is a row of hills
a southern sierra regaining color
or a Mexican range come every summer
my voice from June to September.

—Gabriel Olvera

7. How would you best describe the tone of this poem?

(1) serious
(2) fearful
(3) bitter
(4) depressing
(5) youthful

8. Which statement is true?

(1) The first four lines are all similes.
(2) Every line except the last is a metaphor.
(3) The last line illustrates humor.
(4) The title illustrates personification.
(5) The word *school* is used metaphorically.

9. What is the poet comparing?

(1) himself in two environments
(2) speech and silence
(3) the seasons
(4) plains and hills
(5) Mexico and the United States

10. When is the poet happiest?

(1) when he is at school
(2) in the fall
(3) in summer
(4) in winter
(5) when his voice is a plain

Questions 11–14 refer to the poem below.

I Ask My Mother to Sing

She begins, and my grandmother joins her.
Mother and daughter sing like young girls.
If my father were alive, he would play
his accordion and sway like a boat.

5 I've never been in Peking, or the Summer Palace,
nor stood on the great Stone Boat to watch
the rain begin on Kuen Ming Lake, the picnickers
10 running away in the grass.

But I love to hear it sung;
how the waterlilies fill with rain until
they overturn, spilling water into water,
then rock back, and fill with more.
15 Both women have begun to cry.
But neither stops her song.

—Li-Young Lee

11. What are the phrases "sing like young girls" and "sway like a boat" examples of?

(1) simile
(2) metaphor
(3) exaggeration
(4) personification
(5) symbolism

12. What can you infer about the meaning of the song?

(1) It is about young girls.
(2) It is about a man playing an accordion.
(3) It is about mothers and daughters.
(4) It is about beautiful places in China.
(5) It is about great sadness.

13. Who is "daughter" (line 2)?

    (1) the poet
    (2) the poet's daughter
    (3) the poet's mother
    (4) the poet's grandmother
    (5) a picnicker at Kuen Ming Lake

14. How does the poet feel as she hears the song?

    (1) angry
    (2) embarrassed
    (3) pleased
    (4) bitter
    (5) confused

Answers are on page 232.

READING EFFICIENCY G

Directions: This activity will help you to improve your reading efficiency. Before you start to read, write the present time at the top of the page. When you have completed the reading and all 5 questions, write your finishing time. Subtract to find how long you took. Score your answers. Then turn to page 234 to find your E-Factor and graph your progress.

Finishing Time	
Starting Time	−
Reading Time	=
Number of Answers Correct	

"ON THE GRASSHOPPER AND THE CRICKET"

John Keats

The poetry of earth is never dead:
When all the birds are faint with the hot sun,
And hide in cooling trees, a voice will run
From hedge to hedge about the new-mown
5   mead;
That is the grasshopper's—he takes the lead
In summer luxury—he has never done
With his delights; for when tired out with fun
He rests at ease beneath some pleasant
10   weed.
The poetry of earth is ceasing never:
On a lone winter evening, when the frost
Has wrought a silence, from the stove there
    shrills
15 The cricket's song, in warmth increasing
    ever,
And seems to one in drowsiness half lost,
The grasshopper's among some grassy hills.

1. What do the grasshopper and the cricket prove to the poet?

    (1) that insects are useful
    (2) that nature provides interesting effects in all seasons
    (3) that they are the noisiest insects
    (4) that people often confuse the sounds of the two insects
    (5) that winter is not as pleasant as summer

2. What is the main characteristic of the grasshopper in the poem?

    (1) noisy
    (2) lazy
    (3) fun-loving
    (4) aggressive
    (5) beautiful

3. What is the best definition of the word *poetry* in the poem?

    (1) changing
    (2) beautiful music
    (3) literature
    (4) rhyming words
    (5) movement

4. In what main way does the cricket differ from the grasshopper?

    (1) It doesn't have a pleasing song.
    (2) It sleeps most of the time.
    (3) It doesn't remind the poet of nature.
    (4) It sings in winter instead of summer.
    (5) It bothers the poet.

5. What is the poet's attitude toward nature?

    (1) He enjoys many aspects of it.
    (2) He finds parts of it annoying.
    (3) He doesn't pay attention to it.
    (4) He appreciates it in summer but not in winter.
    (5) He is disturbed by the extremes of summer and winter.

Answers are on page 232.

READING EFFICIENCY H

Directions: This activity will help you to improve your reading efficiency. Before you start to read, write the present time at the top of the page. When you have completed the reading and all 5 questions, write your finishing time. Subtract to find how long you took. Score your answers. Then turn to page 234 to find your E-Factor and graph your progress.

Finishing Time	[ ]
Starting Time –	[ ]
Reading Time =	[ ]
Number of Answers Correct	[ ]

"MEETING AT NIGHT"

Robert Browning

The gray sea and the long black land;
And the yellow half-moon large and low;
And the startled little waves that leap
In fiery ringlets from their sleep,
5 As I gain the cove with pushing prow,
And quench its speed in the slushy sand.

Then a mile of warm sea-scented beach;
Three fields to cross till a farm appears;
10 A tap at the pane, the quick sharp scratch
And blue spurt of a lighted match,
And a voice less loud, through its joys and
    fears,
Than the two hearts beating each to each!

1. What main action is described in the poem?

    (1) The sea flows onto the beach and into the fields.
    (2) Two people row in the ocean.
    (3) The moon rises over the sea.
    (4) A person rows across the sea and walks across fields to visit someone.
    (5) A thief travels on sea and land to rob a house.

2. Who is the speaker of the poem?

    (1) a policeman
    (2) a person in love
    (3) a sailor
    (4) a farmer
    (5) a thief

3. To what senses do the images in the poem appeal?

    (1) sight
    (2) sight and sound
    (3) touch and smell
    (4) sight, sound, and touch
    (5) sight, sound, smell, and touch

4. "The startled little waves that leap/In fiery ringlets from their sleep" is an example of what?

    (1) exaggeration
    (2) literal comparison
    (3) comparison of an object to a person
    (4) repetition
    (5) dialogue

5. Which of the following do the first eight lines of the poem *not* do?

    (1) set a mood
    (2) describe a setting
    (3) provide suspense
    (4) explain the speaker's intention
    (5) appeal to the reader's senses

Answers are on page 232.

CHAPTER 8

Drama

What separates drama from other types of literature? **Drama** is written to be performed. Dramatists, or playwrights, write their stories in the form of dialogue for actors to speak aloud onstage. The best place to appreciate drama is in a theater. There you can watch and listen as actors bring their characters to life. You can see every detail of the physical setting.

Dramatic works generally take one of three forms: comedy, tragedy, or social drama. **Comedy** takes a light approach toward its subject, although the subject itself may be serious. Generally, comedies have happy endings. The dialogue tends to be funny or satirical, evoking recognition and laughter.

Tragedy tells the story of a character who comes to ruin as the result of a flaw in his nature or forces beyond his control. **Social drama** deals with familiar problems in true-to-life situations. Arthur Miller's *Death of a Salesman,* the story of the emotional breakdown of an ordinary working man, is one of the best-known social dramas of all time.

The Elements of Drama

Every drama is built upon the same basic elements:

- stage directions and punctuation

- dialogue

- character

- action

- idea

As you read the following scene, look for the basic elements. The *stage directions* appear in *italic* type between brackets or parentheses. The *dialogue* consists of the words that the characters speak. Remembering the stage directions, try to hear the words of the dialogue as the characters might actually speak them. Notice when the punctuation calls for a pause or a change in the volume or tone of a character's voice.

Use the stage directions and dialogue to form a mental picture of the *characters,* or people in the play. If this were a live production, how would the stage look? Once you can picture the characters and the setting, try to visualize the *action* as it takes place.

After you understand the scene, try to think beyond it. What does the playwright have to say apart from the literal content? What additional *idea,* or message, does the scene convey?

The Interview

[The scene opens in the reception room of the Wurtz Manufacturing Company. Noisily chewing a wad of bubble gum, Henry Johnson walks aimlessly around. Sometimes he sits down for a few seconds before jumping up again. He wears a gray sweater over a white shirt with a ragged collar. A big round button pinned to his sweater says "I Like Girls" in red letters.]

HENRY: [*nervously, in a low voice*] Do I have to wait much longer?

SECRETARY: No, Mr. Harvey should be finished in a minute.

HENRY: I'm a little nervous about interviews, you know.

SECRETARY: [*in a sympathetic tone*] Everyone is, so don't feel
5 bad. Better take that gum out of your mouth. Mr. Harvey hates the sound of popping. [*HENRY quickly removes his gum and drops it, unwrapped, in the secretary's ashtray. She frowns. Meanwhile, MR. HARVEY comes out of his office. He steps up to greet HENRY. They shake hands; Henry has a light grip.*]

10 MR. HARVEY: [*In a firm, commanding voice*] Hello, Henry. William Harvey.

HENRY: [*Softly*] Hello, William. Nice to meet you.

MR. HARVEY: [*Taken aback*] Step into my office, Henry, and we'll talk. [*HENRY sits down across from Mr. Harvey's desk. MR. HARVEY
15 looks over Henry's application and then sits down.*] Well, Henry, I see you have applied for the machinist's position. Tell me about your qualifications.

HENRY: [Slightly confused] Well, I can do anything. I've been a factory worker, a stock boy, an usher, a zookeeper's helper . . .

20 MR. HARVEY: Let's stick to the position you've applied for, Henry. Do you have any experience as a machinist?

HENRY: Not really.

MR. HARVEY: Well, what about a training program?

HENRY: [*Brightening*] I did go to trade school.

25 MR. HARVEY: Well, then.

HENRY: Uh-huh. For one solid week. [*HENRY looks serious. He closes his lips tightly.*]

MR. HARVEY: Is something wrong?

HENRY: No, I'm just trying to keep my teeth from showing. It's a
30 habit I have in interviews.

MR. HARVEY: [Hurriedly] Oh—Well, we'll keep your application on file and call you if we need you. Thank you for coming.

HENRY: You can call me at my sister's place. That's where I usually hang out, just waiting for the phone to ring. [*HENRY exits.*]

This simple scene illustrates the basic elements of drama. It is presented in the form of dialogue framed by stage directions. Characters meet and interact. There is an underlying idea that goes beyond the scene itself.

All of the conversation in this scene happens to be between characters. But there is also a type of dramatic scene in which a single character gives a speech alone upon the stage. Such a scene is called a *soliloquy*.

Stage Directions and Punctuation

Stage directions and punctuation provide clues to a character's emotions and actions. Stage directions are set off from dialogue by *italics*. When Henry discards his used chewing gum in the ashtray, the stage directions call for the secretary to frown, indicating her displeasure.

The stage directions involving Henry reveal his discomfort. He appears confused. He is serious about something that is laughable. He purses his lips nervously.

The punctuation in a play consists of the same marks used in prose. In addition, dashes and ellipsis points often appear in dialogue.

The *dash* (—) indicates a break, a change of direction, or an interruption. Notice how the dash following the "Oh" in line 31 emphasizes the importance of what Mr. Harvey says next. It signifies a definite change in his train of thought. It marks the moment when he decides to waste no more of his valuable time with Henry.

Ellipsis points (. . .) indicate that a character's voice just trails off. When Henry's voice stops after "zookeeper's helper" in line 19, the points of ellipsis tell you that he has lost his way. He knows he's talking too much, but he doesn't quite know how to stop. His voice just fades away into an awkward silence.

Dialogue

Dialogue refers to the spoken words of a play. Together, the dialogue and physical action form the basic structure of drama.

The dialogue between Henry and the secretary tells us about Henry's situation and some of his problems. The dialogue between Henry and Mr. Harvey reveals more of Henry's failings and much about Mr. Harvey's strengths. Henry is impolite, unqualified, ill at ease, and not very bright. Mr. Harvey is poised, direct, and decisive.

No less important than the dialogue in a play is just how the words are spoken. Try to hear the voices of the characters. What do they sound like? Henry's voice is unsure and shy. At first, the secretary's voice is sympathetic.

Stage directions often specify the characteristics of a voice. These include volume, pitch, and tone. The **volume** of a voice is how loud or soft it is. **Pitch** refers to a musical quality. Is the voice pitched high or low? What does a high-pitched voice suggest or reveal about a person? What about a deep voice? **Tone** is an emotional quality that reflects a character's mood. The tone of someone's voice determines whether a simple sentence like "This is great!" means exactly what it says or just the opposite.

Character

As you already know, a character's personality and motives are revealed by the person's words and actions, thoughts and feelings, and by the author's description of the character.

A playwright reveals dramatic character through dialogue, action, and description. In a play, everything you see and hear onstage is important. You are supposed to draw inferences from the appearance of the characters, from their voices, costumes, manner of speaking, and even from the sets. You miss out on some important elements of a play when you read it instead of seeing and hearing it performed. When you read drama, it's important to pay close attention to the stage directions and dialogue.

The stage directions in *The Interview* reveal how unattractive Henry is. He dresses tastelessly. His manners are poor. His appearance and conduct reveal him to be immature and lacking in common sense. Even Mr. Harvey, a model of poise and tact, is visibly "taken aback" when Henry addresses him by his first name. Mr. Harvey's statements and actions reveal him to be friendly, self-assured, and businesslike.

When you see a play onstage, you learn what a character's thoughts and feelings are by how that character speaks and acts. Body language, tone of voice, and visual and vocal expression reveal a character's true thoughts and feelings. The acting is crucial.

When you read a play, however, you must rely on the dialogue and stage directions. You also need to recognize scenes that have special importance. When, for example, a character speaks to a confidant (someone he trusts), he is more likely to reveal his real predicament or his true feelings. In *The Interview*, the secretary functions as Henry's confidant. Henry tells her how nervous he is, something he would not express to Mr. Harvey.

A character's *motivation* explains why he behaves as he does. When the secretary gives Henry reassurance and good advice, she is motivated by sympathy. She understands how uncomfortable a job interview can be. But, like many dramatic characters, she never explains her motives; you have to infer them.

A character's *response* is his reaction to a situation, event, or remark. How did Mr. Harvey respond when Henry addressed him rudely? Responses are often less immediate than Mr. Harvey's shock. They can develop gradually and culminate, or end, in a crucial scene.

EXERCISE 1

Directions: Read the following excerpt from a play. Then put a check in front of the correct answer to the questions that follow.

RICHARD: [*rising*] Bunt? Two runs behind, the bases loaded and they send Hodges up to bunt! [*Shaking his head, he goes into the kitchen. He reappears carrying a bottle of raspberry soda. Still appalled.*] Bunt, for God's sake! Well, what you going to do? [*He*

5 *looks around aimlessly for a moment.*] I'm hungry. Well, that's what comes of having dinner at Schrafft's! Schrafft's! I wanted to have dinner in the saloon across the street—but you can't have dinner in a saloon and then not . . . They don't like it. Oh, I suppose I could have ordered a drink and then not drunk it. . . . But I figure it's

10 easier just to eat at Schrafft's. [*He drops wearily onto the chaise {chair}.*] It's hard on a man when the family goes away. It's peaceful, though, with everybody gone. It's sure as peaceful. [*He settles back in the chaise and grins. Music sneaks in softly, and the light on him dims to a spot.*] Ricky was really upset this morning when they

15 left for the station. It was very flattering. I thought the kid was going to cry. . . . [*He sits, smiling, remembering the scene. Dream lighting by the front door picks up Helen and Ricky leaving.*]

RICKY: But what about Daddy? Isn't Daddy coming with us?

HELEN: Daddy'll come up Friday night.

20 RICKY: But, Mommy, why can't Daddy come up with us now?

HELEN: Poor Daddy has to stay in the hot city and make money. We're going to spend the whole summer at the beach, but poor Daddy can only come up weekends.

RICKY: Poor Daddy . . .

25 HELEN: Daddy is going to work very hard. He's going to eat properly and not smoke like Dr. Murphy told him, and he's going to stay on the wagon for a while like Dr. Summers told him, to take care of his nervous indigestion. . . .

[*In the spot,* RICHARD *drinks from the bottle of raspberry soda. He*
30 *is somewhat awed by the taste. He looks curiously at the label and then reads it.*]

RICHARD: "Contains carbonated water, citric acid, corn syrup, artificial raspberry flavoring, pure vegetable colors, and preservative." Since I've been on the wagon, I've had one

35 continuous upset stomach. [*He looks sadly at the bottle and drinks some more.*]

helen: And just to make sure Daddy's all right, Mommy is going to call Daddy at ten o'clock tonight. . . .

RICKY: Poor Daddy . . .

40 [*The music fades and so does the dream light by the door. Helen and Ricky disappear. The lighting returns to normal.*]

RICHARD: [*coming out of his reverie {dream}*] Ten o'clock! I don't even know how I'm going to stay awake till ten o'clock! [*He stares moodily off into the growing dusk. Suddenly he notices something* 45 *in an apartment across the court. He is momentarily fascinated and rises for a better look.*] Hey, lady! I know it's a hot night but . . . You sit out on this terrace, it's like having a television set with about thirty channels all going at once. . . . Don't give me any dirty look, lady. I pay rent for this terrace. If you don't like it, pull your blind 50 down! [*as she apparently does so*] Oh. Well, that's life.

—Excerpted from *The Seven Year Itch*, by George Axelrod

1. As the scene opens, what is Richard doing?

_____ (1) listening to a baseball game

_____ (2) having dinner

_____ (3) recalling a scene from earlier in the day

2. To what does the phrase "stay on the wagon" (line 27) refer?

_____ (1) driving to work

_____ (2) avoiding alcohol

_____ (3) working late

3. In what context does the conversation between Ricky and Helen occur?

_____ (1) over the telephone

_____ (2) in another location

_____ (3) in Richard's memory

4. What does Richard think about Dr. Summers' advice?

_____ (1) He wishes he had taken it sooner.

_____ (2) He can hardly wait to tell Helen about it.

_____ (3) He thinks it has made him sick.

5. Why does Richard have to stay awake until ten o'clock?

_____ (1) He wants to hear the end of the ball game.

_____ (2) That's when Ricky and Helen will be home.

_____ (3) He expects a phone call from Helen.

Answers are on pages 232–233.

Action

The *action* of a play is comparable to the plot of a novel. As the characters interact, the story begins to unfold and dramatic conflict develops. The action builds upward, with tension increasing, to a high point, or *climax,* from which the story turns downward again, toward a conclusion.

The opening scene of *The Interview* presents Henry and the secretary in the first of a series of related events, culminating in the interview itself, which you know is destined to go badly because Henry is hopelessly unprepared.

As you follow the developments of a play, look for clues about what the *outcome*, or result, will be. Henry's admission of minimal job training practically guarantees that Mr. Harvey will reject him. Usually, however, indications of the outcome are not so obvious.

Idea

Just as nonfiction has a main idea, and fiction has a theme, drama has an underlying message that the playwright wants to communicate to the audience. This is the *idea* of a play.

As you already know, main ideas and themes in prose are rarely, if ever, spelled out. You must infer them from the details. Likewise, in dramatic works, there is no direct statement of the underlying idea. You must infer it from the dialogue, stage directions, characterization, and action.

The dramatic elements of *The Interview* point to the idea without stating it directly. The stage directions fill out the characters of both Henry and Mr. Harvey. The purpose of the scene is told in the dialogue. The characters' interaction moves events along toward the outcome. The idea of the scene is that lacking social skills and experience, Henry has no hope of being offered a job.

Remember, though, that the idea of a play can be as complex as the play itself. *The Interview* is straightforward and uncomplicated and it is not too difficult to draw inferences from it. Most drama, however, requires that you give serious thought to understanding a play's content and meaning.

EXERCISE 2

Directions: Read the following passage from a play. Then put a check in front of the correct answer to the questions that follow.

[*In the back room of Dave's Dive, DAVID, CINDY, and MOLLY argue.*]

DAVID: You skipped out on me again Friday night.

CINDY: [*In a pleading voice*] You know that's my prayer-meeting night.

DAVID: Beer and whiskey buy the bread in this house, you know.

CINDY: But we agreed—Friday would be my day off.

DAVID: Friday is our busiest night, and your pretty little face gets a lot of guys to buy a lot of drinks. I need you here on Friday nights.

CINDY: [*Turning to her mother*] Tell David what it says in the Bible. Man does not live by bread alone. You know what Daddy used to say.

MOLLY: Honey, Daddy is gone, and we've got to make a living now. You ate hand-to-mouth as a preacher's daughter.

CINDY: Maybe so—we were poor, but we were happy. Mama, why did you have to marry him anyway . . .

MOLLY: Stop it, Cindy. David saved us from losing everything.

DAVID: [*Smiling at CINDY*] You'll be just as happy drinkin' and havin' fun with the customers.

CINDY: [*Crying*] I hate this place, the booze, the smoke, everything. Mama, these people are lost souls and he [Pointing to *DAVID*], he's the devil.

1. How is David related to Cindy?

   _____ (1) He is her ex-husband.

   _____ (2) He is her stepfather.

   _____ (3) He is her husband.

2. What can you infer about Molly?

   _____ (1) She does not care about her daughter's feelings.

   _____ (2) She thinks Cindy is unreasonable.

   _____ (3) She sympathizes with her daughter.

3. How would you describe David's attitude toward Cindy?

_____ (1) violent

_____ (2) manipulative

_____ (3) fatherly

4. Why is Cindy upset with David?

_____ (1) He broke an agreement

_____ (2) He mocked her pretty face

_____ (3) He forced her to work overtime

Answers are on page 233.

Writing Activity 9

Choose a character from one of the play excerpts you read in this chapter. Write a description of the character that includes his or her name, approximate age, physical features, and personality traits. Try to make the person's thoughts and feelings come alive through your description.

Answers will vary.

Chapter Review

Questions 1–4 refer to the following excerpt from a play.

MEL: I'm not through with my life yet . . . I still have value, I still have worth.

EDNA: What kind of a life is this? You live like some kind of a caged animal in a Second
5 Avenue zoo that's too hot in one room, too cold in another, over-charged for a growth on the side of the building they call a terrace that can't support a cactus plant, let alone two human beings. Is this what you call a
10 worthwhile life? Banging on walls and jiggling toilets?

MEL: [*shouts*] You think it's any better in sunny Spain? Go swimming on the beach, it'll take you the rest of the summer to
15 scrape the oil off.

EDNA: Forget Spain. There are other places to live.

MEL: Maine? Vermont maybe? You think it's all rolling hills and maple syrup? They have
20 more people on welfare up there than they have pancakes. Washington? Oregon? Unemployed lumberjacks are sitting around sawing legs off chairs; they have nothing else to do.

25 EDNA: I will go anywhere in the world you want to go, Mel. I will live in a cave, a hut, or a tree. I live on a raft in the Amazon jungle if that's what you want to do.

MEL: All right, call a travel agency. Get two
30 economy seats to Bolivia. We'll go to Abercrombie's tomorrow, get a couple of pith helmets and a spear gun.

EDNA: Don't talk to me like I'm insane.

MEL: I'm halfway there, you might as well
35 catch up.

EDNA: I am trying to offer suggestions. I am responsible. I am not the one who's doing this to you.

MEL: I didn't say you were, Edna.

40 EDNA: Then what do you want from me? What do you want from anyone?

MEL: [*buries his face in his hands*] Just a little breathing space . . . just for a little while.

—Excerpted from *The Prisoner of Second Avenue*, by Neil Simon

1. What is the main idea of this passage?

   (1) Mel's asthma
   (2) Mel's desire to travel
   (3) Mel's unhappy marriage
   (4) Mel's mental anguish
   (5) Mel's aches and pains

2. Which one of the following statements about Mel is true?

   (1) He is indifferent about his living situation.
   (2) He feels trapped.
   (3) He is dying to travel.
   (4) He wants to move to another country.
   (5) He is reckless.

3. Edna reacts to Mel's ramblings with which emotion?

   (1) frustration
   (2) encouragement
   (3) love
   (4) indifference
   (5) humor

4. Why is this play called *The Prisoner of Second Avenue*?

   (1) Mel is desperate for a little escape.
   (2) Mel is a prisoner in a New York jail.
   (3) Edna wants a divorce.
   (4) New Yorkers live behind double-locked doors.
   (5) Living in Mel and Edna's building is like living in a zoo.

Questions 5–10 refer to the following excerpt from a play.

ASTON: Sleep well?

DAVIES: Yes. Dead out. Must have been dead out.

ASTON: [*goes downstage right, collects*
5   *the toaster and examines it*] You . . . er . . .

DAVIES: Eh?

ASTON: Were you dreaming or something?

DAVIES: Dreaming?

ASTON: Yes.

10   DAVIES: I don't dream. I've never dreamed.

ASTON: No, nor have I.

DAVIES: Nor me. [*pause*] Why you ask me that, then?

ASTON: You were making noises.

15   DAVIES: Who was?

ASTON: You were.

DAVIES: [*Gets out of bed. He wears long underpants.*] Now, wait a minute. Wait a minute, what do you mean? What kind of
20   noises?

ASTON: You were making groans. You were jabbering.

DAVIES: Jabbering? Me?

ASTON: Yes.

25   DAVIES: I don't jabber, man. Nobody ever told me that before. [*pause*] Nobody ever told me that before. [*pause*] You got hold of the wrong bloke, mate.

ASTON: [*crossing to the bed with the*
30   *toaster*] No. You woke up. I thought you might have been dreaming.

DAVIES: I wasn't dreaming. I never had a dream in my life. [*pause*]

ASTON: Maybe it was the bed.

35   DAVIES: Nothing wrong with this bed.

ASTON: Might be a bit unfamiliar.

DAVIES: There's nothing unfamiliar about me with beds. I slept in beds. I don't make noises just because I sleep in a bed. I slept in
40   plenty of beds.

—Excerpted from *The Caretaker,* by Harold Pinter

5. According to Aston, how was Davies' dreaming?

   (1) pleasant
   (2) funny
   (3) sad
   (4) interesting
   (5) disturbing

6. In line 22, what does the word *jabbering* mean?

   (1) punching
   (2) listening
   (3) screaming
   (4) babbling
   (5) dreaming

7. How would you characterize Davies' reaction to Aston's remarks?

   (1) defensive
   (2) quiet
   (3) predictable
   (4) perceptive
   (5) indifferent

8. The conversation probably takes place in which of the following contexts?

   (1) in the morning
   (2) during the night
   (3) in a small town
   (4) in a large city
   (5) in the parlor

9. What does the British term *bloke* (line 28) mean?

(1) fellow
(2) idea
(3) bed
(4) dream
(5) clothing

10. What does the phrase *dead out* (line 2) mean?

(1) murdered
(2) sleeping soundly
(3) correct
(4) quiet
(5) dark

Answers are on page 233.

READING EFFICIENCY I

Directions: This activity will help you to improve your reading efficiency. Before you start to read, write the present time at the top of the page. When you have completed the reading and all 5 questions, write your finishing time. Subtract to find how long you took. Score your answers. Then turn to page 234 to find your E-Factor and graph your progress.

Finishing Time	
Starting Time −	
Reading Time =	
Number of Answers Correct	

from THE FACTORY LAD

John Walker

Scene: Outside of a factory, lighted.

As the curtain rises the clock strikes eight, and the men enter from Factory.

ALLEN: Now my lads, the glad sound—eight o'clock, Saturday night. Now for our pay, and for the first time from our new master, the son of our late employer.

5 WILSON: The poor man's friend!

ALLEN: Aye; who, as he became rich by the industry of his men, would not desert them in a time of need. He would not prefer steam machinery and other inventions to
10 honest labor.

WILSON: May his son be like him!

ALLEN: Aye; he was a kind man, truly. Good as good could be, an enemy to no man! Ah, a tear almost starts when I think of him! May
15 he be happy, may—. He must be as happy above as he made those on this earth. But come, come, we won't be sad tonight. Saturday night! We won't put a dark side upon things. We'll hope his son, our present
20 master, may be like his father, eh?

HATFIELD: Ah, half like, and I shall be content!

ALLEN: Hush! He comes.

Enter WESTWOOD, from Factory.

25 WESTWOOD: Gentlemen!

HATFIELD: Gentlemen! There's a pleasing way.

ALLEN: Gentlemen, sir! We're only poor, hard-working men, at your service.

30 HATFIELD: Hard-working and honest, we hope.

WESTWOOD: Well, well, what you are is not what I've come about.

ALLEN: No complaint, I hope? Work all
35 clean and right?

WESTWOOD: It may be.

HATFIELD: It may be! It is, or I'll forfeit my wages. Your father, sir, never spoke in doubt, but always looked, spoke his mind,
40 and—

WESTWOOD: And that's what I've come to do. I've come to speak my mind. Times are now altered! To compete with my neighbors—in plain words, in the future I
45 have decided to have my looms propelled by steam.

THE MEN: By steam!

WESTWOOD: Which will dispense with the necessity of manual labor. It will save me
50 some three thousand a year.

READING EFFICIENCY I

1. How did the factory workers feel about their previous boss?

    (1) They felt he made them work too hard.
    (2) They liked and respected him.
    (3) They resented his being rich.
    (4) They feared he would change the factory.
    (5) They felt he mistreated lazy people.

2. When and where does the play most likely take place?

    (1) London in the Middle Ages
    (2) America in colonial times
    (3) England during the Industrial Revolution
    (4) America during World War II
    (5) Canada in the 1960s

3. What is the play's conflict?

    (1) The factory workers do not want a new boss.
    (2) The boss's son does not want to take over the factory.
    (3) The factory boss has died and left the factory in bad shape.
    (4) The factory workers do not like to work hard.
    (5) The factory workers do not want to lose their jobs due to new technology.

4. How can Westwood best be described, based on his speeches?

    (1) practical and insensitive
    (2) mean and cruel
    (3) sympathetic and understanding
    (4) pleasant and charming
    (5) intelligent and demanding

5. What will probably happen next?

    (1) The workers will wish Westwood well and leave.
    (2) The workers will return to their jobs.
    (3) Westwood will find new jobs for all the men.
    (4) The factory will fail.
    (5) The factory workers will lose their jobs and be upset.

    Answers are on page 233.

R E A D I N G   E F F I C I E N C Y   J

Directions: This activity will help you to improve your reading efficiency. Before you start to read, write the present time at the top of the page. When you have completed the reading and all 5 questions, write your finishing time. Subtract to find how long you took. Score your answers. Then turn to page 234 to find your E-Factor and graph your progress.

Finishing Time	
Starting Time −	
Reading Time =	
Number of Answers Correct	

from A WOMAN OF NO IMPORTANCE
Oscar Wilde

Scene: Lawn in front of the terrace. Sir John and Lady Caroline and Miss Worsley, on chairs under large yew tree.

LADY CAROLINE: I believe this is the first English country house you have stayed at, Miss Worsley?

HESTER: Yes, Lady Caroline.

LADY CAROLINE: You have no country houses, I am told, in America?

HESTER: We have not many.

LADY CAROLINE: Have you any country? What we should call country?

HESTER: (smiling) We have the largest country in the world, Lady Caroline. They used to tell us at school that some of our states are as big as France and England put together.

LADY CAROLINE: Ah! you must find it very drafty, I should fancy. (To SIR JOHN): John, you should have your scarf. What is the use of my always knitting scarves for you if you won't wear them?

SIR JOHN: I am quite warm, Caroline, I assure you.

LADY CAROLINE: I think not, John. Well, you couldn't come to a more charming place than this, Miss Worsley. Even though the house is excessively damp, quite inexcusably damp. And dear Jane is sometimes a little

lax about the people she asks down here.

HESTER: Mr. Arbuthnot is very charming.

LADY CAROLINE: Ah, yes! the young man who has a job in a bank. Jane is most kind in asking him here. I am not sure, however, that Jane is right in taking him out of his position. In my young days, Miss Worsley, one never met any one in society who worked for their living. It was not considered the thing.

HESTER: In America those are the people we respect most.

LADY CAROLINE: I have no doubt of it.

READING EFFICIENCY J

1. Where does the play take place?

   (1) in a public park
   (2) at a middle-class American home
   (3) at a wealthy English country home
   (4) at an English farm
   (5) at a ritzy country club

2. What is the mood of the passage?

   (1) depressing
   (2) thoughtful
   (3) suspenseful
   (4) serious
   (5) amusing

3. Which word best describes Hester's character?

   (1) outgoing
   (2) timid
   (3) polite
   (4) self-involved
   (5) resentful

4. Which of the following elements does **not** create humor in the passage?

   (1) Lady Caroline's snobbery
   (2) Sir John's response
   (3) cultural differences between England and America
   (4) Lady Caroline's flightiness
   (5) Lady Caroline's critical attitude

5. What is the author's purpose in the passage?

   (1) to teach people not to be snobbish
   (2) to criticize English people
   (3) to prove that America is more democratic than England
   (4) to show that Americans are more naive than English people
   (5) to make fun of certain character traits.

   Answers are on page 233.

Posttest

The Posttest consists of 40 multiple-choice questions. It should give you a good idea of how well you have learned the material in this book. You should take the Posttest only after you have completed all the chapters. Work as quickly and as carefully as you can. If a question seems too difficult, make an educated guess.

Record your answers on the answer grid on this page. Choose the best of five answer choices by filling in the corresponding circle on the answer grid.

Using the Evaluation Chart on page 218, circle the number of each question that you missed to determine which areas you might need to review before you move on to Contemporary's *GED Language Arts, Reading*.

Pretest Answer Grid

1 ① ② ③ ④ ⑤	15 ① ② ③ ④ ⑤	29 ① ② ③ ④ ⑤
2 ① ② ③ ④ ⑤	16 ① ② ③ ④ ⑤	30 ① ② ③ ④ ⑤
3 ① ② ③ ④ ⑤	17 ① ② ③ ④ ⑤	31 ① ② ③ ④ ⑤
4 ① ② ③ ④ ⑤	18 ① ② ③ ④ ⑤	32 ① ② ③ ④ ⑤
5 ① ② ③ ④ ⑤	19 ① ② ③ ④ ⑤	33 ① ② ③ ④ ⑤
6 ① ② ③ ④ ⑤	20 ① ② ③ ④ ⑤	34 ① ② ③ ④ ⑤
7 ① ② ③ ④ ⑤	21 ① ② ③ ④ ⑤	35 ① ② ③ ④ ⑤
8 ① ② ③ ④ ⑤	22 ① ② ③ ④ ⑤	36 ① ② ③ ④ ⑤
9 ① ② ③ ④ ⑤	23 ① ② ③ ④ ⑤	37 ① ② ③ ④ ⑤
10 ① ② ③ ④ ⑤	24 ① ② ③ ④ ⑤	38 ① ② ③ ④ ⑤
11 ① ② ③ ④ ⑤	25 ① ② ③ ④ ⑤	39 ① ② ③ ④ ⑤
12 ① ② ③ ④ ⑤	26 ① ② ③ ④ ⑤	40 ① ② ③ ④ ⑤
13 ① ② ③ ④ ⑤	27 ① ② ③ ④ ⑤	
14 ① ② ③ ④ ⑤	28 ① ② ③ ④ ⑤	

POSTTEST

Questions 1–4 refer to the following passage.

Statistics form the spine of the legend of Babe Didrikson Zaharias. This is true of nearly all athletes: the results of sporting events are finite [measurable], almost never
5 abstract. In most other human pursuits, in art, music, literature, and so forth, greatness is a matter of intangibles. But in sports there are winners and losers; the results are unmistakable; the statistics are immutable
10 [unchangeable]. In the case of Babe, the statistics that define her greatness are so impressive they seem almost too good to be true.

Between 1930 and 1932 she held
15 American, Olympic, or world records in five different track and field events. During the A.A.U. national meet of 1932, she entered as the sole member of the Golden Cyclones, a team sponsored by the Employers
20 Casualty Company of Dallas; Babe scored thirty points in the meet. The next best team, the Illinois Women's Athletic Club, had twenty-two members who scored a total of twenty-two points.

25 In the Olympics at Los Angeles, she won gold medals and set world records in the 80-meter hurdles and the javelin—breaking the javelin record by an astounding eleven feet. She tied for first place in the high jump,
30 setting another world record; officials ruled, however, that she had dived illegally during her last successful jump and she was awarded the silver medal instead of the gold.

—Excerpted from *Whatta Gal: The Babe Didrickson Story,*
by William O. Johnson and Nancy P. Williamson

1. What is the best title for this passage?

   (1) The Los Angeles Olympics
   (2) Babe Didrikson's Greatest Accomplishment
   (3) Sexism in Sports
   (4) Babe Didrikson: Star Athlete
   (5) Famous Female Athletes

2. The word *intangibles* (line 7) refers to what type of things?

   (1) things that can be easily measured
   (2) things that cannot clearly be perceived or identified
   (3) things that people should not believe
   (4) things that involve mistakes
   (5) things that involve financial sacrifice

3. In the high jump at the Los Angeles Olympics, why did Babe Didrikson win a silver medal instead of a gold?

   (1) She had the second-highest jump in the event.
   (2) She broke a world record.
   (3) The officials ruled that she had dived illegally.
   (4) She could not break the record of 11 feet.
   (5) She failed in her final jump.

4. With which of the following statements would the author of this passage most likely agree?

   (1) Sports are more important than arts and literature.
   (2) The results of sporting events are often misunderstood.
   (3) Statistics alone do not tell the story of Babe Didrikson.
   (4) Greatness is easier to measure in sports than in the arts.
   (5) It is easier to excel in the arts than in athletics.

POSTTEST

Questions 5–8 refer to the following passage.

He stopped the car and studied the opening with his field glasses. Then he motioned to the driver to go on and the car moved slowly along, the driver avoiding
5 wart-hog holes and driving around the mud castles ants had built. Then, looking across the opening, Wilson suddenly turned and said,

"By God, there they are!"

10 And looking where he pointed, while the car jumped forward and Wilson spoke in rapid Swahili to the driver, Macomber saw three huge, black animals looking almost cylindrical in their long heaviness, like big
15 black tank cars, moving at a gallop across the far edge of the open prairie. They moved at a stiff-necked, stiff-bodied gallop and he could see the upswept wide black horns on their heads as they galloped heads
20 out; the heads not moving.

"They're three old bulls," Wilson said. "We'll cut them off before they get to the swamp."

—Excerpted from "The Short Happy Life of Francis Macomber," by Ernest Hemingway

5. What does Wilson see across the open field?

(1) black tank cars
(2) another car and driver
(3) three bulls
(4) three cylinders
(5) a jumble of mud castles

6. How many people can you assume are in the car?

(1) only one
(2) two
(3) at least three
(4) four
(5) six

7. What kind of language is used in lines 12–16?

(1) literal
(2) persuasive
(3) informative
(4) descriptive
(5) informal

8. Based on the passage, what can you infer about Wilson and Macomber?

(1) They are visiting an urban zoo.
(2) They are working on a cattle farm.
(3) They are on safari in Africa.
(4) They are trying to escape from dangerous bulls.
(5) They are touring Europe.

P O S T T E S T

Questions 9–11 refer to the following form.

GRANT MANUFACTURING COMPANY PERFORMANCE ASSESSMENT AND EMPLOYEE DEVELOPMENT FORM

Employee Name _____

ID # _____ Date of Review _____

Job Title _____

Performance Assessment Period from_____ to _____

Manager _____

The assessment of your on-the-job performance is based on the ratings assigned to you by your manager (or supervisor), who compares your performance to the responsibilities and duties stated within your job description. The purpose of a performance assessment is to provide workers and supervisors with a clear and permanent record of the worker's job performance on an annual basis.

The Grant Manufacturing Company performance assessment system uses the following rating system to assess each employee.

EXEMPLARY	Worker's job performance exceeds expectations and goals every day.
GOOD	Worker's job performance meets and frequently exceeds expectations and goals.
AVERAGE	Worker's job performance is average, and occasionally exceeds expectations and goals.
BELOW AVERAGE	Worker's job performance is insufficient, and does not meet the expectations of the company.

Employee's Performance Assessment
(Manager: Check one box in each category.)

	EXEMPLARY	GOOD	AVERAGE	BELOW AVERAGE
PRODUCTIVITY				
TEAMWORK				
CREATIVITY				
ATTITUDE				
PROFESSIONALISM				
ATTENDANCE				

9. How frequently is an employee's perfomance assessed using this form?

   (1) every six months
   (2) once a month
   (3) once a year
   (4) twice a year
   (5) on an as-needed basis

10. Based on the information on the form, which statement is true of an employee who receives a BELOW AVERAGE rating?

    He or she
    (1) might be promoted
    (2) is absent from work frequently
    (3) is meeting the expectations of his or her job
    (4) will be fired
    (5) is not doing his or her job efffectively

11. What is the purpose of a performance assessment?

    (1) to provide evidence of a worker's poor performance so he or she can be fired
    (2) to satisfy a manager's need to help his or her employees
    (3) to allow one employee to critique a coworker
    (4) to provide a record of a worker's job performance on an annual basis
    (5) to reward good workers with financial incentives

POSTTEST

Questions 12–15 refer to the following passage.

"Where do they get vegetables like this?" Minnie asked. She saw other women feeling the tomatoes, sampling the lush bunches of grapes. "The prices are the same
5 as we pay, but what a difference."

Mrs. Jameson laughed a little. "It's worth driving over here, isn't it?" she said. "We used to live not far from here. That's how I happen to know about it." But
10 Mariana suspected this store was not unique, that in the gringo neighborhoods everything was a little better.

At the meat counter, Minnie was even more impressed. She examined carefully all
15 the meat behind the glass, and then asked the butcher to cut some filet mignon. Mariana couldn't ever recall hearing her mother order that, and she noticed it was the most expensive meat. She thought she
20 understood why her mother ordered it.

On the way back to East Los Angeles, Mariana sensed her mother felt defensive and perhaps a little offended because the gringa had shown her a better way to do
25 something, had shown that shopping near home was not good enough for someone with taste.

She heard her mother say, "Next week Pete's buying me a new Cadillac. Then I'll
30 take you shopping with me," and Mariana had never seen such a forced smile on her mother's face.

"Oh, that'll be nice," Mrs. Jameson said.

—Excerpted from *Chicano*, by Richard Vasquez

12. Who is Mariana?

(1) Minnie's friend
(2) Minnie's daughter
(3) Minnie's mother
(4) Minnie's neighbor
(5) Minnie's aunt

13. What can be inferred about the store the women visited together?

(1) It is located in Minnie's neighborhood.
(2) It is where Minnie usually shops.
(3) It is part of a discount food chain.
(4) It is located a distance from Minnie's neighborhood.
(5) It is owned by the Jameson family.

14. Why might Minnie feel defensive and a little offended (lines 22–23)?

(1) She had to travel a long way to buy the same food she could buy at home.
(2) She discovered that the food sold in her neighborhood was inferior by comparison.
(3) She could not afford to shop in fancy grocery stores.
(4) Mrs. Jameson insulted her.
(5) Mrs. Jameson misinformed her.

15. You can infer that Minnie ordered filet mignon for which of the following reasons?

(1) She wanted to impress Mrs. Jameson.
(2) It was her husband's favorite food.
(3) She always liked to try new things.
(4) It was much cheaper than at her regular market.
(5) Mariana recommended it.

POSTTEST

Questions 16–20 refer to the following poem.

I'M JUST A STRANGER HERE, HEAVEN IS MY HOME

The first sign was your hair,
unstraightened, shortened from worry,
and it had only been a year since the
   wedding,
5   but you had grown older, Mama.
I felt your usual care
in the mustard greens, sweet potatoes and
   chicken,
yet you smelled of whiskey and prayer.
10   I showed you the pictures,
asked which ones you'd like remade
and watched you fidget, unable to see
them. Raising your arm, you spoke of your
   rheumatism,
15   it seems like life left your arm first,
like crumbs given to front yard robins.
Age and need, those simple weeds,
were gathering around and taking you away.
                              —Carole Clemmons

16. What is the tone of this poem?

   (1) ironic
   (2) pleasant
   (3) sorrowful
   (4) humorous
   (5) angry

17. What is the main idea of this poem?

   (1) An elderly alcoholic woman is likely to neglect herself.
   (2) People with elderly parents should visit them regularly.
   (3) Mothers continue to act like mothers even after their children are all grown up.
   (4) Age and need have caused noticeable changes in Mama.
   (5) Elderly women tend to suffer from depression.

18. What does line 15 suggest?

   (1) Mama will probably lose her arm before she dies.
   (2) Mama's life has lost value.
   (3) Mama's needs have lessened with age.
   (4) Mama can live as simply as a little robin.
   (5) Mama's health is steadily declining.

19. What does the word *fidget* (line 12) mean?

   (1) to compare closely
   (2) to move nervously
   (3) to laugh loudly
   (4) to look on with interest
   (5) to speak quickly

20. To what does the phrase "those simple weeds" (line 17) refer?

   (1) the yard inhabited by robins
   (2) whiskey and prayer
   (3) Mama's life
   (4) age and need
   (5) rheumatism

POSTTEST

Questions 21–25 refer to a passage from The Glass Menagerie, *a play by Tennessee Williams. Laura, the main character, is extremely shy and very self-conscious about a brace that she wears on one leg. She spends most of her time caring for a collection of small glass figurines.*

[*JIM lights a cigarette and leans indolently {lazily} back on his elbows smiling at LAURA with a warmth and charm which lights her inwardly with altar candles {pleases her very*
5 *much}. She remains by the table, picks up a piece from the glass menagerie collection, and turns it in her hands to cover her tumult {confusion}.*]

JIM: [*After several reflective puffs on his*
10 cigarette] What have you done since high school? [*She seems not to hear him.*] Huh? [*laura looks up.*] I said what have you done since high school, Laura?

LAURA: Nothing much.

15 JIM: You must have been doing something these six long years.

LAURA: Yes.

JIM: Well, then, such as what?

LAURA: I took a business course at business
20 college—

JIM: How did that work out?

LAURA: Well, not very—well—I had to drop out, it gave me—indigestion—

[*JIM laughs gently.*]

25 JIM: What are you doing now?

LAURA: I don't do anything—much. Oh, please don't think I sit around doing nothing! My glass collection takes up a good deal of time. Glass is something you have to
30 take good care of.

JIM: What did you say—about glass?

LAURA: Collection I said—I have one. [*She clears her throat and turns away again, acutely shy.*]

35 JIM: [*abruptly*] You know what I judge to be the trouble with you? Inferiority complex! … Yep—that's what I judge to be your principal trouble. A lack of confidence in yourself as a person. You don't have the proper amount
40 of faith in yourself … For instance that clumping you thought was so awful in high school. You say that you even dreaded to walk into class. You see what you did? You dropped out of school, you gave up an
45 education because of a clump, which as far as I know was practically non-existent! A little physical defect is what you have. Hardly noticeable even! Magnified thousands of times by imagination! You
50 know what my strong advice to you is? Think of yourself as superior in some way!

21. What has Laura been doing since high school?

(1) caring for her collection of little glass statues
(2) working toward her business degree
(3) keeping house for Jim and raising their children
(4) volunteering at a school
(5) undergoing therapy for an inferiority complex

22. Why does Laura pick up a glass figurine (lines 5–6)?

(1) to prevent Jim from breaking it
(2) to show Jim how fragile it is
(3) because she is nervous and confused
(4) because she is angry
(5) because Jim's smoking irritates her

23. What do the dashes in lines 22–23 and 32 indicate about Laura?

   (1) She stutters.
   (2) She is afraid that Jim will make fun of her glass collection.
   (3) She has trouble sharing her thoughts with others.
   (4) She is confined indoors with a serious medical condition.
   (5) She is suffering another bout of indigestion.

24. When Jim says Laura gave up an education "because of a clump" that was "practically non-existent," what does he mean?

   (1) Laura left school to tend a small garden.
   (2) Laura didn't have to wear her brace all the time.
   (3) Laura was self-conscious about a handicap that others hardly noticed.
   (4) Laura's brace was noisy.
   (5) Most of Laura's classmates ignored her.

25. Which of the following conclusions can you draw from this passage?

   (1) Women are more likely than men to have an inferiority complex.
   (2) Shyness is a sign of an inferiority complex.
   (3) An inferiority complex is a sign of shyness.
   (4) Someone who feels inferior probably is inferior.
   (5) An inferiority complex is a lack of self-confidence.

POSTTEST

Questions 26–29 refer to the following review.

Playwright A. R. Gurney calls *Later Life* a comedy, and it has the witty dialogue to live up to the billing. But at its heart, this story of a man in his middle years who can't bring
5   himself to seize one last chance at happiness is no laughing matter.

If the play is to succeed, the audience had better feel for the anguished Austin, a Boston Brahmin so caught in the spiderweb
10 of his bloodline and upbringing that he can't let the free-spirited Ruth into his life even the second time around.

Regrettably, Northlight Theater's production of the work … does not achieve
15 the desired effect …

The story unfolds on an apartment building terrace overlooking Boston Harbor. Inside, a party is going on, but outside, Austin and Ruth are becoming reacquainted.

20 They met years ago on Capri. He was a young naval officer fresh out of Harvard; she was vacationing with friends from Southern Illinois University. The attraction was mutual and instantaneous, but after one idyllic afternoon,
25 Austin walked away from the relationship.

They both have gone on to marriages, but at the time of their second meeting, he is divorced and she is separated. They could help each other, but Austin again is
30 incapable of pressing forward. At the play's end, his life is effectively over, and Ruth's prospects are not much better.

Kristine Thatcher … captures Ruth's resilience, warmth and zest for life. It is easy
35 to understand why everyone at the party is rooting for Austin to nab her.

Michael Gross … has the tougher assignment. He must make the aloof Austin not only understandable but sympathetic,
40 but the actor never reveals what is going on beneath the seemingly smooth surface.

Linda Kimbrough and Greg Vinkler, however, are convincing and terrifically comical in multiple roles as insensitive party
45 guests who wander onto the terrace, interrupting the couple's conversation.

—Excerpted from a review of *Later Life*, by Virginia Gerst.

26. What is the subject of this review?

    (1) a struggling regional theater company
    (2) the Northlight Theater's production of *Later Life*
    (3) the playwright A. R. Gurney
    (4) a made-for-television comedy
    (5) a romantic film

27. How is the character of Austin best described?

    (1) free-spirited
    (2) snobbish
    (3) warm
    (4) sympathetic
    (5) dignified

28. With which of the following would the reviewer most likely agree?

    (1) Kristine Thatcher is miscast in the role of Ruth.
    (2) Michael Gross delivers a complex, sensitive portrait of Austin.
    (3) The character of Austin is poorly written.
    (4) The supporting actors turn in splendid performances.
    (5) The overall quality of the acting rescues a mediocre script.

29. How can the ending of *Later Life* be characterized best?

    (1) bittersweet
    (2) joyful
    (3) satisfying
    (4) hopeful
    (5) surprising

POSTTEST

Questions 30–33 refer to the following passage.

It was June and long past time for buying the special shoes that were quiet as a summer rain falling on the walks. June and the earth full of raw power and everything
5 everywhere in motion. The grass was still pouring in from the country, surrounding the sidewalks, stranding the houses. Any moment the town would capsize, go down and leave not a stir in the clover and weeds.
10 And here Douglas stood, trapped on the dead cement and the red-brick streets, hardly able to move.

"Dad!" He blurted it out. "Back there in that window, those Cream-Sponge Para
15 Litefoot Shoes ..."

His father didn't even turn. "Suppose you tell me why you need a new pair of sneakers. Can you do that?" "Well ..."

It was because they felt the way it feels
20 every summer when you take off your shoes for the first time and run in the grass. They felt like it feels sticking your feet out of the hot covers in wintertime to let the cold wind from the open window blow on them
25 suddenly and you let them stay out a long time until you pull them back in under the covers again to feel them, like packed snow. The tennis shoes felt like it always feels the first time every year wading in the slow
30 waters of the creek and seeing your feet below, half an inch further downstream, with refraction, than the real part of you above water.

"Dad," said Douglas, "it's hard to
35 explain."

—Excerpted from *Dandelion Wine,* by Ray Bradbury

30. Which statement best expresses the main idea of the passage?

(1) Douglas wants to run and be free.
(2) The coming of summer worries Douglas.
(3) New sneakers would help Douglas experience the joy of summer.
(4) Douglas needs orthopedic sneakers for hiking in the back country.
(5) Douglas is a summer athlete.

31. How can the style of the paragraph beginning "It was because" best be described?

(1) informative
(2) persuasive
(3) descriptive
(4) formal
(5) sequential

32. It can be inferred that Douglas and his father are speaking as they walk in which location?

(1) on a wooded path
(2) on a mountain trail
(3) on a country road on the outskirts of town
(4) on a sidewalk in town
(5) on a beach

33. Why is it hard for Douglas to explain his desire for new sneakers?

(1) His father is uncaring.
(2) Some feelings are just hard for him to put into words.
(3) Douglas knows his family cannot afford to buy luxuries.
(4) Douglas is afraid of his father.
(5) There's nothing wrong with his old sneakers.

Questions 34–37 refer to the following passage from a newspaper story.

SINATRA BEFORE SWING: EARLY MATERIAL REVEALS QUIETER SIDE OF THE STAR

To most listeners today, he's the singer who crooned his way to stardom singing "My Kind of Town," "New York, New York," The Lady Is a Tramp" and "I Get a Kick Out
5 of You."

To most listeners, he's all about swagger and strut, the perennial tough guy in a tux, a shot glass in one hand, a microphone and a smoldering cigarette in the other, the
10 enduring symbol of an era when swing still was king.

Peel away the mythology, however; look past the high-life facade [surface] and the hard-edged repertoire [body of work], and
15 you'll find the Frank Sinatra that most of the world doesn't know, or doesn't want to.

Listen past his biggest hits, the anthems that every audience demands, and you'll hear facets of Sinatra's music that shatter
20 universally held perceptions.

It's that repertoire [mixture of songs]— brooding ballads, songs of alienation [separation] and loss, aching love poems, tunes that Sinatra sang before he became a
25 swinger, and long after—that finally is coming to light in a series of long-awaited releases and rare reissues.

Much of this material hasn't been heard in 25 years or more; some of it never has
30 been released before.

—Excerpted from a review by Howard Reich,
Chicago Tribune

34. What is the subject of this passage?

  (1) the era of swing
  (2) new releases and rare reissues of Frank Sinatra's music
  (3) Frank Sinatra's tough-guy image
  (4) audience perceptions of Frank Sinatra
  (5) changing tastes in popular music

35. You can infer that "My Kind of Town" and "New York, New York" are examples of which of the following?

  (1) brooding ballads
  (2) songs of loss
  (3) aching love poems
  (4) the kinds of songs usually identified with Frank Sinatra
  (5) the writer's favorite type of music

36. The writer suggests that the "long-awaited releases and rare reissues" (line 27) reveal what information?

  (1) why Frank Sinatra was viewed as a symbol of swing
  (2) a softer side to Sinatra's music
  (3) the singer's best-known repertoire
  (4) the reasons for his popularity
  (5) a familiar aspect of Sinatra's musical style

37. To what does the word *mythology* (line 12) refer?

  (1) Frank Sinatra's image as a tough guy living the high life
  (2) songs that audiences demand
  (3) Sinatra's biggest hits
  (4) the way that ordinary people look up to celebrities
  (5) music that shatters common perceptions

POSTTEST

Questions 38–40 refer to the following excerpt from an index to a cookbook.

38. On which page would you find a recipe for nut pancakes?

(1) 22
(2) 51
(3) 125
(4) 124
(5) 126

39. Which of the following sets of pasta recipes can be found on the same page?

(1) Lasagna Casserole and Macaroni and Ham
(2) Lasagna Casserole and Spaghetti Meat Sauce
(3) Two-layer Italian Macaroni and Macaroni, Cheese, and Tomato Casserole with Ground Beef
(4) Spaghetti Casserole and Rita's Noodle Ring
(5) Noodle Nests and Macaroni and Ham

40. Which pages tell you whether to freeze oven-fried chicken in waxed paper or in Saran Wrap?

(1) 342
(2) 31
(3) 34 and 35
(4) 342 and 34
(5) 33 and 34

Answer Key

1. (4) This passage focuses on Babe Didrikson's star performances in different sporting events. At best, the other choices are only partially correct.

2. (2) Lines 3–5 state that the results in sports are finite and almost never abstract. The author contrasts this with art, music, and literature. *Intangibles*, therefore, are things that are abstract or beyond human measurement.

3. (3) Although Babe Didrikson tied for the highest jump, she was awarded second place because officials ruled that she had dived illegally.

4. (4) The first paragraph says that in the arts, literature, and music, "greatness is a matter of intangibles" but that, in sports, statistics define greatness.

5. (3) This is stated in the last paragraph.

6. (3) You can count three people in the car: Wilson, Macomber, and the driver. Therefore, you can assume that there are at least three people.

7. (4) The author says the animals looked "like big black tank cars" and "almost cylindrical." These are examples of vividly descriptive language.

8. (3) You can infer that Wilson and Macomber are driving somewhere in the great outdoors. They are most probably in Africa, since Swahili is an African language.

9. (3) The form states that an employee's job performance is evaluated on an annual basis.

10. (5) A BELOW AVERAGE rating indicates that an employee isn't fulfilling his or her duties effectively, but does not indicate that he or she will be fired.

11. (4) As it states, the form serves as a clear and permanent record of a worker's job performance.

12. (2) Mariana uses the word mother in the third paragraph when she thinks about Minnie. This tells you that she must be Minnie's daughter.

13. (4) Since the women had to drive a distance, and Minnie is surprised by what she sees, you can infer that the store is not in Minnie's neighborhood.

14. (2) Mrs. Jameson had shown her a store much bigger and better than the markets in Minnie's neighborhood.

15. (1) Minnie wanted Mrs. Jameson to think that she wasn't dazzled by the beautiful store and that buying expensive items was as natural for her as for the "gringa."

16. (3) The poet is obviously saddened by her mother's failing condition.

17. (4) The poet sees how much her mother has declined from age and need.

18. (5) The poet says that "life left your arm first," meaning that Mama's health is continuing to weaken. First implies more to come.

19. (2) This is the best choice in this context.

20. (4) You can infer that age and need are "those simple weeds" collecting around Mama.

21. (1) Laura tells Jim that her "glass collection takes up a good deal of time" (lines 28–29).

22. (3) The stage directions tell you that Laura turns the figurine in her hands "to cover her tumult." You can infer that this is also part of the reason she picked it up.

23. (3) Dashes indicate interruptions. Laura is interrupting herself because she is unsure of herself and has difficulty expressing her thoughts.

POSTTEST

24. (3) Something that is "practically non-existent" is noticed very little or not at all.

25. (5) Jim says, "Inferiority complex! . . . Yep—that's what I judge to be your principal trouble. A lack of confidence in yourself as a person." (lines 36–39)

26. (2) The first paragraph identifies the play. The third paragraph names the theater company.

27. (2) You can infer that Austin is snobbish from the description of him as a "Boston Brahmin so caught in the spiderweb of his bloodline and upbringing . . ."

28. (4) The last paragraph praises the supporting cast as "convincing and terrifically comical."

29. (1) The sixth paragraph says that at the end of the play, Austin's life "is effectively over, and Ruth's prospects are not much better."

30. (3) The main idea is the connection Douglas makes between new sneakers and his anticipated enjoyment of summer.

31. (3) This paragraph describes in great emotional detail Douglas's feelings about summertime.

32. (4) Line 11 refers to cement. "Back there in that window" (lines 13–14) suggests a storefront, which would most likely be in town.

33. (2) Most of the passage is about what new sneakers feel like to Douglas and what they mean to him. But his response to his father shows that he doesn't know how exactly to explain these feelings or translate them into a practical argument for getting new shoes.

34. (2) This information is given in the last two paragraphs.

35. (4) The first paragraph identifies such songs as the kind of music "most listeners" associate with Frank Sinatra.

36. (2) The fifth paragraph identifies the newly released material as a collection of ballads and other sad songs. These suggest a softer side to the singer's work.

37. (1) Since the mythology can be peeled back, it must be on the outside. Sinatra, on the surface, has long had the image of a tough character leading a wild life in the fast lane.

38. (4) Under "Pancake recipes," find the sub-heading "Nut."

39. (3) Look under "Pasta recipes." Only two pasta recipes appear on the same page.

40. (5) Under "Oven-Fried Chicken," you will find only a recipe. If you look under "Packaging foods for freezer," you can find Saran Wrap on page 34 and waxed paper on page 33.

Evaluation Chart

Use the chart below to help you identify any areas in which you need additional practice. Circle the number of any questions you answered incorrectly. Then note the corresponding skill and content areas. Read across the rows for content areas and down the columns for skills. If your mistakes cluster in any one row or column, it means that you need more work in that particular area.

Skill Area/ Content Area/	Comprehension (pages 13–25)	Application (pages 27–34)	Analysis (pages 35–56)	Synthesis (pages 57–69)
Nonfiction Prose (pages 73–130)	2, 3, 9, 11, 26, 34, 37	29, 38, 40	10, 28, 35, 36, 39	1, 4, 27
Prose Fiction (pages 131–164)	5, 12		7, 14, 31, 32	6, 8, 13, 15 30, 33
Poetry (pages 165–184)	17, 19		16, 20	18
Drama (pages 185–201)	21		22, 24	23, 25

Answer Key

Chapter 1

COMPREHENSION

Exercise 1, Pages 18–19

1. Paragraph 1: (d)
   Paragraph 2: (c)
   Paragraph 3: (a)
   Paragraph 4: (b)
2. (3) From the second paragraph on, the passage focuses on opportunities for adults.
3. (2) The passage provides information about adults returning to college.

Exercise 2, Page 20

1. 1832. This is stated in the second sentence of the second paragraph.
2. He believed the chiefs had been tricked into giving up the land. This information is provided in the last sentence of the first paragraph.
3. He refused to surrender the land. This is explained in the first two sentences.
4. Indian tribes of Illinois. This information is found in the first paragraph.
5. He was sent to a reservation at Fort Des Moines. This is stated in the last sentence of the second paragraph.

Exercise 3, Pages 21–22

1. To *equivocate* means to use unclear language either to mislead someone or to avoid committing oneself to a particular position. The key words *instead of* point to the opposite of *straightforward*.
2. A *flashback* is an intense, emotional memory of a past time or event. The meaning is given after the key word *or*.
3. A *surrogate* is a substitute. The key words *that is* point to the meaning.
4. To have *charisma* means to have extraordinary powers. The word is defined by the sentence directly following it.
5. *Modular* refers to self-contained parts—in this case, computer parts. The comma introduces the definition.

6. A *proverb* is an old, popular saying that expresses a well-known truth or bit of wisdom. The key word yet signals the explanation.
7. A *bellwether* is a leader. The definition is given in the second sentence.
8. A *quarantine* is an enforced period of isolation to prevent the spread of disease. The key word *means* points to the definition.

Chapter Review, Pages 23–25

1. (2) The passage traces the history of New Mexico from prehistoric times to the present. The phrase "the memory of New Mexico's fiery past" indicates that the subject of the discussion is history.
2. (5) The second paragraph specifically says that the Spanish arrived after the Apaches and Navajos.
3. (3) The second paragraph states that Coronado was "compelled by rumors of gold."
4. (2) The first paragraph defines ristras as "strands of blazing red chili peppers, hung from ranch house porches."
5. (1) The paragraph is about the start of the modern era, which began when the railroad came in.
6. (3) See the last paragraph. A hamlet is a small settlement essentially unchanged by time.
7. (1) The last paragraph describes the air in Lamy as fresh and clean in 1880 and still today.
8. (4) Lines 7–8 tell you that prehistoric hunters came to New Mexico as long as 11,500 years ago.
9. (2) Washington persuaded his mother to get him a book.
10. (2) The passage is about the author's first experiences with reading.
11. (4) The author expresses no opinion about his stepfather's job or about the kind of job he himself would one day like to have.
12. (2) When he moved with his family to a new cabin in West Virginia, he persuaded his mother to get him a book to learn from.
13. (1) Washington's mother *procured*, or *got possession of*, an old spelling book for him.

14. (3) Washington *devoured,* or *enjoyed greatly,* the spelling book his mother gave him.
15. (4) The number "18" is an identification number that is marked on the barrels his stepfather packs.

Chapter 2

APPLICATION

Exercise 1, Page 28

1. in the newspaper, according to the second paragraph
2. in magazines and on television, according to the last sentence of the second paragraph
3. direct mail
4. twenty cents, according to the chart

Exercise 2, Pages 29–30

1. (5)
2. (3)
3. (3)
4. (2)

Exercise 3, Pages 30–31

1. Blend in the chocolate and vanilla.
2. Four. Since one pie calls for two eggs, two pies would require four.
3. Pour the mixture into a pastry shell and chill it.
4. One stick of margarine equals one-half cup.

Exercise 4, Pages 31–32

1. T The entire passage is about the Great Depression.
2. F The passage is not critical. Its purpose is simply to provide information.
3. T The last sentence in the second paragraph says that Roosevelt's reforms "helped ease the depression."
4. T The last paragraph gives several examples of the long-term effects of the depression.

Exercise 5, Page 32

1. 2 minutes
2. Dial the number to which you will be sending the fax.
3. Press the FAX button.
4. back

Chapter Review, Pages 33–34

1. (3) The author merely guesses that the doctor was from India, whereas she directly states in her first paragraph that the doctor had a thick accent.
2. (5) The entire passage, and particularly the last paragraph, is about how confused and upset she is.
3. (5) The young woman is a sympathetic character, and the events of the story are told from her point of view.
4. (4) From the events mentioned in lines 11–14, you can infer that Sue grew up quickly at age 15.
5. (3) Lines 14–15 tell you that Sue moved back with her mother after Sue and Larry had a fight.
6. (5) The passage doesn't say why Larry left town. Sue assumes Larry left because of her pregnancy, but she's not sure.

Chapter 3

ANALYSIS

Exercise1, Page 37

1. (1) This is not stated, but it is the best summary of all the details in the passage.
2. (2) He continues despite his great surprise.
3. (3) It is a sign of their courage that they continue toward the strange planet.

Exercise 2, Page 38

1. (2) The eating binge at the bakery is the focal point of the passage. All of the events in the story build toward it. It ends not only the passage but also Vana's diet.
2. (1) The details are presented from the least important to the most important, culminating in Vana's eventual surrender to sweets.

Exercise 3, Page 40

1. (3) Paul is probably older, because his children are much older than Tom's.

2. (1) Paul ends the conversation by saying he must return to his office. Of all the answer choices, an insurance salesman is most likely to work out of an office.

3. (5) The whole conversation is about Tom's divorce; he has had the "worst day" of his life and "split for good."

4. (2) Paul's advice is to try kindness. Tom won't hear of it. "Impossible," he says.

5. (5) Tom describes his job as a "dead-end job."

6. (3) The term *alimony* refers to the payments Tom must make to his ex-wife after the divorce.

Exercise 4, Page 42

1. 2, 1, 4, 3, 5

2. (1) Jake should probably secure his remaining food and supplies before deciding what to do next.

Exercise 5, Page 44

1. T The second paragraph discusses in detail the limitations of Norberto's formal schooling.

2. F Carmen never saw the reading specialist until after she had helped him learn to read a little. She helped Norberto because she wanted to and because he was agreeable.

Exercise 6, Page 46

1. Both were originally from the same neighborhood, former basketball stars, and Vietnam veterans.

2. The last paragraph mentions they each promise better jobs, schools, roads, and lives for citizens in the district.

3. John is a wealthy Republican backed by professionals, white-collar workers, farmers, and businesspeople. Peter is a steelworker and a Democrat closely identified with labor and minorities.

Exercise 7, Page 48

1. (3) The globe is grouped with educational items. In the third paragraph, the author says, "Never one to neglect his schooling, my sleepyhead cuddled up to his world globe. . . ."

2. (4) The last paragraph places the dirty sock in the mixed category.

3. (1) The second paragraph lists batteries with the toys.

Exercise 8, Pages 50–51

1. (3) Sentence fragments and the exclamation *Whoa* are characteristics of informal speech. Merely talking to oneself is informal.

2. (2) Cheri becomes increasingly tense and rattled by the sequence of frightening events and disturbing coincidences.

Exercise 9, Page 51

1. Formal. This passage uses more difficult words and larger sentences than would be used in an informal passage.

2. Forceful. The speaker presents the message in a vigorous, confident manner.

Exercise 10, Pages 52–53

1. (1) The books are listed alphabetically by author.

2. (1) Rountree's book, *On Women Turning 50*, presents profiles of 18 women over the age of 50.

3. (2) Friedan's *The Fountain of Age* was published in 1993, and so was Rountree's book, *On Women Turning 50*. Although 1994 is one of the choices given, none of the books listed was published in that year.

4. (2) From the title and short description, Berman's book, with its inspirational essays, would have the most comfort to offer a person struggling with fear of aging.

5. (3) *The Golden Years: Fit for Life* gives tips on exercise and finances.

Exercise 11, Page 54

1. F The passage is about a military figure, but there is nothing military about the writing style, which is somewhat formal.

2. F The passage does not criticize any persons or events. It is simply informative, in a literary way.

3. T Elizabeth's skirt "billowed like a balloon, flew out in front, then lifted over her head" (lines 7–8).

4. T The last sentence says that other women took up the practice of sewing lead bars into their skirt hems.

5. T This is the subject of the whole passage.

6. T In line 12, Mrs. Custer is described as taking constitutionals about the post; line 6 mentions the walks she takes around the area.

7. F The passage states that Mrs. Custer's dresses are "five yards around."

8. F The passage says that "a dozen years later all were wearing bar lead in their skirt hems on the windy western plains."

Chapter Review, Pages 55–56

1. (1) The first paragraph quotes Aunt Rosie directly about not letting the anger take over.

2. (1) Nothing in the passage indicates that Aunt Rosie pushes her way into situations where she is not wanted. The other choices are all reasonable inferences.

3. (3) The main idea is presented in the very first sentence. Inconsiderate behavior can certainly ruin a marriage, but it is not the main idea of this selection.

4. (5) This is most in keeping with Aunt Rosie's advice to keep anger under control and express one's true feelings in a calm fashion.

5. (3) This passage is written in an informal prose style.

6. (4) In the first paragraph, Aunt Rosie specifically says that nothing is solved by letting anger take over.

7. (2) The writer prevented a fight by following Aunt Rosie's advice. Instead of an angry outburst, she simply told her husband how she felt and why.

8. (2) Lines 12–13 describe Les as standing hesitantly, as if his wife might throw something. From this you can infer that he expected his wife to be angry.

9. (4) Lines 20–24 explain why Les came home late from work.

10. (3) The passage says that Les had to settle a change of plans with the foreman at a construction site and that he carried a briefcase. From this it seems most likely that Les is an architect.

11. (2) Lines 14–16 describe Les as apologizing softly with tired eyes and his shoulders drooping. From this you can infer that he felt sorry and hesitant.

12. (1) The writer seems to be optimistic since things worked out better than expected with her husband. Part of this is due to a change in the writer's attitude about her husband's behavior.

Chapter 4

SYNTHESIS

Exercise 1, Page 58

1. (3)
2. (2)

Exercise 2, Page 59

1. (P)
2. (O)
3. (P)
4. (O)
5. (P)

Exercise 3, Page 60

1. (4) The conversation seems to indicate that the speaker is in love with Estella.
2. (1)
3. (5) The speaker states that on at least two different occasions, Estella made the speaker cry, or "broke his heart."

Exercise 4, Pages 61–62

1. (2)
2. (5)
3. (2)

Exercise 5, Pages 63–64

1. answers will vary
2. answers will vary
3. answers will vary
4. answers will vary
5. (3)

Chapter Review, Pages 67–69

1. (2) The fact that Mama says she would not send him out alone indicates that she is reluctant.
2. (1)
3. (1)
4. (2) His mother is reluctant to send him out alone, so he wants to reassure her.
5. (3) Mama tells Pepé to burn a candle for Papa. This indicates that he has died.
6. (4) The story is told in the third person, using "he" and "she" as subjects, indicating it is from an outside observer's point of view.
7. (5)
8. (3)
9. (1)
10. (2) The fact that the narrator and Joan share a bedroom and a son indicates that they are most likely husband and wife.
11. (1)

Chapter 5

NONFICTION PROSE

Exercise 1, Page 74

1. T This is indicated in the first paragraph.
2. T This is stated in the third paragraph.
3. F No reference is made to to other youth shelters.
4. F The subject of the piece is Covenant House itself and the services it offers.
5. F Scan the article for children's ages. The fourth paragraph mentions a child of 11.
6. F The second paragraph says, "No child is ever turned away."
7. F According to the second paragraph, covenant House has 200 part-time workers.
8. F Sanctuary is safe haven. Troubled teens too rarely find sanctuary from the harsh world of the street.

Exercise 2, Page 75

1. Murder by arsenic poisoning. This is explained in the second and third paragraphs.
2. Sleepiness, insomnia, swollen feet, excessive weight gain. See the last sentence of the third paragraph.
3. The autopsy revealed an enlarged liver, a symptom of arsenic poisoning. This is stated in the second sentence of the third paragraph.
4. A well-reserved body in death. See the last paragraph.
5. He analyzed strands of Napoleon's hair. See the fourth paragraph.
6. On the island of St. Helena, to which he had been exiled. See the first and third paragraphs.

Exercise 3, Page 76

1. F The last paragraph says that a better basic understanding of these diseases is needed.
2. F NIAID's program calls for more scientific research into the disease processes. The third paragraph says that contact-tracing has been of only limited benefit.
3. T This is explained in the last paragraph.

4. T The first paragraph links complications to suffering, which implies negative effects.
5. T The third paragraph mentions new drug-resistant strains of disease.

Exercise 4, Page 78

1. (2) This is the theme of the entire passage.
2. (1) This is stated in the second sentence of the second paragraph.
3. (2) In the first sentence of the third paragraph, the author introduces his personal opinion with the words *I believe*.
4. (1) The last two sentences of the passage quote the graduate who has just been promoted.

Exercise 5, Page 80

1. (3) The first paragraph stresses the drawbacks of the other diets.
2. (1) *Anemic* and *homesick* are examples of biased language here. The other choices present information in neutral terms.

Exercise 6, Page 82

1. (b)
2. (c)
3. (d)
4. (a)
5. (e)
6. (f)
7. (g)

Exercise 7, Pages 83–84

1. (3) The purpose of any editorial is to persuade.
2. (2) The third paragraph quotes the constitutional "right of the people to keep and bear arms."
3. (3) Lines 11–14 tell why a ban on handguns will not solve the crime problem. The fourth paragraph explicitly mentions illegal gun sales, and the sixth paragraph protests a tax increase.
4. (1) The last two paragraphs support the writer's point of view about how defenseless law-abiding citizens would be without handguns.

Exercise 8, Pages 85–86

1. (1) This is plainly stated in the last sentence.
2. (1) The mention of an "angry husband" and the fact that a police officer was shot indicate that a fight took place.
3. (2) The editorial argues that violent crime declined in England after handguns were outlawed and implies that a ban here would have a similar effect.
4. (3) Both editorials urge increased protection against crime. They cannot agree on what real protection is or should be.

Exercise 9, Pages 87–91

1. (2) The first paragraph suggests the title by mentioning the different groups present at the dedication. The article goes on to describe their respective concerns.
2. (4) This is a factual account written in the style of straight news.
3. (3) This is stated in the last paragraph.
4. (2) The passage discusses the many changes that electric technology has brought to people's lives.
5. (4) In this sentence, the phrase refers to a process of unconscious learning.
6. (3) Since electric technology implies the use of electricity, television is the correct answer.
7. (5) The statement that "the older training of observation has become quite irrelevant in this new time" (lines 30–31) implies that we must learn new ways of relating to today's technology.
8. (1) The second paragraph states that the Cornish miners introduced the Wisconsin miners to better methods of extracting ore, with the result that old mines were reopened and new ones were discovered.
9. (1) The subject of the passage is the history of mining in southwest Wisconsin. All of the information falls under this general topic.
10. (3) The last paragraph explains how, whenever market prices fell, hundreds of miners found themselves unemployed.

11. (3) The purpose is to salute the memory of two people whose joint legacy has enriched an entire community.

12. (5) The fourth paragraph states that Walter and Lavinia fell in love with the same idea. They shared a common vision and the will to realize it.

13. (1) A stereotype is a generalization. Lavinia Phelps did not conform to the stereotype, or common image, of an old woman quietly at home, no longer a productive member of her community.

14. (2) The language emphasizes Representative Palmer's wealth, ignorance, and obvious insensitivity to the farmers' plight.

15. (2) The third paragraph sharply contrasts the almost cartoonishly overdressed politician enjoying public attention with the many farmers who must go into debt just to keep their land.

16. (5) Representative Palmer's actions, words, and even her wardrobe are all calculated to draw attention from the press. Her only real goal is re-election. She shows no interest in farmers' problems, no understanding of them, and no desire to meet or hear from real voters with real concerns.

17. (3) *Festooned* means decorated.

18. (2) Palmer spoke first at the Spring Agriculture Convention in Torrence.

19. (3) Palmer promised to seek more federal aid for agriculture (lines 20–21).

Exercise 10, Page 93

1. the highest quality mattress
2. to be the top manufacturer of mattresses in the world
3. Employees must be courteous, proud of their work, committed to producing superior and innovative products, determined, honorable, and philanthropic (charitable).

Exercise 11, Pages 94–95

1. (4)
2. (2) The form states that managers submitting forms may sign their own submissions.
3. (3)

Exercise 12, Pages 96–97

1. (3) The excerpt states that the leave of absence is available to full-time employees after six months of employment.
2. (2)
3. F, T, T, T, F

Exercise 13, Pages 98–99

1. (2)
2. (5)
1. (4)
2. (4)

Exercise 14, Pages 100–101

1. (3)
2. (2) He states that he was very happy because of the "favorable account you give me of all the Family."
3. (5)

Exercise 15, Pages 102–103

1. (2) The author uses phrases such as "Here one of them is passing . . . "and "He clicks his . . . boots, " which indicates that he is writing as events unfold.
2. (4)
3. (1)

Exercise 16, Pages 103–104

1. (3) Stephen King (the author) seems surprised by the amount of money, and says his apartment rent was $90 a month. This implies that he was not familiar with the prices books could sell for, and was poor at that time.

2. (5) He states that "the strength ran out of my legs" and "I whooshed down to a sitting position there in the doorway."

3. (2) He stated that he wanted to buy something "wild and extravagant," but there was nothing wild and extravagant at La Verdiere's, so "I did the best I could. I got her a hair-dryer."

4. (4)

Exercise 17, Pages 107–108

PART A

1. (1) F
  (2) O
  (3) F
2. (1) O
  (2) F
  (3) F
3. (1) F
  (2) F
  (3) O
4. (1) F
  (2) O
  (3) F

PART B

1. 3
2. 1
3. 4
4. 1

Exercise 18, Page 109

You should have listed the following words or phrases: (1) *strikes out*, (2) *simpy*, (3) *bad timing*, (4) *cardboard characters*, and (5) *witless plots*.

Exercise 19, Page 110

Your answer should have included the following: (1) *remarkable*, (2) *richly imagined*, (3) *daring*, (4) *bold*, (5) *ruthlessly comical*, (6) *intellectually stimulating*, (7) *finest*, and (8) *effective*.

Exercise 20, Page 111

1. *smart, spunky*
2. *heart-pounding*
3. "I wouldn't be surprised if she is nominated for a raft of honors."
4. "superior thriller," "brilliant performances"

Exercise 21, Pages 112–113

1. (3) Benny recounts several unuseful pieces of advice his friends gave him once they learned he was going to do television.

2. (3) Benny praises the competence of the technicians who "face the problems that are constantly cropping up with speed, skill, and imagination."

3. (5) In the last sentence of the article, Benny notes that "the movie industry would do well, even at this early stage, to adapt many of the steamlined methods of television."

4. (2) The entire passage is lighthearted (humorous) but informative as well.

5. (2) In this sentence Benny is saying that it would take Hollywood weeks to duplicate, or copy, the stage scenes that television directors set up each day.

6. (4) In this sentence Benny is discussing the phenomenal, or remarkable, progress which the television industry had already made.

7. (3) This is a very funny line—a good example of Benny's ability to create a comedic expression.

Exercise 22, Pages 114–115

1. (1) Paul Robeson's acting career is the theme that unites all the details in the passage.

2. (2) Robeson starred in *The Emperor Jones*. He became closely identified with the role of Brutus Jones. You can infer from these two facts that Brutus Jones was the title character in the London play.

3. (2) His role as Othello is mentioned in the fifth sentence of the final paragraph.

4. 4, 2, 5, 3, 1

5. Your answer should include any five of the following: *expressive features, resonant voice, tremendous sensitivity, dignity, simplicity, true passion, very experienced, mature, dignified, unforgettable, a high point in the history of American theater.*

Exercise 23 , Pages 116–117

1. Van Gogh was in the town of Arles, in southern France. This is stated in the first sentence.
2. Van Gogh. The second paragraph mentions that the description was taken from his letters to his family.
3. Your answer should include two of the following: "nearly half-dead"; "I have just slept sixteen hours at a stretch"; "I am all right again"; "my eyes are still tired." See paragraphs 3 and 4.
4. Complete or absolute restfulness. This is stated in the last sentence.
5. Answers will vary.
6. new uses of color, different styles and subjects
7. white
8. illness and long hours spent painting

Exercise 24, Page 118

1. (2) "Poetry is like the bird's song" is the only simile among the choices because it uses the word *like* to compare two things.
2. (1) That the best poems have music and magic in common is stated in the last sentence of the second paragraph.
3. (5) The main idea of the passage is that reading poetry should be a joyful experience. This idea is stated in the first sentence.
4. (4) The fact that the delight of poetry will be lost can be inferred from the first paragraph.

Chapter Review, Pages 119–122

1. (4) The first and second paragraphs specify the subject of the exhibit: various kinds of work by Latino artists.

2. (2) Castillo's studio includes his own sculpture, and the exhibit includes contemporary art. These facts alone make it false to say that the studio is devoted to ancient art.
3. (4) The rough and powerful retablos are described in the last sentence.
4. (1) Bou and Uribe are described as contemporary painters in the second sentence of the next to last paragraph.
5. (1) This is a very favorable review.
6. (2) The passage makes no mention of Honduras.
7. (1) You can infer from context clues that *riveting* means "exciting."
8. (2) That the information was received from the *Apollo* astronauts is stated in the third sentence.
9. (4) This statement is a personal judgment. All the other statements are facts that can be proved.
10. (1) This is what the reviewer means when he says that the writer "brings the astronauts to life."
11. (2) Hanging from a cliff implies great danger; so does the in-flight explosion of an oxygen tank.
12. (5) You can tell from the first paragraph that the reviewer has the highest possible opinion of this film. The top rating is four stars.
13. (5) All of the choices are mentioned in the second paragraph.
14. (5) The first sentence of the second paragraph names the main subjects of this documentary: William Gates and Arthur Agee.
15. (1) When a reviewer says that a particular film "is what the movies are for," you can conclude that he is recommending it for all audiences.
16. (3) The long commute and the change to a largely white school imply that William and Arthur face difficulties ahead.

READING EFFICIENCIES

Reading Efficiency A, Pages 123–124

1. (5)
2. (2)
3. (4)
4. (4)
5. (2)

Reading Efficiency B, Pages 125–126

1. (3)
2. (5)
3. (1)
4. (2)
5. (3)

Reading Efficiency C, Pages 127–128

1. (4)
2. (4)
3. (3)
4. (4)
5. (2)

Reading Efficiency D, Pages 129–130

1. (3)
2. (5)
3. (4)
4. (2)
5. (4)

Chapter 6

PROSE FICTION

Exercise 1, Pages 135–136

1. (3) The first sentence of the paragraph states that "he knew he must explore this island quickly." The last sentence of the first paragraph refers again to an island.
2. (3) The second paragraph mentions "midsummer shells." July is the only midsummer month listed in the choices.

3. (1) A bob-white is a bird. There is no evidence that Pentaquod is running away from anyone. From his name and the simile "eat like a chieftain," it can be inferred that he is an Indian.
4. (1) Pentaquod's observations of the surroundings reassure him that he will be able to provide for himself.
5. (2) The phrase "if he could but catch it" indicates the availability of food.

Exercise 2, Pages 140–141

1. (3) Johnny resents Mack. He talks back to him and won't cooperate. He describes the detective as fat and stupid. His behavior shows hostility.
2. (1) In these lines, Johnny is thinking things over. He expresses self-hatred and an urgent need to conceal his fear. These are evidence of a deep conflict within him.
3. (2) When Johnny learns of Eddie's death, he begins to doubt himself and becomes afraid. This is why he tries to escape.
4. (1) Clues that reveal the setting include the detective, the two cops at the door, the plainclothesman, and the female officer.
5. (2) Johnny's friend Eddie has been fatally stabbed. We know Johnny witnessed the stabbing because he says he knew Eddie was dead when the officers came to the door and because he regrets not having stayed away.

Exercise 3, Pages 142–143

1. (1) Although damage to the aircraft is mentioned, the action centers around the loss and restoration of oxygen in the cabin.
2. (2) The fourth paragraph states that Harris accepted the risk, which is another way of saying that he took a gamble. He gambled because he believed that the odds were worth the risk.
3. (3) The passengers were able to breathe again when the plane reached 12,000 feet and regained consciousness at 10,000 feet.

4. (1) The fourth paragraph mentions "further structural damage," implying that some damage was already done.

5. (2) This is the point toward which the action builds and from which it begins to resolve itself. The pilot risks possible destruction of the plane for a chance to restore oxygen to the passengers.

Exercise 4, Page 145

1. He felt faint. He was trying to keep himself from fainting.

2. He is determined. He forces away thoughts of weakness or failure.

3. Himself. He is encouraging and reassuring himself out loud. He tells himself, "You have to last." There is no sign that anyone else is in the boat with him.

4. The forward part of a boat. See line 7.

Exercise 5, Page 146

1. D   The narrator felt, in turn, "nearly smothered," "squeezed," "cramped," and "perfectly miserable," which all make for an extremely uncomfortable trip.

2. D   The adults did not speak to him except to complain or scold.

3. A   The narrator is a child. He is seated between two men so he doesn't fall. The woman refers to his "young" bones.

4. D   The boy is described in lines 10–11 as having short legs.

5. D   The woman was cruel. She poked him with her shoe and scolded him if he moved.

Exercise 6, Pages 147–148

1. (3) A first-person narrator is telling the story. See lines 10 and 13.

2. (2) Boggs says, "Come out and meet the man you've swindled." To swindle means to cheat.

3. (1) Lines 29–30 describe Sherburn as "a heap the best dressed man in that town."

4. (2) This is stated in line 13.

5. (2) He threatens to come after Boggs if Boggs "opens his mouth against him" after one o'clock (lines 36–37).

6. (3) The townspeople yell at Boggs, laugh at him, and sass him. One of them says Boggs doesn't mean anything by his behavior and would never hurt anyone. All this adds up to a colorful but harmless character.

7. (2) The misspelling is deliberate. The author wants the reader to hear the regional speech.

Exercise 7, Page 150

1. (d)
2. (g)
3. (h)
4. (a)
5. (j)
6. (b)
7. (f)
8. (c)
9. (e)
10. (i)

Exercise 8, Page 150

1. L
2. L
3. F   The expression refers to great happiness, not acrobatics.
4. L
5. L
6. L
7. F   The world doesn't actually smile. The expression refers to happiness or good luck.
8. F   The marriage was not literally made in heaven; it was a happy, promising union.
9. F   People do not literally walk upon the air. But happiness is a feeling of joy mixed with lightness.
10. F   The expression refers to great eagerness and impatience. People cannot physically be beside themselves.

Exercise 9, Pages 151–152

1. (2) The paragraph uses vivid figurative speech to describe tractors digging up the earth.
2. (3) Insects do not move at great speed or kick up huge clouds of dust. They crawl along the ground.
3. (1) The tractors are depicted as plowing through everything—fences, dooryards, hills, gulches, water courses, and houses—causing destruction.
4. (1) This is figurative language, transforming machines into the image of pigs.
5. (2) Line 13 describes the man as a "robot in the seat."

Exercise 10, Pages 152–153

1. (3) The first sentence says that a moth flew into a candle. The rest of the paragraph is built around this event.
2. (2) To ignite means to catch fire. The moth's wings caught fire like tissue paper would have—extremely fast.
3. (2) Crackling and pistol fire are both sounds.
4. (1) "Green leaves" and "red trunk of a pine" (lines 9–10) suggest a forest setting.

Exercise 11, Pages 155–156

1. (2) The first paragraph says Pete "could just see himself in a new home." The passage describes his experiences with real estate salespeople.
2. (3) The second paragraph says that Pete believed his financial success would enable him to live wherever he chose.
3. (1) Both men avoid answering Pete's questions or telling him the truth—that, because of his race, he is not welcome in the development. Their responses to Pete evade the point of his questions.
4. (3) Although Pete can afford to live where he wants, racial descrimination still keeps him out of this neighborhood.

Chapter Review, Pages 157–160

1. (5) His feeling of being like an outsider is expressed in the first sentence of the third paragraph.
2. (2) The second paragraph describes how the narrator crossed over a fence to get to an area strewn with clothes and weapons and bodies under a hot sun. The third paragraph specifically refers to a battle ground.
3. (4) The image of such a machine is used to convey the inhumanity of war.
4. (3) The passage is about the pain and misery of war. Words such as "terrible," "grim," "littered with clothes and guns," "mournful company," "swollen forms," "agitated bodies," "blood-stained crowd," "cursing, groaning, and wailing" all show the agony of war.
5. (3) The whole passage is about Simple's long life of suffering.
6. (1) In the first paragraph, Simple speaks of having been "born young, black, voteless, poor, and hungry, in a state where white folks did not even put Negroes on the census." He resents having had to work so hard for so little in return.
7. (4) Simple lists the ways in which being black has led to his poverty and his hard life.
8. (1) The first several sentences show that this scene takes place in the kitchen at breakfast time.
9. (3) Everything the young man says throughout the passage is said in a sarcastic tone, even the passage in which he tells his grandmother, "I'm nuts about you."
10. (2) Her reference to a good night's sleep and her advice to avoid a chill show that she is concerned about her grandson's physical health.
11. (5) This is stated in line 34.
12. (3) Rain helps establish the gloomy mood.
13. (1) Yossarian is embittered and overwhelmed by the injustice and poverty he sees around him.
14. (4) The last line, "What a lousy earth!" sums up the passage. Yossarian takes a very negative, pessimistic view of the world.

READING EFFICIENCIES

Reading Efficiency E, Pages 161–162

1. (3)
2. (1)
3. (3)
4. (4)
5. (2)

Reading Efficiency F, Pages 163–164

1. (3)
2. (4)
3. (1)
4. (5)
5. (2)

Chapter 7

POETRY

Exercise 1, Page 167

1. Stanza 1: stair, care
   Stanza 2: smell, tell
   Stanza 3: near, hear
   Stanza 4: ago, know
2. (3) The last line of each stanza indicates that the woman is lonely and lives alone.

Exercise 2, Pages 170–171

1. (1) The author is sad that her mother missed out on so much of the beauty and gaiety in life. She also feels love and gratitude because her mother tried to give her something beautiful to hold on to.
2. (2) Lines 9 and 10 say, "My mother reached for beauty and for its lack she died."
3. (2) We do not know the mother's occupation, but line 4 says "the tenement her orbit." The poem also mentions "the broken molding" (line 7) and the "filthy street" (line 8); so we know that she lived in a gloomy environment.

4. (2) The daughter remembers her mother as having tried to rise above their gloomy circumstances for something better.
5. Answers will vary. Possible meaning: The duty and hard work of raising a child in the bleak environment of the tenement house simply overwhelmed the mother, despite her best efforts.
6. The rhyming words in lines 1 and 3 are *beauty* and *duty;* in lines 2 and 4, the words *died* and *pride* rhyme.

Exercise 3, Page 173

1. S Note the word *like.*
2. M
3. M
4. S Note the word *than* (two times).
5. M

Exercise 4, Page 174

1. ball of dark yarn
2. *gathers, loosens, spreads,* and *unravel*
3. fog and blue strands

Exercise 5, Page 176

1. (5) The theme of the poem is the cramped, impersonal environment of a large apartment building.
2. (3) This simile uses the word *like* to compare people living in a large apartment building to bees swarming in a hive.
3. (4) *Comb* and *home* rhyme; the ending of each word sounds alike.
4. (4) The poet uses the words *identical* and *cramped* to describe the living spaces.

Exercise 6, Page 177

1. (1) This comparison is made in lines 9 and 10, "stars are great drops of golden dew."
2. (3) This is a metaphor, a comparison made without the use of the words *like, as,* or *than.*
3. (3) Music. The poet refers to a band playing and, twice, to singing.

4. (5) The poet is expressing the happiness of one who is in love. He uses the phrase *I love you* twice.

Exercise 7, Pages 178–179

1. (1) Without using *like, as,* or *than,* the poet compares the crows' voices to thunder.
2. (3) Simile. In lines 1 and 2, crows "speak *like* men to one another."

Chapter Review, Pages 180–182

1. (2) New York City. The last line says the bus has New York license plates.
2. (3) *Escapism* describes the poet's mood. The passenger seems angry and wants to escape from his urban surroundings.
3. (3) You can assume that the driver is African American. In race-torn cities, the driver and passenger will switch places so that the bus will have an African-American passenger and a white driver.
4. (4) Lines 14 and 15 explain the passenger's need to show others that the driver has done well up North.
5. (5) The passenger wants to go to a small fishing village in an unknown part of Florida.
6. (1) The poet wants to escape from the big city to a smaller place "more suitable to the heart" (line 8).
7. (1) The tone is serious. The poet may be youthful, but that doesn't mean that the mood of the poem is. This poem is a serious expression of the poet's feelings about his voice (his identity).
8. (2) Every line except the last compares the poet's voice to an aspect of geography, but without the use of *like, as,* or *than.*
9. (1) The poet is using his voice as a symbol of how different he feels when he is away at school and when he is home in the land he loves.
10. (3) He is happiest when he is at home during summer months, when school is out and he can truly be himself.
11. (1) They are both similes, making comparisons using the word *like.*

12. (4) The second stanza names the places about which the poet's mother and grandmother sing.
13. (3) "Daughter" is the poet's mother. The mother and daughter in the poem are the poet's grandmother and mother.
14. (3) Line 11 says that the poet loves to hear the song sung.

READING EFFICIENCIES

Reading Efficiency G, Page 183

1. (2)
2. (3)
3. (2)
4. (4)
5. (1)

Reading Efficiency H, Page 184

1. (4)
2. (2)
3. (5)
4. (3)
5. (4)

Chapter 8

DRAMA

Exercise 1, Pages 190–191

1. (1) "Bunt? Two runs behind, bases loaded and they send Hodges up to bunt!" (lines 1–2) obviously refers to a baseball game.
2. (2) To "stay on the wagon" is most likely a health measure since it is mentioned along with two other health measures: not smoking and proper diet. Richard also refers to being on the wagon when he drinks the soda.

3. (3) The stage directions tell you that Richard has settled back in the chaise where "he sits, smiling, remembering the scene" of the conversation.

4. (3) Richard complains that he has had "one continuous upset stomach" since he quit drinking (lines 34–35).

5. (3) In his memory sequence (lines 37–38), Richard recalls that Helen said she would call at ten o'clock.

Exercise 2, Pages 193–194

1. (2) There are several clues in the passage. Cindy's father, the preacher, is gone, and her mother is now married to David.

2. (2) Molly feels that she and Cindy owe a debt of gratitude to David. She does not want to hear Cindy criticize the man who saved them from losing everything.

3. (2) David needs Cindy to attract more business to the bar, especially on Friday nights, when her "pretty little face gets a lot of guys to buy a lot of drinks" (lines 6–7). He flatters her in an attempt to get what he wants.

4. (1) David had previously agreed that Cindy could have Friday nights off to attend her prayer meetings.

Chapter Review, Pages 195–197

1. (4) Mel is in a state of mental anguish. In the opening lines, he says that he is not through with life and that he still has value and worth. Later, he alludes to being "halfway" to insanity (lines 33–34). In the final two lines, he expresses a desperate need for breathing space.

2. (2) Edna says that Mel lives like a "caged animal" (lines 3–4). Mel himself says he needs "just a little breathing space" (lines 42–43), and he knows that travel is not the answer.

3. (1) Edna's words show how frustrated she is. She says: "I am not the one who's doing this to you" (lines 37–38); "Don't talk to me like I'm insane" (line 33); Then "what do you want from me?" (line 40); and "What do you

want from anyone?" (line 41).

4. (1) This scene is all about Mel's desire to escape. Edna describes him as living like "a caged animal in a Second Avenue zoo." Mel is obviously the main character in a play that takes its name from his predicament (problem).

5. (5) The dialogue tells us that Davies' dreaming, groaning, and jabbering woke Aston up.

6. (4) You can determine the meaning from the context. The word *groans* (line 21) provides the best clue. *Jabbering* refers to gibberish, or unintelligible talk.

7. (1) Davies takes pains to deny that he dreamed, jabbered, or was unaccustomed to sleeping in a bed.

8. (1) Aston asks Davies if he slept well and then gets the toaster, so you can infer that their conversation takes place in the morning.

9. (1) Aston is referring to himself in lines 27–28 when he says, "You got hold of the wrong bloke, mate."

10. (2) The phrase "dead out" refers to sleeping well (line 2).

READING EFFICIENCIES

Reading Efficiency I, Pages 198–199

1. (2)
2. (3)
3. (5)
4. (1)
5. (5)

Reading Efficiency J, Pages 200–201

1. (3)
2. (5)
3. (3)
4. (2)
5. (5)

Using the Reading Efficiency Activities

Contemporary's Reading Efficiency Activities will help increase your reading speed and your comprehension accuracy. The activities are similar to the reading passages and questions you will find on the GED Test.

Your goal is to complete each exercise in less than 10 minutes. You should also answer at least 4 of the questions correctly. If you can always score within this range (within the shaded areas of the Efficiency Factor Chart), you should be successful with the readings and the number of questions on each GED Test.

Once you know the amount of time it took you to complete the activity and the number of questions you answered correctly, look at the Efficiency Factor Chart. Find your time along the left side and your number of correct answers along the top. If your time falls between two of the times on this chart, round up to the higher time. Move across and down until your time and number correct meet. This is your E-Factor.

Find where your E-Factor fits on the Efficiency Factor Grid. Make a dot to the right of that number on the line below the number of the Reading Efficiency Activity you completed.

As you read other Activities, mark your E-Factor and connect the dots to create a line graph. You should see a line that moves upward as it crosses the grid. If your E-factor is not improving, ask your teacher what you can do to increase either your speed or your accuracy.

EFFICIENCY FACTOR (E-FACTOR) CHART

Number Correct

Reading Time	0	1	2	3	4	5
6.0	0	33	67	99	133	167
6.5	0	31	62	92	123	154
7.0	0	29	57	86	114	143
7.5	0	27	53	80	107	133
8.0	0	25	50	75	100	125
8.5	0	24	47	71	94	118
9.0	0	22	44	67	89	111
9.5	0	21	42	63	84	105
10.0	0	20	40	60	80	100
10.5	0	19	38	57	76	95
11.0	0	18	36	55	73	91
11.5	0	17	35	52	70	87
12.0	0	17	33	50	67	83

READING EFFICIENCY

EFFICIENCY FACTOR GRID

	A	B	C	D	E	F	G	H	I	J	Reading #
170											
165											
160											
155											
150											
145											
140											
135											
130											
125											
120											
115											
110											
105											
100											
95											
90											
85											
80											
75											
70											
65											
60											
55											
50											
45											
40											
35											
30											
25											
20											
15											

E-Factor ____ ____ ____ ____ ____ ____ ____ ____ ____ ____

Glossary

A

action: the sequence of events in a drama—comparable to the plot of a novel

analyze: to break something down into its parts to understand the whole, as in a passage, paragraph, or graphic

application: taking information from one source and applying it to another situation

atmosphere: the mood or general feeling in which a story is rooted

B

bias: a writer's personal opinions that give the writing a positive or negative slant

C

character: a fictional person in a work of literature

characterization: the writer's presentation of a character through description, action, dialogue, thoughts, and feelings

classify: to put information into categories that enhance understanding

climax: the turning point in the action of a play or the plot of a novel

comedy: a drama that takes a light approach to its subject; characterized by funny or satirical dialogue and a happy ending

commentary: a review or essay about popular culture

comparison: the presentation of similarities between people, things, or ideas

conflict: the struggle between opposing forces in a story, such as a person against others, himself or herself, society, or nature

context: the surrounding words or sentences that help explain the meaning of a particular word or expression

contrast: the presentation of differences between people, things, or ideas

critical essay: a subjective and sophisticated type of commentary on the arts

D

descriptive language: writing characterized by vivid, colorful words and phrases

dialect: a regional variation of standard speech

dialogue: the words spoken by the characters in a drama

drama: a story, written in the form of a dialogue, to be performed onstage

drawing a conclusion: making an interpretation based on facts or supporting details

E

editorial: a column in a newspaper or magazine expressing the opinion of the publication's editor

effects: things that happened as the result of an action or an event

ellipsis points: punctuation consisting of three dots in a row, used to indicate that someone's voice has trailed off or that words in a sentence have been omitted

essay: an informative article about a book, play, or specific topic

F

fact: a true statement that can be proved through research

fiction: novels, short stories, and other literature that deals with imaginary characters and events

figurative language: words chosen for effect, not literal truth, to express a speaker's message

first-person point of view: a type of writing in which the author is also the narrator or main character in the story

G

Great Depression: a worldwide business slump when the U.S. stock market crashed in the 1930s

I

idea: in drama, the underlying message of a play

imagery: the mental pictures suggested by descriptive language in prose or poetry

inference: an educated guess about something that is not directly stated in a passage but is strongly hinted at or implied

informative essay: a commentary on the arts written for the general reader and designed to inform without judging

irony: a type of humor that implies a difference between what is true and what should be true

L

literal language: words that mean exactly what is stated, with no other meaning implied

M

main idea: a statement that tells what a whole selection is about

metaphor: a comparison made without the use of the words *like*, *as*, or *than*

motivation: in drama, the factors that reveal the reasons for a character's behavior

N

nonfiction prose: reading selections that present factual information or that express a viewpoint

O

opinion: a personal judgment or belief

order of importance: organizing information in a paragraph or passage upward from a small detail to the central idea, or downward from the most important point

P

personification: giving the qualities of a living thing to something that is not alive, or giving human qualities to something that is not human

pitch: the musical quality of a voice

place: the physical setting in which a story occurs

plot: in fiction, the sequence of events leading to the climax and then the conclusion

poetry: writing in verse form designed to appeal to the senses and the imagination; characterized by figurative language, rhythm, and rhyme

point of view: how a particular event or series of events look to a specific individual

propaganda: deceptive writing intended to influence readers by misrepresenting the truth

prose fiction: type of writing that includes novels and short stories and deals with imaginary characters and events

R

reference: a source of objective information, such as an encyclopedia, a telephone directory, an almanac, or a road map

resolution: ending part of a story

response: in drama, the reaction of a character to a situation, event, or remark

review: a personal critique of a movie, book, play, or television or radio program

rhyme: the repetition of sounds

rhythm: the beat or pattern of language or sound

S

sarcasm: a tone of bitter humor, usually directed at a specific target

scan: read quickly but closely to find a specific fact or detail

sequence: the order in which things are presented or arranged

setting: the combination of place or location, time, and atmosphere; the background against which a story takes place

simile: a comparison that uses the words *like*, *as*, or *than*

social drama: a type of drama dealing with familiar problems in true-to-life situations

soliloquy: dialogue spoken aloud by a single actor alone upon the stage

stage directions: in the text of a drama, written material apart from the dialogue that explains a character's thoughts, feelings, or physical movements

stanza: in a poem or song, a verse or several lines that stand together

style: the general category of a piece of writing (formal, persuasive, informative, etc.) based on the type of words and sentences used

subjective: characterized by opinion

supporting details: items of information that support the main idea of a passage

symbolism: having one thing represent something else, such as a heart representing love

synthesis: the integrating of information from different sources to reach a new understanding

T

theme: the implied message that underlies and gives meaning to a work of fiction or drama

time: when a story takes place—in the past, present, or future

tone: the emotional character of a piece of writing or, in drama, of a character's voice

tragedy: a drama in which a leading character comes to ruin as the result of a character flaw or overwhelming outside forces

V

volume: in drama, the loudness or softness of a character's voice movements

Index